AFRICAN VOICES
ON DEVELOPMENT AND
SOCIAL JUSTICE

EDITORIALS FROM
PAMBAZUKA NEWS
2004

Pambazuka Press – www.pambazukapress.org

Pambazuka Press is an imprint of Fahamu Books (www.fahamubooks. org). We are a pan-African publisher of progressive books that aim to stimulate debate, discussion, analysis and engagement on human rights and social justice in Africa and the global South. We publish books and CD-ROMs on Africa, the African Union, capacity building for civil society organisations, China and Africa, conflict, human rights, media, trade, aid & development and women's rights.

Pambazuka News – www.pambazuka.org

We also publish the prize-winning weekly electronic newsletter Pambazuka News. With over 1,400 contributors and an estimated 500,000 readers, Pambazuka News is the authoritative pan-African electronic weekly newsletter and platform for social justice in Africa, providing cutting-edge commentary and in-depth analysis on politics and current affairs, development, human rights, refugees, gender issues and culture in Africa.

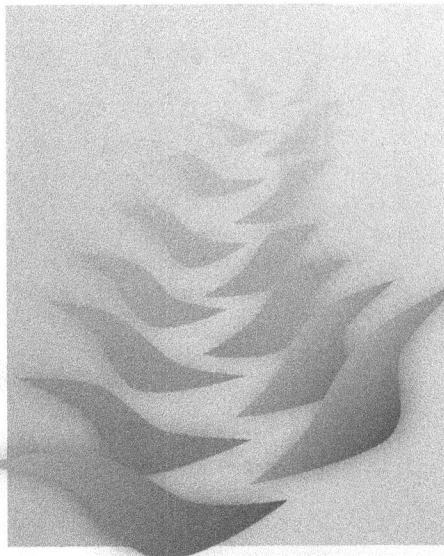

AFRICAN VOICES ON DEVELOPMENT AND SOCIAL JUSTICE

EDITORIALS FROM PAMBAZUKA NEWS 2004

Edited by
Firoze Manji and Patrick Burnett

Pambazuka
Press
An imprint of Fahamu Books

This edition published 2010 by Pambazuka Press, an imprint of Fahamu Books
Cape Town, Dakar, Nairobi and Oxford
www.pambazukapress.org   www.fahamubooks.org   www.pambazuka.org

Fahamu, 2nd floor, 51 Cornmarket Street, Oxford OX1 3HA, UK
Fahamu Kenya, PO Box 47158, 00100 GPO, Nairobi, Kenya
Fahamu Senegal, 9 Cité Sonatel 2, POB 25021, Dakar-Fann, Dakar, Senegal
Fahamu South Africa, c/o 27A Esher St, Claremont, 7708,
Cape Town, South Africa

First published in 2005 by Mkuki Na Nyota Publishers
This edition published in 2010 by Pambazuka Press,
an imprint of Fahamu Books

British Library Cataloguing in Publication Data
A catalogue record for this book is available from the British Library

ISBN: 978-1-906387-75-4 paperback
ISBN: 978-1-906387-60-0 ebook

Manufactured on demand by Lightning Source

CONTENTS

CHAPTER 5
Resource Exploitation in Nigeria

CHAPTER 6

Discussing the Democratic Republic of Congo,

the Heart of Africa

CHAPTER 7

An 'Unhappy Birthday': the World Bank and International

Monetary Fund Turn 60

Acknowledgements
Our thanks to all contributors, who so willingly allowed
us to include their essays in this book. Our thanks also to Fahamu
staff who worked hard on compiling, editing, design and
layout to meet, as always, impossible deadlines.

INTRODUCTION

African Voices
on Development and
Social Justice

Firoze Manji and Patrick Burnett

DESPITE ITS ENORMOUS potential, Africa is today the poorest continent. Malaria, HIV/AIDS and maternal mortality are estimated to kill one million per year (or 2,800 per day) in Africa. According to UNDP, more than 50 per cent of Africans suffer from water-related diseases such as cholera and infant diarrhoea. More than 40 per cent of Africans cannot even obtain sufficient food on a day-to-day basis. For the African farmer – more than 80 per cent of whom are women - conventional fertilisers cost two to six times more than the world market price. More than 40 per cent of women in Africa do not have access to basic education. A woman living in sub-Saharan Africa has a 1 in 16 chance of dying in pregnancy or childbirth. This compares with a 1 in 3,700 risk for a woman from North America.

Add to these the numerous ongoing conflicts, each claiming hundreds of thousands of lives every year (estimated at 3.8 million in the Democratic Republic of Congo (DRC) alone since 1998) and there may be justification in characterising Africa as a wasteland of conflict, disease and poverty.

With the imminent publication of a report from the UK Prime Minister Tony Blair's Commission on Africa, and the UK's presidency of the G8 and European Union, there is likely to be much attention on Africa during 2005. Northern governments and Northern NGOs will no doubt have much to say about how Africa's ills should be dealt with. Africa will once again be the object of pity, a 'basket case', a 'scar on the conscience of the world'. Charity, not justice, governance, not self-determination, will be their watchwords. The danger will be that Africa is likely to face once again an externally driven agenda for social development that combines a narrowly defined programme of privatisation with a broadly defined programme of globalisation – the recipe of structural adjustment programmes and poverty reduction strategy papers that have become so tediously familiar over the last two decades and which, many would claim, exacerbated the destitution of the region.

But as Nelson Mandela so aptly put it at a public rally in Trafalgar Square, London, in February 2005: 'Like slavery and apartheid, poverty is not natural, it is man-made and it can be overcome and eradicated by the actions of human beings. And overcoming poverty is not a gesture of charity. It is an act of justice.'

And that encapsulates the basic premise upon which Pambazuka News, from which this collection of essays originates, was founded: to be a platform for social justice in Africa. But as with all struggles for justice and emancipation, the motive force for change comes not from noblesse oblige, but from the actions of those who are the victims of injustice mobilising in concert with acts of solidarity from without. Since its establishment in December 2000, Pambazuka News has sought to be a vehicle for commentary, debate and information for those committed to the cause of social justice in Africa.

The newsletter came into existence in response to the demands of human rights and other civil society organisations in Africa where access to the internet – and in particular the worldwide web – was limited, slow and expensive. Fahamu, the organisation that publishes Pambazuka News, responded by providing a service which summarises each week current contents from key websites, lists, and other materials sent to the newsletter for publication. From the beginning, we wanted to ensure that we made available not just 'information' but also commentary on key developments in the region. Now approaching its 200th edition, Pambazuka News has established itself as the primary newsletter on social justice in the region. The editorials, comments and analyses published in Pambazuka News have been widely reproduced on other lists, websites and magazines (both electronic and printed).

For the first time, we are making the editorials published over the last year available in a book form (they are also all available free online at www.pambazuka.org). They provide a different perspective about development and social justice in Africa that rarely finds expression elsewhere. They constitute, we believe, a valuable record of the perspective of both African activists and academics on key developments and events in the region during 2004, viewpoints that are neither complacent nor romantic about the conditions created by African governments, nor dismissive about the creative potential of Africa to determine its own future.

As a weekly email publication, and with limited resources at its disposal, Pambazuka News does not pretend to be comprehensive in its commentary on Africa every week. We are aware of the many gaps, and realise that the collection of editorials in this book reflect the unevenness of that coverage. Our intentions, and those of our publishers, are to make this an annual publication. But that will depend on how this book is received.

Chapter 1 sets the global and regional context of 'undevelopment' in Africa, challenging some of the shibboleths of development. 2004 was the 10th anniversary of the genocide in Rwanda that led to close to a million people being slaughtered in the space of a few months. The essays from a special issue of

Pambazuka News published in April constitute the second chapter, highlighting the complicity of the international community in these crimes against humanity. The establishment of the African Union and the attempts to develop regional integration are commented upon in the essays in Chapter 3.

That Pambazuka News has not just been a commentator on the world but also engaged in the struggles for social justice is demonstrated through its support for the coalition of civil society organisations operating under the banner of Solidarity for African Women's Rights to campaign for the ratification of the Protocol to the African Charter on Human and Peoples' Rights on the Rights of Women in Africa. Pambazuka News has published several special issues on the theme, participated in advocacy actions at African Union meetings, and made available technologies that enable people to sign an online petition by sending text messages from their mobile phones. The articles related to this campaign form the content of Chapter 4.

The paradox of Africa is that it has some of the world's greatest mineral resources, making it one of the richest continents. And yet it is the region of greatest impoverishment. Its natural resources have been robbed for the benefit of the few and the destruction of human communities and their environments, a subject addressed in Chapter 5. There is little irony in the fact that those countries with the greatest potential natural resources have also witnessed savage civil wars. While wide-scale slaughter is the subject of international attention in some countries, there has been a deafening silence about the killings in the DRC (Chapter 6).

The Bretton Woods Institutions, the IMF and World Bank, celebrated their 60th anniversaries in 2004, an event that was hardly a cause for celebration in the region. In a series of editorials, their disastrous track record in Africa is assessed (Chapter 7).

Africa has the largest refugee population in the world. The rights of those subjected to forced migration are rarely acknowledged or protected. They are amongst the most impoverished of Africa's people. Poverty is too commonly portrayed as the subject of pity, providing the justification for the huge industry of the 'development machine', a vast institutional and disciplinary nexus of official agencies, practitioners, consultants, scholars, and other miscellaneous experts producing and consuming knowledge about the 'developing world'. But, as Pierre Sané puts it, 'poverty will only cease when it is recognised as a violation of human rights and, as such, abolished' (Chapter 8).

Two countries that have received much attention over the last year have been Zimbabwe and Sudan, and both are a source of continued controversy. Zimbabwe's crisis continued to drag on inextricably in 2004, with no clear solution in sight. 'Four Years on from the Beginning of the Plunge' is the title of one of the editorials contained in Chapter 9, and this speaks of the despair of progressive forces at the state in which Zimbabwe finds itself. Chapter 10 discusses the situation in Darfur and includes the thought-provoking essays by well-known scholars Kwesi Kwaa Prah and Mahmood Mamdani problematising the nature of the Darfur genocide and the historical roots of Arab and African identities.

The concluding Chapter 11 contains a selection of letters submitted by subscribers to Pambazuka News and published in the weekly newsletter, demonstrating the often lively debate that many of these editorials have sparked. We hope that the collection of articles included in this edition will contribute further to that debate.

ABOUT THE AUTHORS

Kafui Adjamagbo-Johnson is the Coordinator of Women in Law and Development in Africa (WiLDAF), West Africa.

Zeinab Kamil Ali is a member of the Commission on Human Rights, Djibouti.

Rudy Amenga-Etego is from the National Coalition Against the Privatisation of Water in Ghana.

Eno Anwana's major interest is the sustainable management of Africa's vast wealth of natural resources by Africans. Since 2002 Anwana has worked in the Niger Delta region of Nigeria on a MacArthur-funded project focusing on the wise use of natural resources and sustainable development. Anwana is affiliated with Nigerian's foremost environmental NGO, the Nigerian Conservation Foundation, a membership-based NGO.

Innocent Balemba works for Amnesty International. His article was written in his personal capacity.

Joel Bisina is a peace activist and founder and Regional Director of the Niger Delta Professionals for Development (NIDPRODEV), a non-profit organisation working on the communal and inter-tribal conflicts in the oil-rich Niger Delta Region of Nigeria.

Patrick Bond is Professor at the University of the Witwatersrand, Johannesburg. He is also the author of *Talk Left, Walk Right: South Afica's Frustrated Global Reforms*, Pietermaritzburg, University of KwaZulu-Natal Press, 2004; and *Against Global Apartheid: South Africa meets the World Bank, IMF and International Finance*, London, Zed Books, 2003.

Patrick Burnett is the News and Information Coordinator for Fahamu and Co-editor of Pambazuka News. He has a background in journalism and is based in Cape Town, South Africa.

Gerald Caplan is the author of *Rwanda: The Preventable Genocide* (2000), the report of the International Panel of Eminent Personalities appointed by the Organisation of African Unity to investigate the 1994 genocide in Rwanda, and the founder of Remembering Rwanda: the Rwanda Genocide 10th Anniversary Memorial Project.

Richard Carver is Director of Oxford Media Research. He wrote 'Broadcasting and political transition: Rwanda and beyond' in Richard Fardon and Graham Furniss (eds), *African Broadcast Cultures: Radio in Transition*, James Currey, 2000.

Tim Concannon is with the Stakeholder Democracy Network.

Eva Dadrian is an independent broadcaster and political and country risk analyst for print and broadcast media. She currently works as a consultant for Arab African Affairs (London) and writes on a regular basis for *Africa Analysis* (London), for *Al Ahram Hebdo Echos Economiques* and *Al Ahram Weekly* (Cairo) and contributes to the BBC World Service's Africa Service (London).

Abdulai Darimani is Programme Officer, Environment Unit, Third World Network-Africa.

Eugenia Date-Bah is Director of the ILO InFocus (International Focus) Programme on Crisis Response and Reconstruction and former manager of the ILO Action Programme on Skills and Entrepreneurship Training for Countries Emerging from Armed Conflict.

Demba Moussa Dembele is Director of the Forum for African Alternatives in Dakar, Senegal.

Sarah Erlichman is the UNHCR Community Services Officer in Kigali. The opinions expressed in her article are entirely her own, and not those of UNHCR.

Hannah Forster is Executive Director of the African Centre on Democracy and Human Rights Studies (ACDHRS).

Vincent Gasana is a Rwandan who lives and works as a broadcast journalist in London.

Barbara Harrell-Bond is Distinguished Visiting Professor, Forced Migration and Refugee Studies Programme, American University in Cairo.

Paul Higate is a lecturer in social policy in the School for Policy Studies at the University of Bristol. His research interests are gendered relations in peacekeeping operations and he has recently started a project to further explore the topic in Liberia, East Timor and Cyprus.

Mike Kagan is a refugee law specialist.

Camille Karangwa survived the genocide in Rwanda and now lives in Pretoria, South Africa, where he works for the African Association of Political Science. He has just published at the 'Editions du jour' a book entitled *Le chapelet et la machette: Sur les traces du génocide rwandais*. He can be contacted at: camijour@yahoo.com

Joseph Yav Katshung is Executive Director of CERDH (Centre d`Etudes et de Recherche en Droits de l`Homme et Démocratie).

Steve Kibble is the Africa/Yemen Advocacy Co-ordinator for the Catholic Institute for International Relations.

Mahmood Mamdani is Herbert Lehman Professor of Government and Director, Institute of African Studies, at the University of Columbia, New York.

Firoze Manji is founder Director of Fahamu and founder and Co-editor of Pambazuka News. He is also Visiting Fellow at Kellogg College, University of Oxford.

Hein Marais is a South African writer and journalist. A former chief writer for the Joint United Nations Programme on HIV/AIDS (UNAIDS), his work is focused largely on AIDS and on political-economic issues. He is the author of *South Africa: Limits to Change – The Political-economy of Transition*, Zed Books/UCT Press.

Henning Melber is Research Director at the Nordic Africa Institute in Uppsala, Sweden. He joined SWAPO of Namibia in 1974 and was Director of the Namibian Economic Policy Research Unit in Windhoek between 1992 and 2000.

James Milner is a Trudeau Scholar and doctoral student at the Refugee Studies Centre, Queen Elizabeth House, University of Oxford. He has formerly worked as a consultant for UNHCR in India, Cameroon, Guinea and Geneva, and the European Council on Refugees and Exiles.

Faiza Jama Mohamed is the Africa Regional Director of Equality Now.

Charles Mutasa is Research and Policy Analyst at the African Forum and Network on Debt and Development (AFRODAD).

Laurie Nathan is Visiting Fellow at the Crisis States Programme, London School of Economics.

Akong Charles Ndika is an energy policy analyst with Global Village Cameroon.

Mary Ndlovu is a Zimbabwean human rights activist who used to work for the Legal Resources Foundation, Zimbabwe.

Antoinette Ntuli is Director of HealthLink and chairs the Co-ordinating Committee of the Global Equity Gauge Alliance.

Adebayo Olukoshi is Professor of International Economic Relations and currently the Executive Secretary of the pan-African Council for the Development of Social Science Research in Africa (CODESRIA), which is headquartered in Dakar, Senegal. His article was based on speaking notes for an address delivered at the third Southern African conference on Equity in Health, Durban, South Africa, 8–9 June 2004.

Kwesi Kwaa Prah is Director of the Centre for the Advanced Studies of African Societies. This article has been used with the permission of the author.

Brian Raftopoulos is Associate Professor at the Institute of Development Studies, University of Zimbabwe.

Sara Rakita is Programme Consultant for TrustAfrica and writes in her personal capacity.

Pierre Sané is UNESCO's Assistant Director-General for Social and Human Sciences, a post he has held since joining the organisation in May 2001. He is responsible for a programme of work that ranges from human rights and the fight against discrimination to philosophy, ethics of science and technology, policy-action research and international cooperation in social sciences. Prior to joining UNESCO he was Secretary General of Amnesty International (1992–2001). At the beginning of his career he worked in the field of regional and international development both in Africa and in Canada. He writes this article in his personal capacity and not as a representative of UNESCO.

Rotimi Sankore is on the editorial board of Pambazuka News and is Coordinator of CREDO for Freedom of Expression and Associated Rights, which focuses on rights issues in Africa.

Riaz Tayob works for the Southern and Eastern African Trade Information and Negotiations Institute (Seatini) in South Africa.

Ernest Wamba Dia Wamba, is a professor and the leader of the Rassemblement Congolais la democratic (RCD-Kingani). He is based in Kinshasa (DRC). He is a recipient of the prestigious Prince Claus Award for Culture and Development in recognition of his 'scholarly contribution to the development of African philosophy and for sparking off the philosophical debate on social and political themes in Africa'. He has taught at a number of universities including Harvard and the University of Dar-es-Salaam.

Mary Wandia is the Advocacy Officer with the African Women's Development and Communication Network (FEMNET).

Everjoice J. Win is a Zimbabwean feminist activist. She is a former Commonwealth Adviser to the Commission on Gender Equality.

Eugenia Zorbas worked in Rwanda for one year in 2002/3 and has since returned to academia as a PhD student in the Development Studies Institute at the London School of Economics and Political Science, with a research focus on post-genocide reconciliation debates in Rwanda.

CHAPTER 1

AFRICA AND THE PROCESS OF 'UNDEVELOPMENT'

Neo-liberal Globalisation and Its Social Consequences

Adebayo Olukoshi
Pambazuka News 165, 15 July 2004

THE ACCELERATED PROCESSES of globalisation that have characterised the last decade and a half in world history and the forces and interests that have emerged to dominate and propel them have brought to the fore a broad range of issues and concerns that touch directly on global and local-level equity and justice both generally as they pertain to the developmental experience and more specifically as they are being played out in the social sectors of which health and education occupy a place of prime importance.

Although, at one level, globalisation appears to promise a great deal of opportunity for progress and advancement, the process, in the way in which it has been shaped in the contemporary period, has also been accompanied, at another level, by a sharpening of socio-economic disparities and inequalities among nations and within countries. Evidence suggests that the main winners from globalisation represent a small and diminishing minority even as millions, including many who once formed part of or aspired to the middle class, have been pushed to the bottom of the social ladder into poverty and misery.

A plethora of explanations have been advanced as to why the process of globalisation has not been accompanied by social gains and has, instead, resulted in the erosion of some of the achievements recorded in an earlier phase of development. While some scholars point to the fact that the current experience of globalisation is driven by the narrow concerns of international financial investors with a strong short-term, speculative orientation that is inimical to the overall interests of the working poor and the real sectors of economies, others have suggested that the problems that have arisen are traceable directly to the neo-liberal ideological principles and doctrinal foundations on the basis of which the process of globalisation is being governed and which has resulted in the enthronement of a narrow and limiting market logic in the policy process.

There is clearly some truth in the various competing explanations which have been offered as to why the problem of inequality would seem to have worsened on the back of globalisation. But over and above these is the question of the state, particularly in the developing countries, and the erosion and delegitimisation not only of its role in the developmental process but also the erosion of its broad policy planning and implementational capacities at the same time as the efforts at supplanting it with the private sector and/or non-governmental organisations have failed to live up to expectations.

When this is taken together with the fact that in the African context, the free market orientation of policy premised on deflationary macro-economic principles has failed to deliver growth and has instead widened the boundaries of poverty, it is easy to begin to understand why the problems of inequality and injustice have worsened. It is here, in my view, that the problem ought to be located in the first place.

The Making of the Post-Colonial African State and Social Policy

The state, whether in developed or developing countries, played an important historical role as a social actor. The high point of the development of the social state came in the period immediately after the Second World War with the emergence and spread of different variants of social democratic and welfare regimes in response both to popular domestic pressures by the working poor in Europe and as a direct response to the challenge of an ascendant socialism/communism most eloquently symbolised by the Bolshevik Revolution and its initial spread across Eastern Europe and Asia.

The post-war context of the consolidation of the social state coincided with the period of late colonialism which also witnessed for the first time in the colonial experience, a deliberate and conscious investment of effort in the promotion of 'development' which included greater attention to the promotion of infrastructure, the nurturing of local industrial processing and the expansion of health and educational facilities and expenditure.

At independence, African states were, not surprisingly, invested with broad-ranging social responsibilities which were integral to the anti-colonial social contract on the basis of which the nationalist politicians mobilised the populace for the independence struggle. Central to the contract was the promise of the expansion of social policy in a direction which would significantly improve the health and nutritional status of the populace, expand access to education and offer greater opportunities for employment. African countries succeeded in varying degrees in achieving the goals which they defined: in the period to 1980, the livelihood prospects of the populace were generally improved – life expectancy maintained an upward trend even as child and maternal mortality showed improvements.

The expansionary economic policies which African governments pursued in the 1960s and 1970s had a great deal to do with the successes which they recorded. With growth rates averaging 5 to 7 per cent and star economic performers like Cote d'Ivioire and Kenya clocking up to 9 per cent average growth rates, it was possible to expand the social expenditure of the state particularly with regard to health and education. Policy was geared to promote the inclusiveness of marginal groups and subsidies were employed to improve the reach and coverage of the educational and health targets of the state.

To be sure, the post-colonial model of social policy formulation and implementation was not without its problems and some of the problems were to become sources of dysfunctionality that eventually weakened the effectiveness of policy and, finally, the onset of socio-economic crises. Still, in comparison to the poor growth records of the 1980s and 1990s, the 1960s and 1970s seemed like golden years.

The Onset of Economic Crisis and the Age of Orthodoxy

The onset of the African economic crisis at the beginning of the 1980s triggered attacks on the social policies of the post-colonial state. While for most African governments, the immediate, almost instinctive response which they had to the crisis in their economies was to curb social expenditures as the core of the austerity measures which they adopted, this attack on the social sectors was carried further and transformed into a dogma in the context of International Monetary Fund(IMF)/World Bank structural adjustment which had a deflationary, market-oriented thrust that saw and treated the post-colonial state as the problem and not a part of the solution.

The economic crisis management and reform strategy promoted by the IMF and the World Bank drew heavily from an ascendant global neo-liberalism which was one-sidedly anti-state and which was committed to 'freeing' the forces of the market under the banner of 'getting prices right', curbing inflation, and promoting the private and/or non-state sector. The consequences of this crisis management strategy were many and devastating from the point of view of the health sector and the health status of the average Africa.

The shift in the structure of incentives which the structural adjustment framework represented and which consisted of efforts at shifting the locus of developmental activities away from the state to market also triggered a brain drain from the social sectors generally and the public health system in particular even as freshly qualified health personnel roamed the streets in many countries unable to find gainful employment.

The immediate post-colonial health system definitely had many problems but there was also a clear vision which underpinned it and which sought to improve livelihood and well-being. During the crisis and adjustment years, this vision was lost and the alternative that seemed to replace it was preoccupied primarily with winning the battle to roll back the frontiers of the state and enthrone the market.

Little initial attention was paid to ways in which the health gains that had been recorded in the lead up to and immediately after independence could be safeguarded. The consequence was that a chaotic situation prevailed in many countries in which the public health system was in a state of collapse and mired in all-round shortages of personnel, equipment and medicaments while the private/non-governmental health system, such as it existed, proved to be inadequate in many ways even as its services were priced beyond the reach of the working poor.

The decline which was registered in the health status of the average African was dramatic and alarming: diseases which were previously under control or which were well on the way to elimination resurfaced while life expectancy suffered reversals as maternal and infant mortality grew at the same time as the nutritional status of many households declined. The wider framework of economic reform and structural adjustment which was being pursued had clearly taken a toll on the health sector and combined with developments in the health system itself to send alarm bells ringing. Across Africa and the rest of the world, the case began to be made for adjustment with a human face.

The pleas for the modulation of economic reforms in order to give adjustment a human face led to the introduction of a series of interventions which came under the rubric of the social dimensions of adjustment. Overall, most of these programmes failed to achieve the objectives for which they were introduced and there is no greater evidence of this than the worsening of the problems of growing exclusion that they were supposed to help tackle.

The shallowness of the interventions was brought into sharp relief by the outbreak of the HIV/AIDS pandemic, which the social dimensions of adjustment were simply unable to address and which accelerated at a time when the capacity of the state and of the public health system had been severely eroded.

Beyond Structural Adjustment and Towards the Social State

One of the fundamental lessons from the failure of the social dimensions of structural adjustment to have an effect, and a factor which is equally relevant for the Poverty Reduction Strategy Papers (PRSPs) which have been put in place across Africa during the last two years, is that no progressive policy of social advancement can be successful if it is treated as a residual category to serve targeting needs while the 'serious' business of macro-economic policy-making is carried on without a clear social objective in mind.

To be truly effective, social policy must be an integral part of macro-economic policy-making, not a residual add-on. This can only be done if there is a conscious effort to avoid the decoupling of social policy from macro-economic policy formulation as has happened over the last two decades. Such an approach will require, as necessary, the harmonisation of economic policies and instruments with the goal of social renewal and advancement built on foundations of equity and justice.

For macro-economic policy-making to succeed in advancing the frontiers of social policy in a manner that is equitable, just and inclusive, it would also require to generate growth without which it will not be possible to expand expenditure. The tragedy for Africa is that the structural adjustment years were characterised by a policy orthodoxy which, by its deflationary logic, stifled growth.

The quest for a social state will necessarily, therefore, involve a revisiting of the macro-economic fundamentals that inform policy with a view to effecting a radical shift from a growth-retarding orthodoxy to a growth-promoting heterodoxy. In sum, the rebirth of a social state in Africa will also simultaneously involve a re-thinking of policy in a direction that could promote what some have conceptualised as developmental democracies on the continent.

How Africa Develops Europe
(and the Rest of the Rich World):
Real Development and Aid

Antoinette Ntuli

Pambazuka News 139, 15 January 2004

INCREASINGLY ATTENTION is being given to documenting the extent to which Africa (and the rest of the developing world) is in fact providing development aid, as opposed to being a recipient of aid. This aid is being provided in myriad ways including financial relations, subsidising ecological resources, provision of ready trained skilled labour and, increasingly, providing holiday resorts of unbeatable value.

The slave trade was the most visceral manifestation of the ongoing exploitative relationship between Africa and the rich world. The haunting images of manacled Africans toiling in the cotton fields of the USA have now been replaced with images of starvation, war, brutality, fecklessness and HIV. These graphic images, beamed throughout the world, perpetuate a sense of need and dependence that serves the purposes of powerful and wealthy states. Such images make it easy to believe that Africa both requires and could benefit from Western aid. This however belies the real relationship between Africa and the West. In reality, in order to understand Africa's relationship with the developed world, it is important to look at figures which show that, far from contributing nothing to the economy of developed countries and taking everything in return, Africa's contribution to developed countries could be considered as its own form of development aid.

According to Jubilee Research the accumulated external debt of the world's richest country, the USA, is $2.2 trillion – almost the same as the $2.5 trillion owed by the entire developing world including India, China and Brazil. They calculate that this means that every American citizen owes the rest of the world $7,333 while every citizen of all the developing countries only owes the rest of the world $500. Meanwhile the poor are financing the debt of the developed world, as capital flows from poor countries, helping to lower rich countries interest rates and inflate the value of their currencies, enable them to purchase goods from the rest of the world far more cheaply than they would otherwise have been able to do.

Jubilee Research have also quantified the economic damage attributable to natural disasters arising from climate change as being more than $300 billion per annum. Industrialised countries (at least historically) are almost entirely responsible for human driven global warming although 96 per cent of all deaths from natural disasters occur in developing countries. The value of economic output built on growing 'carbon debt' (in which carbon debt is calcu-lated according to the amount by which a country exceeded its fair share in the emission of greenhouse gasses) attributable to the G7 countries, was estimated as being in the region of $13–15 trillion for a typical year in the 1990s – while the conventionally indebted poor countries had a carbon credit that could be valued at three times their orthodox debt. Thus if this concept of debt is used, the developing world is subsidising the rich world and should perhaps be considering what structural adjustment processes the rich world needs to put in place in order to meet their debt repayments.

The UNDP calculated that by 1987 nearly one third of Africa's skilled people had moved to Europe – Sudan lost 17 per cent of doctors and dentists, 20 per cent of university teaching staff, 30 per cent of engineers and 45 per cent of sur-veyors in 1978; 60 per cent of Ghanaian doctors trained in the early 80s are now abroad; and Africa as a whole is thought to have lost up to 60,000 middle and high level managers between 1985 and 1990. This reverse subsidy seems set to continue. Some estimates indicate that mechanistic and flawed developed country staff forecasting needs mean that the USA, for example, will require one million additional nurses in the next ten years to meet its shortfall.

Writers on human resources such as Bundred and Martineau put the cost of training a GP as US$60,000, calculating a reverse subsidy from the developing world of US$500m per annum just for health personnel. In South Africa alone, the loss of more than 82,000 skilled personnel over an eight-year period between 1989 and 1997 is estimated to have cost the country US$5 billion. UNCTAD quantified US savings of US$3.86 billion in training costs as a result of importing 21,000 Nigerian doctors over a ten-year period.

Central to these startling statistics are structural adjustment programmes. Rather than providing restitution for the period of formal occupation of African countries that took place between the 1880s and 1960s, the West chan-nelled large sums of monies into newly independent African countries through massive bank loans. In the process a number of banks became severely stretched. With the 1980s came an intense period of structural adjustment pro-grammes, the immediate objective of which, according to Walden Bello, was to rescue banks that had become overextended; the longer-term objective was to further integrate Southern countries into the North dominated world economy. Although initially few countries were keen to take structural adjust-ment loans, as more and more countries ran into difficulty servicing the huge debts made to them, so they had no option but to 'structurally adjust'.

Structural adjustments demanded that, as a pre-condition to receiving aid, developing countries open their markets to globalisation and privatise their utilities such as water and electricity services. Among the other requirements were tightening of state expenditure and devaluation of currencies resulting in an end to free health and education and dramatic cut backs in these services.

The withdrawal of resources for education and health initiated a cycle of deprivation in which working conditions, including salaries deteriorated, triggering an exodus of staff and further debilitating the services. Simultaneously, funding of academic training institutions was reduced, and there was a concurrent flight of intellectuals and decimation of institutions of higher learning. Philip Altbach calculates that roughly 1.5 million students (most of whom leave the South to study in the North) study in countries outside their own, and a significant number do not return.

The net effect has been to strip countries of a significant component of their social capital and create a vacuum of skill, conveniently providing jobs for highly trained Westerners (to be paid for in hard currency) and simultaneously the conditions for Africa to be reduced to providing technical level education and producing a workforce only fit to do the dirty jobs of the rich world.

And just as there seems to be broad agreement that structural adjustment has not been beneficial to Africa, the General Agreement on Trade in Services (GATS) is ready and poised to fill the gap. The combined worth of health and education markets is estimated to be US$5 trillion according to Bertrand and Kalafatides. If the major proponents of GATS have their way, all these services will be up for grabs by powerful transnational corporations, and the right of African states to provide these common goods will be emasculated.

What the figures above show is that, combined with conditions like structural adjustment and GATS, the cycle of development aid from Africa to Europe and the rest will be continued. For African intellectuals, students, political activists and Africanists everywhere this signals a call for international solidarity of the kind inspired by the anti-apartheid movement – as a countervailing force against the new world order that compels Africa to continue to feed the bloated stomach of greed.

World Debt Day: Who Owes Whom?

Interview with Demba Moussa Dembele
Pambazuka News 156, 13 May 2004

THOSE CAMPAIGNING AGAINST Third World debt have long argued that crippling levels of debt have been a severe block to the development of African countries, causing widespread poverty and hardship. Six years ago, over 70,000 Jubilee 2000 supporters formed a human chain in Birmingham to call for the cancellation of the debts of some of the world's poorest nations. To mark this occasion, World Debt Day on 16 May is intended to call attention to the ongoing debt crisis, provide a global rallying point for all those who continue to care about the suffering being caused by debt and encourage campaigners by providing an opportunity for action and advocacy. *Pambazuka News* emailed a list of questions to Demba Moussa Dembele, Director of the Forum for African Alternatives in Senegal, to gauge where Africa stands in the debt stakes.

Pambazuka: Why should people care about World Debt Day?

Dembele: The day commemorates one of the largest gatherings ever held to call world attention to the impact of the Debt Crisis. It was on 16 May 1998, during the G7 Summit in Birmingham (UK) that the call on Western and Japanese leaders to cancel poor countries' debt went out. That day was a turning point in the Jubilee 2000 Campaign and helped put the debt issue on centre stage.

Pambazuka: Briefly, what is the impact of the current levels of debt on the development of African countries?

Dembele:
■ Sub-Saharan Africa's debt accounts for 71 per cent of its GDP
■ The debt represents more than 180 per cent of exports
■ Debt service absorbs 12–13 per cent of exports receipts on average
■ Accumulated arrears (debt service that could not be paid) represents more than 30 per cent of current debt levels
■ Since 1988, sub-Saharan Africa (SSA) is getting very little in terms of new loans. A greater part of some of the loans we hear about is used to service old debts
■ Unsustainable debt deters foreign direct investments.

Pambazuka: If the negative effects of unsustainable debt are so well documented, why are the debt-collecting institutions and countries so reluctant to intervene in an area of such obvious importance?

Dembele:
■ The debt bondage is the new face of colonialism or even slavery
■ Debt is used as an instrument of domination: it is at the heart of the unequal power relations between the North and the South. It is also an instrument used to plunder and exploit indebted countries' resources
■ Debt is an instrument of resource transfer from the South to the North. In 2002, according to the UN, net transfers from the South to the North were estimated at $200 billion. During the four previous years, net transfers from the South amounted $120 billion a year
■ The IMF and the World Bank use debt as a tool to impose their disastrous policies. Without that tool they would have a very limited or no influence in Africa or elsewhere.

Pambazuka: Many people point to the Highly Indebted Poor Countries Initiative (HIPC) as evidence that something is being done to resolve the debt crisis. Others argue that the HIPC is a sham and has not led to significantly improved levels of debt relief. In your opinion, what progress has been made and what more needs to be done?

Dembele:
■ So far 11 countries, including nine in sub-Saharan Africa, have achieved the completion point. But almost all of these countries did not have 'sustainable' debt levels as the World Bank predicted in its debt sustainability analysis (DSA)
■ The amount of debt 'cancelled' for these countries is minimal compared to their overall debt. It is less than 20 per cent
■ At this pace, it would take a quarter century to see all eligible countries achieve the completion point
■ The only solution to the debt crisis is total debt cancellation. Nothing less.

Pambazuka: Many have claimed that much of the debt owed by African countries (for example, the apartheid debt owed by South Africa) is illegitimate and that in actual fact, Western countries owe Africa for centuries of exploitation. Is this view gaining ground?

Dembele: Since the World Conference on Racism in Durban (South Africa) in 2001, the issue of reparations has been accepted by world public opinion. Of course, some European countries and the United States have shunned the conference for fear of being exposed. However, the idea is gaining ground every day. In Africa, more and more voices – intellectuals, policy-makers, activists, etc – use every opportunity to remind the world, especially the West, that it is Africa that is owed an immeasurable debt. In addition, the work of Jubilee South – the international debt network – and other national or regional networks has helped promote the idea of reparations in various forms.

Pambazuka: What's stopping African countries from simply defaulting on their debt and channelling the resources into health and education?

Dembele:

■ Many African leaders are beholden to the West. They are afraid of standing up to them

■ In addition, these leaders are afraid of challenging the World Bank and the IMF. Some of them are even afraid of supporting the call for debt cancellation. I remember a former Tanzanian finance minister saying in Washington, DC, that his country does not support the idea of multilateral debt cancellation because this would 'kill the goose that lays the golden eggs'

■ Collective debt repudiation is a political decision. At this juncture, it is not easy to see a unified political position that would support debt repudiation. But civil society organisations are working on it. We think that by exposing the hypocrisy and bad faith of bilateral and multilateral creditors and showing the disastrous impact of debt on Africa's human development indicators it will be possible some day to convince an enlightened leadership to move toward that decision.

Pambazuka: Recently there has been talk of debt swaps. What are debt swaps and are they an effective method of alleviating the debt crisis?

Dembele: Debt swaps are a mechanism by which part of a country's debt is sold by one or several of its creditors (private creditors) to another entity that invests the proceed in the same country. For instance, a commercial bank that seeks to get rid of its loan to a country like Senegal, will sell that loan – generally at a deep discount – to an investor, a corporation, which will use the face value of the debt to invest in a publicly owned company in Senegal. There are several kinds of swaps, such as debt-equity swaps, whereby a corporation that bought part of Senegal's debt uses it to buy shares in an existing state-owned company. This mechanism has been extensively used in Latin America and in a few cases in sub-Saharan Africa. Another type of swap is debt-for-nature, a case in which an environmental group buys a country's debt and uses the proceeds for environmental protection.

Since swaps involve only private debt, it cannot be an effective mechanism for debt alleviation given that almost 90 percent of poor African countries' debt is public. And swaps are a mechanism for transferring public assets to foreign hands. For this reason, it is not a good solution for those countries that have a substantial commercial debt, like Nigeria.

Pambazuka: If the current levels of debt and debt repayment burdens continue, what is the prognosis for African countries over the next ten years?

Dembele: Right now, many African countries are not servicing their debt. Or they do so by incurring new debts. Therefore, if the current levels of debt burden continue, over the next ten years:
- Many African countries may be totally stripped of their sovereignty
- The levels of poverty will worsen and millions of lives will be at risk
- There will be a total collapse of the state and other public institutions
- The Millennium Development Goals will not be achieved.

Pambazuka: Who do people need to target if they are concerned about the debt issue and want to make an impact? Who are the stakeholders?

Dembele: The targets are:
- G8 leaders (major bilateral creditors and masters of the international financial institutions)
- IMF and the World Bank (multilateral debt has overtaken bilateral debt in many cases)
- The Western credit agencies (that guarantee private debts)
- The parliaments of Western countries
- The United Nations system (to take a clear stand on debt cancellation)
- The African governments (to form a united front and eventually move toward debt repudiation).

Violently Intent on Keeping Us in Poverty: International Trade Policy

Riaz Tayob
Pambazuka News *178, 14 October 2004*

THE NORTH-SOUTH ECONOMIC and political divide is the overriding concern in international trade relations, with the rich North creating conditions that allow for the pillaging and primitivisation of the poor South. Together, the international financial institutions (IFIs) and the World Trade Organisation (WTO) adopt a coherent and comprehensive neo-liberal paradigm for trade and economic management, and this free trade ideology is imposed on developing countries.

There are serious deficiencies in this ideology, which are rarely given any credence, or receive at best grudging acknowledgement. The North uses the free trade ideology as a means of domination over the resources and livelihoods of the people of the South. One does not have to be a radical or a revolutionary to question the merits of their policies; simply looking at the economic history of rich countries is instructive. Do as I say and not as I did is the North's mantra.

The neo-liberal, free trade, Washington Consensus ideology is used as a tool to maintain resource flows from the South to the North. Militarily the colonisers were kicked out of African countries after bloody and horrific struggles. Neo-liberalism replaced military colonial occupation and ensures that resource flows from the South to the North continue. Instead of rule by the gun, it became rule by trade policy. Free trade was used as the ideology to continue to maintain colonial economic relations with the South.

Trade is regulated primarily by the WTO. After the collapse of the WTO Cancun Ministerial meeting, where developing countries refused to be bullied into accepting onerous trade and development terms, the USA and the European Union (EU) indicated that they would pursue regional trading arrangements (RTAs) with countries.

The failure of the economic superpowers to achieve what they desired at the multilateral level must inform our analysis of what they hope to achieve through regional negotiations. Since many issues the North hoped to impose on the South through the WTO were rejected, it is imperative for the South to maintain this consistency in RTA negotiations simply because the issues are not in our interest. However, Southern governments, especially in Africa, are much weaker in regional and bilateral negotiations with the North than they are at the WTO simply because of their extreme (and increasing) dependence on the North.

The rationale for African countries entering into RTAs are complex. There is the overriding perception that RTAs improve a country's economic development because of the alleged link between liberalisation and economic growth. However, a United Nations Development Programme longitudinal study of least developed countries found indications that liberalisation leads to de-industrialisation. One of the main reasons for entering RTAs is that regional bodies have greater representative and market power and may improve parity in bargaining. In order to benefit from the consolidation of representation, one can, wrongly, presume that there is an African regional integration plan that guides efforts in this regard.

The WTO establishes the framework for the implementation of free trade values: liberalisation is the aim of international trade. For an RTA to be WTO compliant it must result in higher levels of economic integration within a reasonable period of time, cover substantially all trade and be more liberalised than the WTO regime. This means that RTAs extend liberalisation commitments even further.

International trade is also impacted upon by the World Bank and the IMF. The IFIs actively promote Washington Consensus values of neo-liberal economics. The principle ideology they impart is that the market allocates resources best and the state should not interfere by creating market distortions. They also promote tariff reductions and trade liberalisation generally, forcing the South to give for free what the North should bargain for in negotiations.

In the context of RTAs it is important to recognise that the combination of these factors indicates that trade policy (and development policy) is externally determined by participation with the IFIs and the WTO. These agreements regulate the development path that is open for countries to follow. The control in many instances is indirect and in many more it is quite direct.

But free trade and liberalisation were not used as policies by the North to reach their current stage of development. The Now Developed Countries (NDCs) used different sets of policies (almost the exact opposite of the Washington Consensus). Free trade and liberalisation are now mantras prescribed under the guise of being pro-development. The North used state power to regulate markets, increase the social wage, create public services, use tariffs as a means of industrial development and controll investment flows amongst other measures.

For evaluation of African policies and global engagement, it is therefore revealing enough for us to begin our analysis in comparing the IFI/WTO prescriptions with the policies used by the North previously (historic capitalism), in order to understand what is happening to the South presently, within this form of neo-liberal globalisation. One need not be a revolutionary to see that things in our countries are getting worse or that the policy prescriptions used are so divorced from reality as to be positively harmful.

Neo-liberalism treats all economic activities alike, whereas the North developed by not treating all economic activities alike. Simply put, the North recognised that investing in a casino would have a different developmental impact from say housing construction. This is a distinction the neo-liberal system does not allow governments to make, so for instance subsidies under the WTO can be made to general sectors and not specific industries, or, GATS treats basic health and water services the same as tourism and gambling, when there are clearly qualitative differences.

The neo-liberal ideology also pushes for perfect competition, which is a utopian ideal that has never existed! In the early stages of development, the Northern countries actually pursued anticompetitive policies to assist with their development. In practice, Northern countries followed the principle of protection of industries including infant industries and only opened their markets once a particular level of market dominance/ economies of scale were achieved. This is in direct contradiction to the arguments against infant industry protection and in favour of the consumer welfare effects of liberalisation based on efficiency, which are being shoved onto African developmental agendas. Tariff liberalisation is promoted by the WTO and the IFIs when high tariffs were the primary tool used to develop manufacturing capacity in the North. In other words, the system forces African governments to prefer cheaper imported goods over job creation at a time when unemployment is rife. The recognition that imported goods contain labour is not obvious, and we continue to import labour contained in our imports and make them cheaper by liberalising tariffs.

By using the economic analysis toolbox that the Northern countries themselves used to develop, we see a world that is violently intent on keeping us in poverty in perpetuity. The term violently is not used lightly because at present even an analysis of Africa's chances of pursuing Schumpertarian increasing return activities is heavily constrained by our international commitments, our so-called level of global integration.

Since regional integration is a reality that must be dealt with, national and regional development agendas should, at the very least (but not only), incorporate the view that different economic activities have different impacts on the economy as Schumpeter pointed out. Some activities generate positive returns (manufacturing), others are return neutral (tourism) while resource extraction and primary commodity production (after a point) generate negative/diminishing returns. In order to generate additional revenue for the state, so that it can serve its distributive function to improve the conditions of citizens, any international trade engagement must prioritise increasing return economic activities to promote revenue generation occasioned in part by tariff income losses due to imposed trade liberalisation. The impact of these losses is not discussed adequately in the public domain and there is a presumption that everything will be all right.

The WTO for instance allows tariff escalation. This means that it is cheaper and easier for Africans to export coffee beans than it is to export processed coffee. Therefore Africa does not develop beyond coffee growing. It also allows for tariff peaks that are used to keep out goods where African countries have particular advantage like leather goods. So any move by Africans to develop manufacturing capabilities or to exploit comparative advantage to benefit meaningfully from their products meets with enormous obstacles and disincentives in Northern markets. These obstacles are legal and continue the colonial legacy of forbidding manufacturing in the colonies.

To bring about a change in the developmental pathway for Africa a number of obstacles have to be overcome, the first being the ideology of free trade that contaminates every level of policy making in many countries. Most officials and ministers do not know they do not know or are politically helpless in the face of free trade ideology.

The principles of free trade which are presented as inherently good are unsurprisingly absent in the North's approach to agriculture. In agriculture free trade is turned on its head, because the WTO allows the North to use trade distorting subsidies – state intervention that distorts the market: the ultimate free trade sin. So the system is schizophrenic: it prescribes a host of ideologies to govern trade in our countries (and thereby our development) but fails to apply it consistently in areas of interest to the South.

Because our governments are being pragmatic, they do not see the systemic and structural violence it creates and unleashes on our people. Over 70 per cent of Africans rely on agriculture as a means of living, yet they are prevented from using this comparative advantage. South Africa in particular is giving the land back to black people but is forcing these farmers to compete with subsidised European and American imports. This is a recipe for disaster.

Many governments in Africa, however, are adopting the view that the more RTAs they belong to, the more beneficial it will be to their economies. But, for instance, the Southern African Development Community (SADC) Free Trade Agreement (FTA) is estimated to reduce Namibia's revenue by between 31 and 50 per cent over the next 12 years (and these exclude the dynamic effects!). A plethora of agreements would further reduce income. This is not simply a matter for trade negotiators; it has serious implications for governmental stability especially at a time when debt levels are rising exponentially. Money for much needed social welfare is simply not going to be available because most governments rely heavily on international trade taxes for revenue.

At present though, the international trade context within which African countries operate is skewed against them because increasing return activities:

■ Do not enjoy meaningful market access in export markets (especially in areas where we have comparative advantage)

▪ Do not have sufficiently protected domestic markets to promote entrepreneurship and local development
▪ Suffer from supply side constraints
▪ Face continually declining commodity/primary goods prices and unfair competition in agriculture
▪ Are prevented through whimsical barriers to market entry in foreign countries.

Africa's openness to foreign goods and services within the domestic market is a problem. Africa is the continent that is most open to global trade. This means that even in the domestic market, local manufacturers must compete with transnational corporations. African manufacturers are expected to survive without protection from the state. We are trying to compete through exports in highly organised foreign markets while surrendering our home turf and losing out in both. The policies imposed on us simply do not make sense. Africa has slavishly followed most of the prescriptions of the former colonial powers with a spectacularly tragic outcome. If most of what we are doing is so different from what the North did and things are getting worse, then it is time to look at alternatives. There are other views on development that are simply not canvassed at all by our governments. If African governments are to prosper economically and politically, we need to at least begin to look at the policies used in the past by the now rich countries. If our governments fail to even consider some of these alternatives, then democratic government or not, it is a sad day. It is even sadder when these free trade conditions are imposed by many honourable and dedicated leaders who suffered greatly to bring us liberation (Nelson Mandela included), only to compound our people's material destitution.

NEPAD: South Africa, African Economies and Globalisation

Henning Melber
Pambazuka News 141, 29 Jan 2004

WITH ITS SUCCESSFUL democratic transition, South Africa emerged during the second half of the 1990s as a new political and economic factor on the continent. Within this process, Thabo Mbeki's foreign policy approach could be characterised as 'a complicated and sometimes contradictory mixture of ideology, idealism and pragmatism' (Gerrit Olivier in *International Affairs*, no. 4/2003). South Africa's Finance Minister Trevor Manuel, in a keynote address to the German Foundation for International Development, characterised as early as December 1998 the emerging South African strategy in a revealing way by asserting 'there is a new resilience and a new will to succeed in the African continent. We in South Africa have called it a renaissance, a new vision of political and economic renewal. It takes the global competitive marketplace as point of departure.'

Such understanding gave birth to the New Partnership for Africa's Development (NEPAD), for which Thabo Mbeki and his team can be considered to be the midwives (if not fathers – due to the absence of women in the male dominated process). NEPAD has managed to obtain – after some diplomatic manoeuvring and a number of strategic compromises – the blessings of the African Union and subsequently the United Nations General Assembly. It can be considered as a blue print for Africa's further socio-economic integration into the dominant global market.

Critical assessments of this strategy, which had been successfully promoted as the development paradigm by a number of African governments with the backing of the G8, have pointed out that its concept blends nicely into the neoliberal mainstream of globalisation. It is fully in line with the economic strategy of South Africa's present government, seeking closer integration into the dominant structures of the world economy. As Ian Taylor and Philip Nel have warned (in *Third World Quarterly*, no. 1/2002), the inherent danger of such a strategic move might lie in the message that it serves to legitimise instead of aiming to restructure the existing global power relations, to which African countries have been a victim. They further articulate the suspicion that the driving force behind such a policy might be the 'linkage between globalisation, export-driven trade policies and a nascent transnational elite', and maintain that 'making neoliberalism somehow "work for all", rather than rethinking the overall global trading system, is the key strategy of South Africa particularly and New Africa more generally'.

As if to confirm this, South Africa's Minister of Finance Trevor Manuel, in his capacity as the chairman of the development committee to the International Conference on Financing for Development in Monterrey on 18 March 2002 stated: 'There is general consensus that globalisation provides an opportunity for countries to improve standards of living, but it's not an end in itself ... The key challenge is to attempt to manage globalisation in such a way that it does lead to poverty reduction' (http://www.dfa.gov.za/docs/ffd253b.htm). But clearly so, NEPAD will not be able to replace demands for a fair share in the world's resources by those who have been the victims of domination and exploitation for far too long. At best it might be able to slightly increase the far too tiny piece shared from the global cake with stakeholders in Africa (stakeholders should in this context of course read as shareholders). Instead of a meaningful radical alternative, NEPAD seems to be much closer to 'more of the same' – namely capitalism as a new form of global apartheid, as Patrick Bond keeps on warning in his recent writings. Along similar lines, Ian Taylor reminds us of the active role elites in the South have played in this recent process of capitalist expansion termed (misleadingly) 'globalisation' by supporting the new Washington Consensus, resulting in the promotion of the liberalisation of trade and capital movements. It remains to be seen, from the point of view of those outside of these elites, if there is any substance in the pragmatism which argues: better this capitalism than no capitalism at all.

Such affirmative response to re-structuring the access to potential resources among others through a 'trade as aid' paradigm has been articulated by the South African Foreign Minister Dlamini Zuma in an address on 22 March 2002 to the University of Alberta, in which she had the following to offer: 'To the private sector, the continent of Africa is endowed with the human capital, mineral wealth and unlimited opportunities for trade, investment and partnership as proposed in the NEPAD programme. Other countries are taking advantage of this burgeoning market; it is imperative that you are not left behind. The opportunities abound in Africa.' (http://www.dfa.gov.za/docs/unal253a.htm) She did not need to send such a message to the capital at home: the windows of opportunity had already been discovered by the big companies operating from a South African base.

There is massive expansion of South African capital into the continent of hitherto unprecedented dimensions. This is illustrated in a chapter written by John Daniel/Varusha Naidoo and Sanusha Naidu to the 'State of the Nation' volume for 2003-2004, published by the Human Sciences Research Council. Its title says it all: 'The South Africans have arrived'. And an article in the Financial Times (17 November 2003) identifies 'a strategic shift by South African businesses' through companies 'striking out in search of bigger profit margins in their backyard'. Already since 1991 South Africa has been the largest foreign direct investor (with an annual average of $ 1.4 billion) within the continent. Large scale operations are undertaken by a variety of private companies as well as (ex-)parastatals, ranging from Spoornet and Portnet via Eskom and Sasol to South African Airways. MTN and Vodacom also compete as operators in the telecommunication business abroad and invest in the potentially huge markets of Nigeria and the DRC. Financial institutions such as Standard Bank join the 'traditional' multinationals in the mining sector, which have a long-standing experience in seeking other profitable opportunities to accumulate further.

Presumably greener pastures are explored and invaded by the local giants in the wholesale and retail business. South African chain stores mushroom all over the continent, South African Breweries owns and controls large parts of the beverage sector elsewhere. This penetration of neighbouring and continental markets goes hand in hand with the particular pro-active role of South Africa in engaging in and addressing international trade issues through a strategic involvement of the ministers for trade and for finance respectively in the current efforts to modify the global economy under the WTO. It is complemented by a parallel intensification of South-South cooperation seeking the consolidation of an alliance between the economically more powerful transitional economies such as South Africa, Brazil, India and China.

The South African economist Stephen Gelb, previously member of Thabo Mbeki's team drafting the original policy documents preceding NEPAD, reminded in a recent analysis published by his Edge Institute of the South African president's earlier approach. In a 1997 speech the then-Deputy President referred to the need for South Africa 'to "walk on two legs" in its foreign policy – to cultivate strong relations with the South, as well as strategic relations with the industrialised countries'. Gelb concludes, that NEPAD:

> is grounded in the full realities of South Africa's relations with
> the continent, including those beyond its immediate regional
> neighbourhood in Southern Africa. At the same time it is also
> grounded in the realities of globalisation, especially the une-
> venness of its impact amongst and within nations, and reflects
> an attempt to shift the continent, including South Africa itself,
> towards a more effective engagement.

More radical critics, who had opted to remain outside of the centres of political and economic power in present South Africa, speak out more directly. This is among others reflected in a number of articles published in the South African Labour Bulletin (no. 3/2003) under the thematic title 'NEPAD – a wish to build a dream on'. They suggest from a more or less critical distance that NEPAD offers the opportunity for South African capital to expand further in Africa by creating new market access. NEPAD is hence considered as a lubricant for a South African expansion into other parts of the continent, which under an Apartheid regime until the early 1990s would have not been conceivable. Almost ironically, only a politically correct post-Apartheid government allows the promotion of and greases a process, which is again (though not exclusively) to the benefit of those who already profited from the previous undemocratic system at home and can now enter spaces abroad.

Confronted with this view on occasion of a public NEPAD seminar in Stockholm (held on 9 October 2003 during the 3rd meeting of the Swedish-South African Binational Commission) the South African Vice President Jacob Zuma and the Deputy Foreign Minister Aziz Pahad seemed not amused. Their responses suggested that they perceive the South African type of capitalism as better suited for African conditions than other forms of capitalism (or no capitalism at all), and by no means a problem. The suggestion that the (class) struggle continues also in democratic South Africa was brushed aside as another example of notorious 'ultra-leftism'. But maybe they should join in with Robert Zimmermann (aka Bob Dylan) to intone the classical refrain 'and the times, they are a-changing' – or, for that matter, admit that they (the times) haven't changed as much as one might have thought a couple of years ago that they would.

From Partition to Re-Unification:
120 Years Since the Partition of Africa

Rotimi Sankore
Pambazuka News 187, 16 December 2004

THE 120th ANNIVERSARY of Africa's partition passed largely unmarked in November 2004. While some no doubt would wonder what the significance of this is today those that are aware of the partition and its implications will be able to see its negative implications for Africa's development and parallels with Cold War era Balkanisation of the world into East versus West spheres of influence. Some would even argue that Hitler's brazen land grab or policy of 'Lebensraum ' in which the Nazis claimed expansionism and conquest was vital for the continued political and economic development of Germany sprang from the objectives of the Berlin Conference. Without doubt, however, the goal of the Berlin Conference was to consolidate expansionism for resources and markets through negotiation rather than war.

Globalisation came to Africa via the transatlantic slave trade about 500 years before the term became 'sexy' or was even coined. This massive plundering and abuse of Africa's most valuable resource – its citizens – provided millions of slave workers and stupendous profits for the forerunners of many of today's multi-million dollar business empires and their countries of origin. The equivalent present day would be to have today's multinationals backed by states forcibly recruiting millions to work in factories and industries as slave labour for 400 years with absolutely no pay beyond food and water supported by floggings, amputations and hangings to keep the workers in line. The idea is not far fetched. The creation of an artificial class of non-persons by way of demonising Jews created the slave labour for the companies behind the Nazi war production machine. If six million perished in Germany and some parts of Europe within six years in a state policy partially hidden from society but subsequently exposed, think what could have happened over a period of 400 years of unrestricted savagery by numerous states and a clearer picture emerges of the most savage, violent, and comprehensive mass violation of rights in human history.

Some 'experts' squabble over whether Africa lost 25, 50 or a 100 million to this bestial policy sanctioned by states, and use various criteria to compute varying figures – abductees that actually arrived alive at slave plantations, those that ended up at the bottom of the ocean, those that died resisting, those that died as a result of displacement and its consequences such as disease and hunger, children that died after loosing their families, etc. This is beside the point. Not only were millions in their youth and productive prime lost, millions more were psychologically destroyed and displaced and most importantly the development of society was more or less suspended for 400 years. We only need to look at the impact of the holocaust on Jews, or the current Darfur crisis to see what state-sanctioned policies of destruction of a people can do to the stability, development and psychology of peoples and their societies.

But this is not the main focus of this write up. The significance of the above is that it was against this background that the partition of Africa – a continuation of the policy of plundering by other means – from human to natural resources – was enforced. The Berlin Conference of 1884 formalised the scramble for and partition of Africa by colonial powers. The conference was hosted by the German government of Otto Von Bismarck and led to Africa being carved up for the exploitation of its resources along the lines of modern day gangsters dividing cities into market spheres of influence to avoid arbitrary gang warfare that is bad for 'business'.

By the end of the conference of 13 European powers and the United States, the template had been laid down for the creation or superimposition of roughly 50 countries, the majority of which cut arbitrarily across the logic of nationality, geography, language or other uniting factors. The then major players were Britain, Germany, France, and Portugal, which between them already controlled most of the coastal territories where forts were established to protect trading companies. Belgium, Italy and Spain played supporting roles with the others haggling in vain for crumbs. The broad division that resulted was:

▪ Hosts Germany grabbed Namibia (German Southwest Africa) and Tanzania (German East Africa), Togoland, some of Cameroon and Benin
▪ Great Britain pressed its naval and military advantage and secured Egypt, parts of Sudan, Uganda and Kenya (or British East Africa), most of southern Africa including South Africa, Zambia, Zimbabwe (or Rhodesia), Botswana and significant areas of West Africa especially Nigeria and Ghana (Gold Coast)
▪ Belgium and King Leopold II held tight to the Democratic Republic of Congo (DRC, then known as the Belgian Congo)
▪ France secured most of western and central Africa, then known as French West Africa and French Equatorial Africa and later some of North Africa
▪ Portugal took Mozambique and Angola
▪ Italy got Somalia (Italian Somaliland) and a portion of Ethiopia
▪ While Spain made do with the smallest territory – Equatorial Guinea (Rio Muni).

The negative impact of the partition on Africa could not have been lost on the colonial powers especially Bismarck of Germany whose entire 40-year political career was devoted to the unification of Germanic states including fighting three wars including the Franco-Prussian war of 1870-71 and executing an endless series of diplomatic manoeuvres that played his neighbours against each other. (The subsequent defeat of Germany in the First and Second World Wars led to the loss of its colonies)

For the 'natives' already disoriented by the slave trade and its consequences, expansionism, protectorates and artificial states not only meant the denial of the right to self determination, it meant suppression and containment by state machineries designed for colonial rule. Colonial economies were not designed to develop the colonies but rather to create wealth for the colonial powers. An entire legislative framework and state apparatus was specifically designed to ensure that 'the law' crushed any signs of dissidence. Sedition, criminal defamation, insult laws, states of emergency, detention without trial, pass laws, etc, became key instruments of control by colonial authorities or white minority governments in southern Africa. These frameworks and culture of intolerance for opposing views were largely inherited by many African states and laid the foundation of the institutional abuse of rights in many modern African countries today.

It is utterly impossible to sustain human rights within the context of unviable states, failed states, or states perpetually in a state of conflict either because they are an artificial construct with ruling elites based very narrowly on ethnic, language, racial or other artificial divisions. Also, the artificial borders created by the partition of Africa broke apart ethnic nationalities and in many cases fused them artificially with others nationalities within new states. Ruling elites were cultivated either from minorities or majorities or artificially created and sustained using the army and or police. These divide and conquer policies were unsustainable indefinitely and it was just a matter of time before conflicts broke out over political or economic domination. In some countries, the process of independence leading to the withdrawal of colonial powers served as the trigger for long suppressed divisions to boil over. Either way, the entire construct of these states was aimed at exploiting and violating the rights of citizens.

By the time of independence, many African countries were stuck with these artificial constructs and a change of guard offered no solution. Not insignificantly, the independence era coincided with the cold war era and any leaders actually asserting independence were promptly labelled communists and dispatched via coups, murder or both. Some countries such as the DRC are yet to recover from the consequences of such interference and disruption that led to the murder of its elected Prime Minister Patrice Lumumba and the imposition of Mobutu. If, as in the case of Ghana's Nkrumah, new leaders actually advocated African unity and a reversal of the colonial borders and fiefdoms of new political leaders then other insecure African governments anxious to maintain the status quo opposed them. Where soldiers were not directly prompted to seize power, the fragile nature of many states and their non-productive nature meant that in the struggle for political power, the most organised and best armed body of men would inevitably become aware of their potential power and sweep squabbling politicians aside. The assumption of power by armies largely trained to serve colonial interests by holding down populations could only lead to more institutional violation of rights. Despite their occasional anti-imperialist posturing and theatrics designed to confuse issues and consolidate their hold on power, this was the true nature of the Mobutus and Idi Amins.

The Cold War also resulted in prolonging the life of white minority rule in southern Africa as the liberation movements were seen as pro-communist or socialist and the white minority governments pro west and pro-capitalist. Cold War rivals sustained all sorts of undemocratic governments of the left, right or centrist kind, as Africa once again became an arena of conflict.

In other words, the interruption of social, economic and political development by four centuries of slavery, the repressive legislative frameworks, state apparatus, institutions and culture created by colonial authorities, the non-productive nature of many economies, the unviability of others, artificially constructed states, long periods of military or civilian dictatorships that plundered the countries, the Cold War fall out and so forth have all combined to create the present political culture and political economy which prevails in much of Africa and makes it difficult if not impossible to uphold human rights in a sustainable form.

Any move away from this past which had as its central feature the institutional violation of rights must therefore have as its new central feature, the institutional promotion of rights. Its not a coincidence that the new African Union has emerged in a decade that has seen more elections in Africa than in the last 40 to 50 years of independence of most Africa countries. In the case of some southern African countries, independence was only won in the last 10 to 20 years. Compared to the relative 600 to 700 years of stability and development in Europe only accelerated or held back by revolution or war for certain periods its easy to see why Africa remains the least developed continent despite its potential. The context becomes clearer in comparison with the Asian colonies which had their civilisations, cultures and developmental trajectories affected by decades of colonialism – but crucially not suspended or destroyed by 400 years of slavery followed by carving up and imposition of mostly artificial states. The result is that Asia has an unbroken sense of history and culture and recovered quickly but not yet completely from colonialism. In the case of China and Japan, the results of the relative lack of disruption are clear to see. Were it not for the immortality of the pyramids, mummification techniques that indicate advancements in medical science and undeniable archaeological evidence of several African civilisations thousands of years older than many European and Asian civilisations, Africa and civilisation would never be mentioned in the same breath. As it stands, Hollywood is still in denial as evidenced by its continuous portrayal of ancient Egypt by white actors. This travesty and violation of historical and cultural rights can only be equalled by a spectacle of African actors portraying ancient Greece, Rome or China without any sense of irony.

The largely unbroken development of Europe over the last few centuries also explains why modern day European military dictatorships such as Franco in Spain, Salazar in Portugal or more recently in Greece and the Balkans did not fundamentally upset the development of those societies even though some of them and Franco in particular lasted over 30 years – longer than most African dictatorships. Even where as in the case of Hitler and Mussolini dictatorship and war led to destruction, the Marshall plan with its more or less free billions of dollars reconstructed and even gave impetus to the further development of those societies.

Most importantly and not surprisingly, major European governments sub-sequently came to the conclusion that the creation of a European Union would help break the cycle of wars and conflict in Europe and create the develop-mental basis for future socio-economic and political stability. At the heart of this today is the promotion of European-level core rights instruments, which provide more protection to citizens than the rights regimes in many individual countries hence the tendency to resort to the European Courts for the protec-tion of rights, denied in-country. 'I will go to Europe' has become a fashionable slang by many that feel cheated and unprotected.

The adoption of several rights based treaties and protocols by the new African Union is a step in the right direction and the recent declaration of a treaty signing week within the last month shows that the Commission of the African Union in particular clearly understands the role that promotion of rights can play in the development of modern society. The mission, vision and strategic plan promoted by the commission's current Chair Professor Alpha Konare are evidence of this. It is far from clear, however, that many African governments understand this as evidenced by the lethargy towards signing, ratifying and institutionalising instruments that will enhance the protection of rights such as the African Court of Human Rights / Court of Justice and the Protocol for the Protection of Rights of Women. This trend must be reversed. The broad sketches of African and world history and development above demonstrate that nowhere on the planet is the institutionalisation of rights more crucial to development than in Africa.

The political integration of Africa is aimless and doomed unless done on a rights basis that reverses hundreds of years of a largely imposed political culture of rights abuses, which can in turn unleash its creative and develop-mental potential. The protection of rights can also not be sustained on the basis of underdevelopment. Governments largely based on exploitation and the preservation of ruling elites, or that preside over underdeveloped societies tend to deny free expression and core rights of association, assembly, political participation and ignore key economic and social rights such as health care, housing, food security and so forth. The summary and core of the rights imperative is that all societies need these rights to develop and cannot develop further without the protection of these rights.

The Challenges Before
Africa and the African Union

Rotimi Sankore and Firoze Manji
Pambazuka News 112, 29 May 2003

THE CHALLENGES FACING the African continent are enormous. On every front – economic and industrial development; scientific and technological know how; electrification; agriculture; education; healthcare; housing; tele-communications; transport; peace and stability; institutional respect for social, economic, political and human rights – and on all other indices of modern society the continent is yet to fulfil its potential. The reasons for this have been articulated extensively – 400 years of vicious slavery and colonisation includ-ing the murder of millions of Africans in their prime, decades of military coups and dictatorships of all sorts backed by both 'Eastern and Western bloc' countries in the Cold War battle for strategic interests and resources, etc. These are terrible events, which would have undermined the development of any continent

Nevertheless, present day African governments are still failing in their duty to break the shackles imposed on their countries by the injustices of the past and guide their countries into the 21st century.

On 25 May the African Union celebrated the 40th anniversary of Africa Liberation Day and the formation of the Organisation of African Unity. The 26 May was also the second anniversary of the formal creation of the African Union. In his anniversary message, the current chair of the union President Thabo Mbeki of South Africa saluted:

> the distinguished leaders of the continental struggle such as Kwame Nkrumah, Gamel Abdel Nasser, Haille Selassie, Mmandi Azikiwe, Sekou Toure, Modibo Keita, Kenneth Kaunda, Mwalimu Julius Nyerere, Augostino Neto, Samora Machel, Amilcar Cabral, Albert Luthuli, Oliver Tambo, Walter Sisulu, Nelson Mandela and many others … [and their] Pan-Africanist vision of a Union of African States sharing common aims of multicultural unity, socio-economic and political co-operation and development, the promotion of human rights, the protection of human rights and freedoms, the promotion of peace and stability and the removal of the remaining yokes of colonialism and apartheid on the continent.

He also acknowledged that 'there are new issues on our agenda today such as democracy, peace and stability, human security, good economic governance as well as sustainable development, human rights, health, gender equality, information and computer technology, integrated regional development, cultural and heritage preservation and promotion.'

More importantly, he admitted that:

> The international community is eager to see whether we will be able to live up to the conditions that we have set ourselves in NEPAD and its African Peer Review Mechanism (APRM) in which we have designed measures to assist states where capacity gaps exist and to set benchmarks of excellence for a vibrant and progressive Africa ... We, in Africa'are optimistic that a new dawn is breaking and that prosperity, peace and human security will be a reality rather than a figment of our imagination.

But rather disappointingly, the first tasks that African Union has set for itself do not take account of President Mbeki's fine words. Instead, the Executive Council meeting of the AU attended by foreign ministers of all 53 member-states of the African Union met last week to 'consider issues' relating to the implementation of decisions taken by heads of state and government during the launch of the African Union regarding 'Common African Defence and Security Policy; the new structure of the Commission; progress report on the election of the AU Commissioners; scale of assessment for member-states; and the link between the AU and the African Diaspora.'

This distinguished gathering of ministers did not think it necessary to respond to the urgent issues such as warnings by the World Food Programme of looming food shortages and famine in several African countries including Angola, Congo Brazzaville, DRC, Eritrea, Ethiopia, Lesotho, Liberia, Malawi, Somalia, Sudan, Swaziland, Zambia, and Zimbabwe, where various estimates of between 30 million and 40 million people are at risk of starvation.

By no coincidence, the governments of these countries have been identified by several international and African organisations as suppressing press freedom and freedom of expression. In almost all cases, the rights to association, assembly and political participation have also been curtailed.

There also seems to be no collective awareness of other grim facts and statistics hanging like a sword of Damocles over of millions of Africans:

▪ Of the ten countries in the world spending the least on healthcare, only one – Tajikistan – is not African. Liberia, Burundi, Somalia, Niger, Sierra Leone, Ethiopia, Madagascar, Central African Republic and Chad top this list

▪ Of the ten most undernourished nations in the world only three – Afghanistan, North Korea and Haiti – are not African. The other seven are Somalia, Burundi, Eritrea, Dem Republic of Congo, Liberia and Niger

▪ The ten countries in the world with the highest death rate, and lowest life expectancy are all African: Botswana; Mozambique; Zimbabwe; Swaziland; Angola; Namibia; Malawi; Niger; Zambia; and Rwanda make up the first list with Sierra Leone, Burundi, Djibouti, swapping places with Angola, Namibia and Zimbabwe on the second list

■ Of the ten countries in the world with the youngest populations (normally characterised by high death rates and high birth rates) nine are African: Uganda; DRC; Chad; Niger; Sao Tome and Principe; Ethiopia; Burkina Faso; Mali and Benin

■ Of the ten most corrupt countries in the world, five – Nigeria, Uganda, Cameroon, Kenya and Tanzania – are African

■ The ten countries in the world that are worst for education are all African: Niger; Burkina Faso; sierra Leone; Guinea; Ethiopia; Angola; Mali; Mozambique; Senegal; Burundi and Guinea Bissau

■ Not surprisingly, eight of the ten countries on the planet with the highest rates of illiteracy are African: Niger, Burkina Faso; Gambia; Ethiopia; Senegal; Mali; Mauritania and Sierra Leone (the other two being Afghanistan and Haiti)

■ Yet, Africa seems to be heading full steam towards a housing catastrophe with ten of the fastest growing countries in the world being African: Niger; Somalia; Angola; Uganda: Liberia; Burkina Faso; Mali; Ethiopia and DRC.

It is therefore no surprise that malaria is estimated to kill one million people per year (or 2,800 per day) in Africa. HIV/AIDS kills an estimated two million people each year. Add to these the numerous ongoing conflicts claiming hundreds of thousands of lives every year (estimated at more than three million in DRC alone over the last three years) and it will be no exaggeration to say that Africa may well descend into a wasteland of conflict, disease and poverty if the trend is not reversed over the next few decades. But 2020 or 2040 are not so far away. It was only 'yesterday' that the 1970s and 1980s targets for 'everything for all' by the year 2000 were set without any clear arrangement to achieve these targets, and today it is 2003.

The ongoing SARS epidemic is yet to take a thousand lives globally but was placed at the fore of a recent meeting of Asian countries. The Canadian authorities were reported on 29 May to have decided to quarantine 5,000 persons at risk from the SARS virus. Yet the AU does not think the healthcare crisis facing Africa deserves to be fast tracked to the fore of its agenda. The right to life is after all the most important of all. To describe the African healthcare crisis as a result of criminal negligence would not be an exaggeration.

To anyone familiar with the political and economic history of Africa, the surprise is not that these statistics exist. The surprise is that there is no cohesive plan to reverse the trend.

The task of rebuilding the continent must therefore begin immediately. Improved education, healthcare, dealing urgently with the tragedy of HIV/AIDS, agriculture, scientific and technological development, housing, conflict resolution, peace and stability, and so forth must be accelerated to the fore of the AU's agenda. Unfortunately, this seems unlikely to happen unless African civil society makes every effort to ensure it is done.

But before any of these can happen, freedom of expression and freedom of association needs to be institutionalised. Nothing can happen without these. Only last week we witnessed the absurdity of a Moroccan editor being sentenced to four years in jail for publishing a satirical weekly which 'insulted the King of Morocco.' Such absurdities belong in the feudal past of humanity and have no place in the modern world. Yet Morocco is not alone. Eritrea one of the first few countries to sign the constitutive act of the African Union has imprisoned 18 editors and journalists and banned the entire private media. In July, 53 African heads of state will gather in Maputo for a meeting of the African Union. At least two thirds of them possess a plethora of anti-media and anti-freedom of expression laws in the armouries employed to stifle debate and alternative opinion.

Last week, on the occasion of the 40th anniversary of Africa Liberation Day, CREDO wrote to President Mbeki asking him to 'call on fellow African leaders to release all incarcerated journalists, repeal all anti-media and anti-free-expression laws and legislation in their countries and end the persecution of journalists, civil society and peaceful democratic opposition.' The letter also urged him to 'act speedily and decisively on these issues and to ensure they are firmly on the agenda of the 2nd Ordinary Session of the Assembly of the African Union planned for Maputo, Mozambique in July 2003.' The letter stressed that 'an end to the suppression of press freedom, freedom of expression and the rights to assembly, association and political participation will be a first and crucial step' towards solving the problems facing Africa.

CHAPTER 2

REMEMBERING RWANDA

Rwanda Ten Years after the Genocide: Some Reminders of the International Response to the Crisis

Gerald Caplan
Pambazuka News 150, 1 April 2004

AROUND THE WORLD, commemorations of the 10th anniversary of the Rwanda genocide are about to be launched. The central actors responsible for allowing Hutu extremists to perpetrate the genocide are well known: the government of France, the United Nations Security Council led by the USA with British backing, the UN Secretariat, the government of Belgium, and, by no means least, the Roman Catholic Church. The Organisation of African Unity also refused to condemn the genocidaires and proved to be largely irrelevant throughout the crisis. As a consequence of these acts of commission and omission, 800,000 Tutsi and thousands of moderate Hutu were murdered in a period of 100 days. Reviewing the events of those days, I find myself thinking not once but repeatedly: It's almost impossible to believe that any of this actually happened. The following is a selection of some of those events. They, and the lessons they suggest, are worth bearing in mind as we who refuse to let the memory of the genocide dissipate begin our commemorations of the 10th anniversary.

1. Time and again in the months prior to and during the genocide, the Commander of the UN military mission to Rwanda (UNAMIR) pleaded with the UN Department of Peacekeeping Operations in New York to expand his very limited mandate. The only time his request was ever approved was in the days immediately after the Rwandan president's plane was shot down, triggering the genocide. UNAMIR was then authorised to exceed its narrow mandate exclusively for the purpose of helping to evacuate foreign nationals, mainly Westerners, from the country. Never was such flexibility granted to protect Rwandans.

2. Heavily armed Western troops began materialising at Kigali airport within hours to evacuate their nationals. Beyond UNAMIR's 2,500 peacekeepers, these included 500 Belgian para-commandos, 450 French and 80 Italian troops

from parachute regiments, another 500 Belgian para-commandos on stand-by in Kenya, 250 US Rangers on stand-by in Burundi, and 800 more French troops on stand-by in the region. None made any attempt to protect Rwandans at risk. Besides Western nationals, French troops evacuated a number of well-known leaders of the extremist Hutu Power movement, including the wife of the murdered president and her family. All non-UNAMIR troops left within days, immediately after their evacuation mission was completed.

3. From the beginning of the genocide to its end, no government or organisation other than NGOs formally described events in Rwanda as a genocide.

4. From beginning to end, all governments and official bodies continued to recognise the genocidaire government as the legitimate government of Rwanda.

5. The months of the genocide happened to coincide with Rwanda's turn to fill one of the non-permanent seats on the Security Council. Throughout those three months, the representative of the government executing the genocide continued to take that seat and participate in all deliberations, including discussions on Rwanda.

6. Almost all official bodies remained neutral as between the genocidaires and the Rwandan Patriotic Front, the mostly Tutsi rebels in the civil war that was being fought at the same time as the genocide. As if they were morally equivalent groups, both the genocidaire government and those fighting to end the genocide were called upon by the UN, the Organisation of African Unity and others to agree to a ceasefire. They did not call on the genocidaires to stop the genocide. Had the Rwanda Patriotic Front (RPF) agreed to a ceasefire, the scale of the genocide behind government lines would have been even greater.

7. Only days after the genocide began, 2,500 Tutsi as well as Hutu opposition politicians crowded into a Kigali school known as ETO, where Belgian UN troops were billeted; at least 400 of them were children. They were seeking protection against menacing militia and government soldiers outside the compound. In the midst of the stand-off, the Belgian soldiers were ordered to depart ETO to assist in evacuating foreign nationals from the country. They did so abruptly, making no arrangements whatever for the protection of those they were safeguarding. As they moved out, the killers moved in. When the afternoon was over, all 2,500 civilians had been murdered.

8. After 10 Belgian UN soldiers were killed by Rwandan government troops the day after the Rwandan president's plane was shot down, Belgium withdrew all its troops from the UN mission. So that Belgium would not alone be blamed for scuttling UNAMIR, its government then strenuously lobbied the UN to disband the mission in its entirety.

9. Two weeks after the crisis had begun, with information about the magnitude of the genocide increasing by the day, the Security Council did come very close to shutting down UNAMIR altogether. Instead, led by the USA and the United Kingdom, it voted to decimate the mission, reducing it from 2,500 to 270.

10. After the deaths of 18 American soldiers in Somalia in October 1993, the United States decided to participate in no more UN military missions. The Clinton administration further decided that no significant UN missions were to be allowed at all, even if American troops would not be involved. Thanks mostly to the delaying tactics of the US, after 100 days of the genocide not a single reinforcement of UN troops or military supplies had reached Rwanda.

11. Bill Clinton later apologised for not doing more to stop the genocide. However, his claim that his administration had not been aware of the real situation was a lie.

12. French officials were senior advisers to both the Rwandan government and military in the years leading to the genocide, with unparalleled influence on both. Virtually until the moment the genocide began, they gave unconditional support as well as considerable arms to the Hutu elite. Throughout the 100 days and long after, French officials and officers remained hostile to the 'Anglo-Saxon' RPF, whose victory ended the genocide. To this day the French have never acknowledged their role nor apologised for it.

13. After six weeks of genocide, France, which offered no troops to the UN mission, suddenly decided to intervene in Rwanda. Within a week of the decision, Operation Turquoise was able to deploy 2,500 men with 100 armoured personnel carriers, ten helicopters, a battery of 120 mm mortars, four Jaguar fighter bombers, and eight Mirage fighters and reconnaissance planes – all for an ostensibly humanitarian operation. The French forces created a safe haven in the southwest of the country, which provided sanctuary not only to fortunate Tutsi but also to many leading Rwandan government and military officials as well as large numbers of soldiers and militia – the very Hutu Power militants who had organised and carried out the genocide. Not a single person was arrested by France for crimes against humanity. All were allowed to escape across the border into then-Zaire, entirely unrepentant and often still armed. Predictably, these genocidaires were soon launching murderous excursions back into Rwanda, beginning a cycle that led to the subsequent bloody conflict that destabilises central Africa still.

14. France long remained hostile to the post-genocide government in Rwanda and sympathetic to the previous French-speaking Hutu regime. Many of the leaders of the new government were from English-speaking Uganda and were considered the 'Anglo-Saxon' enemy by the French government. In November 1994, barely four months after the end of the genocide, Rwanda was deliberately excluded from the annual Franco-African summit hosted by France. Zaire's President Mobutu, who had been ostracised by the French government in recent years, was invited, as was Robert Mugabe, the anglophone president of anglophone Zimbabwe.

15. The Roman Catholic Church in Rwanda was the largest and most influential denomination in the country, with intimate ties to the government at all

levels. It failed to denounce the government's explicit ethnic foundations, failed to denounce its increasing use of violence against Tutsi, failed to denounce or even name the genocide, failed to apologise for the many clergy who aided and abetted the genocidaires, and to this day has never apologised for its overall role. The Pope has refused to apologise on behalf of the church as a whole.

16. Within months of the end of the genocide, relief workers and representatives of the international community in Rwanda were telling Rwandans they must 'Quit dwelling on the past and concentrate on rebuilding for the future' and insisting that 'Yes, the genocide happened, but it's time to get over it and move on.'

17. George W. Bush, during the campaign for the 2000 Republican presidential nomination, was asked by a TV interviewer what he would do as president if, 'God forbid, another Rwanda' should take place. He replied: 'We should not send our troops to stop ethnic cleansing and genocide outside our own strategic interest. I would not send US troops into Rwanda.'

18. The new Rwanda Patriotic Front government inherited a debt of close to $1 billion, some of it incurred by the previous government in genocide preparations – expanding its army and militias and buying arms. After the genocide, the RPF was obligated to repay in full the country's debt to its Western lenders.

19. Following the genocide, the World Bank was left with a $160 million programme of aid to Rwanda that it had extended to the previous government. . Even though the new government was penniless, the bank refused to activate that sum until the new government paid $9 million in interest incurred by its predecessor. A bank official told a UN representative: 'After all, we are a commercial enterprise and have to adhere to our regulations. ' The sum was eventually paid by some donors.

20. In the first nine months after the genocide, the donor community provided $1.4 billion in aid to the Hutu refugee camps in eastern Zaire and Tanzania. Since, as was universally known, genocidaires had taken over the camps, a good part of these funds went to feed and shelter them and to fund their retraining and rearming as they planned cross-border raids back into Rwanda. For Rwanda itself, while donor funds for reconstruction were generously pledged, in the first year after the genocide only $68 million was actually disbursed. To this day, Rwanda has never received reparations remotely commensurate with the damage that the international community had failed to prevent.

21. Once the genocide ended, the UN military mission was finally expanded. As UNAMIR II, it remained in Rwanda for almost two more years as a peacekeeping force, costing the UN $15 million a month. But the main challenge had become less one of peacekeeping and more one of peace-building – the recon-

struction of a totally devastated country. UNAMIR had the equipment, the skills and the will to play a major role in reviving the country's shattered structures. What it lacked was the mandate and modest funding from the Security Council to perform such a role. But UN headquarters never sought such authorisation from the Security Council, nor did the council ever initiate such a move.

22. When a UN mission leaves a country, it follows a formula to determine how much of its equipment should be left behind. UNAMIR owned much desperately needed equipment, from computers to vehicles to furniture. When the mission wrapped up in April 1996, both UN officials in Kigali and members of the Security Council urged UN headquarters to interpret the formula with maximum generosity and flexibility; they believed that 80 per cent of all non-lethal equipment should remain in Rwanda. UN headquarters announced that 93 per cent of all equipment was to be transported out of the country for storage or use elsewhere. After much pressure was applied, the UN bureaucracy decreed finally that 62 per cent of all equipment be removed.

23. So far as is known, not a single person in any government or in the UN has ever been fired or held accountable for failing to intervene in the genocide. In fact, the opposite is true. Some careers flourished in the aftermath. Several of the main actors were actually promoted. We can consider this the globalisation of impunity.

24. Despite the unanimity of every major study undertaken and in the face of the testimonies of survivors and the first-hand accounts of international humanitarian workers in Rwanda at the time, denial of the genocide persists. Deniers include Hutu Power advocates, many of them still active in Western countries, as well as lawyers and investigators working for Hutu clients at the International Criminal Tribunal for Rwanda. Denying the Rwandan genocide is the moral equivalent of denying the Holocaust.

Why We Must Never Forget
the Rwandan Genocide

Gerald Caplan
Pambazuka News 150, 1 April 2004

THOSE OF US WHO are preoccupied, even obsessed, with commemorating in 2004 the 10th anniversary of the Rwanda genocide are often taken aback when we are asked what all the fuss is about. After all, just today I received from the Holocaust Centre of Toronto an invitation to join in commemorating the 60th anniversary of the Holocaust in Hungary. Not the entire Holocaust, just the terrible Hungarian chapter. Yet memorialising the genocide in Rwanda is never taken for granted in the same way.

Is it not already ancient history? Are there not all kinds of human catastrophes that no one much bothers with? Did it not take place in faraway Africa, in an obscure country few people could find on a map? Was it not just another case of Africans killing Africans? What does it have to do with us, anyway?

These questions deserve answers, not least because some are entirely legitimate. Above all, it is fundamentally true that there would have been no genocide had some Rwandans not decided for their own selfish reasons to exterminate many other Rwandans. But once this truth is acknowledged, a powerful case for remembering Rwanda remains, and needs to be made.

The Responsibility to Remember

First, Rwanda was not just another ugly event in human history. Virtually all students of the subject agree that what happened over 100 days from April to July 1994 constituted one of the purest manifestations of genocide in our time, meeting all the criteria set down in the 1948 Geneva Convention on the Prevention and Punishment of Genocide. Genocide experts debate whether Cambodia or Srebrenica or Burundi were 'authentic' genocides; like the Holocaust and (except for the Turkish government and its apologists) the Armenian genocide of 1915, no one disagrees about Rwanda. And since genocide is universally seen as the crime of crimes, an attack not just on the actual victims but on all humanity, by definition it needs to be remembered and memorialised.

Second, it was not just another case of Africans killing Africans, or, as some clueless reporters enjoyed writing, of Hutu killing Tutsi and Tutsi killing Hutu (or Hutsi and Tutu, for all they knew or cared). The Rwandan genocide was a deliberate conspiratorial operation planned, organised and executed by a small, sophisticated, highly organised group of greedy Hutu extremists who believed their self-interest would be enhanced if every one of Rwanda's one million Tutsi were annihilated. They came frighteningly close to total success.

Third, the West has played a central role in Rwanda over the past century. Just as no person is an island and there is no such thing as a self-made man, so every nation is the synthesis of internal and external influences. This is particularly true of nations that have been colonies, where imperial forces have played a defining role. To its everlasting misfortune, Rwanda is the quintessential example of this reality. The central dynamic of Rwandan history for the past 80 years, the characteristic that allowed the genocide to be carried out, was the bitter division between Hutu and Tutsi. Yet this division was largely an artefact created by the Roman Catholic Church and the Belgian colonisers.

Instead of trying to unite all the people they found in Rwanda 100 years ago, Catholic missionaries invented an entire phoney pedigree that irreconcilably divided Rwandans into superior Tutsi and inferior Hutu. When the Belgians were given control of the country following the First World War, this contrived hierarchy served their interests well, and they proceeded to institutionalise what amounted to a racist ideology. At independence in the early 1960s, this pyramid was turned on its head, and for the next 40 years Rwanda was run as a racist Hutu dictatorship. None of this would have happened without the church and the Belgians.

The Culprits

Last, but hardly least, the 1994 genocide could have been prevented in whole or in part by some of the same external forces that shaped the country's tragic destiny. But without exception, every outside agency with the capacity to intervene failed to do so. My own list of culprits, in order of responsibility, is as follows:

- The government of France
- The Roman Catholic Church
- The government of the United States
- The government of Belgium
- The government of Britain
- The UN Secretariat.

I name the French and the church first since they both had the influence to deter the genocide plotters from launching the genocide in the first place. Rwanda was the most Christianised country in Africa and the Roman Catholics were far and away the largest Christian denomination. Catholicism was virtually the official state religion. Catholic officials had enormous influence at both the elite and the grassroots level, which they consistently failed to use to protest against the government's overtly racist policies and practices. Indeed, the church gave the government moral authority. Once the genocide began, Catholic leaders in the main refused to condemn the government, never used the word genocide, and many individual priests and nuns actually aided the genocidaires.

Rwanda was a French-speaking country, and France replaced Belgium as the key foreign presence. When the RPF, a rebel group of English-speaking Tutsi refugees from Uganda, invaded Rwanda in 1990, the French military flew in to save the day for the Hutu government. For the following several years, right to the very moment the genocide began, French officials had enormous influence with both the Rwandan government and army. They failed completely to use that leverage to insist that the government curtail its racist policies and propaganda, stop the increasing massacres, end the widespread human rights abuses, and disband the death squads and death lists.

Two months after the genocide began, a French intervention force created a safe haven in the southwest of the country through which they allowed genocidaire leaders and killers, fleeing from the advancing RPF, to escape across the border into Zaire. From Zaire they began an insurgency back into Rwanda with the purpose of 'finishing the job'. Eventually this led to the Rwandans invading Zaire/Congo to suppress the insurgency, which in turn soon led to the vicious wars in the Congo and the subsequent appalling cost in human lives throughout eastern Congo.

Once the genocide was launched after 6 April 1994, the American government, steadfastly backed by the British government, were primarily responsible for the failure of the UN Security Council to reinforce its puny mission to Rwanda. Under no circumstances were these governments prepared to budge. The commander of the UN force – UNAMIR – repeatedly pleaded for reinforcements, and was repeatedly turned down.

Two weeks into the genocide, the Security Council voted to reduce UNAMIR from 2500 to 270 men – an act almost impossible to believe 10 years later. Six weeks into the genocide, as credible reports of hundreds of thousands of deaths became commonplace and the reality of a full-blown genocide became undeniable, the Security Council voted finally to send some 4,500 troops to Rwanda. Several contingents of African troops were put on standby, but deliberate stalling tactics by the USA and Britain meant that by the end of the genocide, when the Tutsi-led rebels were sworn in as the new government on 19 July, not a single reinforcement of soldiers or material ever reached Rwanda. This was one of the darkest moments in the history of the United Nations.

As for Belgium, notwithstanding the racist attitudes and colonial behaviour of its soldiers, their contingent was the backbone of UNAMIR. When ten Belgian soldiers were murdered by Rwandan government troops on the very first morning of the genocide, the Brussels government immediately decided to withdraw the remainder of its forces and to lobby the Security Council to suspend the entire Rwandan mission. Its motive was simple: they did not want to be seen as the sole party undermining UNAMIR. At the Security Council, of course, it found eager allies.

The role of the UN Secretariat is somewhat ambiguous. To a large extent, its failure to support the pleas of its own UNAMIR force commander reflected its lack of capacity to cope with yet another crisis combined with its understanding that the US and Britain would not alter their intransigent positions. Still, there were many occasions when the secretariat failed to convey to the full Security Council the dire situation in Rwanda, and many opportunities when it failed to speak up publicly in the hope of influencing world opinion.

A Multitude of Betrayals

It is not far-fetched to say that the world has betrayed Rwanda countless times since its first confrontation with Europeans in the mid-1890s. This account has presented several of these betrayals before and during the genocide: by the Catholic Church, by the Belgian colonial power, by the French neo-colonial power, by the international community.

To exacerbate further this shameful record, we need to look at the past decade. First, the concept that the world owed serious reparations to a devastated Rwanda for its failure to prevent the genocide has been a total non-starter.

Second, there has been precious little accountability by the international community for its failure to prevent. The French government and the Roman Catholic Church have to this moment refused to acknowledge the slightest responsibility for their roles or to apologise for any of their gross errors of commission or omission. President Bill Clinton and Secretary-General Kofi Annan have both apologised for their failure to offer protection, but have both falsely blamed insufficient information; in fact what was lacking was not knowledge – the situation was universally understood – but political will and sufficient national interest. No one has ever quit their jobs in protest against their government's or their organisation's failure to intervene to save close to one million innocent civilian lives.

Those We Must Not Forget

Finally, the very existence of the genocide has largely disappeared from the public and media's consciousness. This is the latest betrayal. Marginalised during the genocide, Rwanda's calamity is now largely forgotten except for Rwandans themselves and small clusters of non-Rwandans who have had some connection with the country or specialise in genocide prevention. That is why I founded the Remembering Rwanda movement in July 2001. I had four targets for remembering: the innocent victims; the survivors, many of whom live in deplorable conditions with few resources to tend to their physical or psychological needs; the perpetrators, most of whom remain free and unrepentant scattered around Africa, Europe and parts of North America; and the so-called 'bystanders', the unholy sextet named earlier. Rather than being passive witnesses, as the word 'bystander' implies, all were active in their failure to intervene to stop the massacres, and all remain unaccountable to this day. It is time the Rwandan genocide is treated with the concern and attention it so grievously earned.

Towards Justice and Reconciliation in Rwanda: Taking Stock

Eugenia Zorbas
Pambazuka News 150, 1 April 2004

JUSTICE AND RECONCILIATION are concepts difficult to define, let alone achieve. What may seem 'just' for a community or a country may be very unjust for the individual victim. There seems to be a tension between reconciliation, implying a kind of moral compromise, and justice in the strict, Western, prosecutorial sense it is usually used.

In the wake of violence on a societal scale, finding the right balance between justice and reconciliation, or between retribution and forgiveness, is an extremely delicate process and this is all the more so in cases of genocide. In the Great Lakes region, where today's oppressors tend to perceive themselves as yesterday's victims, justice and reconciliation become even more subjective and difficult goals.

In Rwanda, the RPF-dominated Government of National Unity is prioritising, as its name implies, the reconciliation of its citizens chiefly through a prosecutorial (trial-based) approach. However, since 1998 there has been a recognition among the highest government echelons that working with a penal and legal system that is completely overstretched – at the beginning of 2003, there were an estimated 115,000 prisoners in Rwandan jails and communal lockups (*cachots*) – will require some innovative thinking and a move away from the 'white man's' standards of justice. This is why the much talked about *gacaca* traditional conflict resolution mechanism was adapted and revived.

Moves Towards Justice – Arrests, Courts, Trials and the Legacy of Genocide

Despite the opening of a press office in Rwanda and the establishing of some important precedents in international criminal law, the International Criminal Tribunal for Rwanda's (ICTR) contribution to justice and reconciliation within the country is very limited.

Domestically, the ICTR's work remains virtually unknown and when it is, the tribunal's reputation may have been irreparably damaged by early scandals regarding endemic corruption and bureaucratic inefficiency.

The tribunal's relationship with the government itself has been a tormented one; the ICTR's mandate covers the period of January to December 1994, during which RPF soldiers allegedly carried out several massacres. The ICTR's insistence that these crimes should be investigated led to moral outrage from the RPF leadership, accusing the court of putting the RPF on the same level as the genocidaires.

Rwanda's national courts operate in parallel with the ICTR. From having a rumoured 10 lawyers left in the country, no equipment, damaged buildings and no money to pay their staff in 1994, the national courts had by early 2004 tried upwards of 5,500 individuals. Though many of the early trials were severely flawed, the national legal system's performance arguably did more to restore some kind of confidence that (some) perpetrators were being brought to trial – by comparison, the ICTR and its hundreds of staff and multi-million dollar annual budgets had at the beginning of 2004 completed 18 cases and arrested 66 individuals.

Even at this accelerated pace, it was thought that the Rwandan formal judicial system would require more than a century to process the hundred thousand plus detainees. The adaptation of a traditional, grassroots conflict resolution mechanism – the *gacaca* tribunals – represents an affordable and expedient alternative. After a pilot phase, deemed a success by the government, *gacaca* courts are due to open across the country in 2004.

Innovative Thinking – Justice and Reconciliation Combined through the Gacaca Courts

The goal of *gacaca* is to promote reconciliation through providing a platform for victims to express themselves, encouraging acknowledgements and apologies from the perpetrators, facilitating the coming together of both victims and perpetrators every week on the grass. *Gacaca* courts are also empowered to hand down sentences that include community work schemes that can directly benefit the most destitute families of victims. While *gacaca* is a potential source of 'truth' on how the genocide was implemented, its provisions for confessions and guilt pleas represent one of *gacaca* 's most cited shortcomings.

Under these provisions, if someone confesses before being denounced, he or she is liable for a substantial decrease in the length of the sentence. Importantly, confessions are only acceptable if they include the incrimination of one's co-conspirators.

Some argue that this system of confessions creates rife conditions for vendetta-settling. Others estimate that an additional 200,000 people could see themselves imprisoned for genocide-related crimes. Others still say that intimidation of potential witnesses is widespread in the countryside in particular, where perpetrators presumably far outnumber survivors. Lastly, participation in *gacaca* is mandatory, implying that subsistence farmers and petty traders must give up a day of labour per week (on average) with no compensation in cash or kind; this mandatory character has fomented some resentment about *gacaca* .

Despite what may seem like insurmountable problems, *gacaca* represents the only workable solution for bringing those responsible for atrocities to trial promptly. It is difficult to judge the public perception of the *gacaca* tribunals. Presumably, Rwanda's tens of thousands of prisoners would favour a system that would help speed up their hearings. Also presumably, survivors would want to see perpetrators punished, and in the spirit of 'restorative' justice, may welcome replacing long prison sentences with more useful community work schemes. Having said that, the genocide survivor organisations remain extremely apprehensive of *gacaca* .

The real test will be when the tribunals begin working nationwide this year. If judges are incompetent or biased, if communities conspire to silence a witness, or if *gacaca* is used as a means to settle scores, neither justice nor reconciliation will be served.

Other Measures Promoting Reconciliation: the National Unity and Reconciliation Commission (NURC)

Since its inception in 1999, the NURC has organised conferences and work-shops on the theme of unity and reconciliation, culminating in two national summits, where Rwandans from all levels of society were represented. The NURC has also held workshops for segments of the population attending 'civic re-education' or 'solidarity' camps (ingandos) – such as provisionally released prisoners and demobilised soldiers (from the national army as well as from former Armed Forces of Rwanda (FAR) and Interahamwe combatants repatriated from the Democratic Republic of Congo (DRC)). Despite the NURC's all-encompassing mandate, it is still perceived as being an instrument of the central authorities and as being too 'vertical' in its activities, not doing enough grassroots work on 'the hills'.

Collective Memory

Monuments and memorials are institutional embodiments of collective memory and as such, part of the reconciliation process. In Rwanda, genocide memorials pepper the country and new ones continue to be created. Often memorials are housed in churches – sites of many group massacres. Another institution created to foster collective memory is the national day of mourning for the victims of the genocide. The month of April more generally is consid-ered to be a month of mourning and parties or celebrations of any kind are discouraged.

It is insightful to reflect on how different groups interpret these memorials and annual mourning periods. Some Rwandans consider the national day of mourning in particular as an obstacle to unity perhaps implicitly taking the view that forgetting the past is the best way to 'move on'. But if those who cannot remember the past are condemned to repeat it, then memory may be the best safeguard against a recurrence of violence. Others see the annual periods of mourning as a 'Tutsi affair', claiming that the commemorations are only for Tutsi victims, the moderate Hutu who perished in 1994 having been forgotten. They touch upon an important issue, to which we now turn.

Victors' Justice? Are the Hutu being Collectively Stigmatised?

There is a real danger that the RPF are, or will come to be, perceived as a party run by, and for, les Ougandais – an inner circle of anglophone Tutsi refugees born in Uganda. In light of this, and despite the official party line that all citizens of Rwanda are Banyarwanda ('not Tutsi, nor Hutu, nor Twa') and therefore equal before the law, many Hutu may feel that the justice being meted out is a form of victor's justice.

The official refusal to recognise alleged (Hutu) victims of RPF atrocities in Rwanda and eastern DRC in particular buttress such feelings. And because the national courts – and presumably this will hold true for the *gacaca* tribunals and the ICTR as well – are focusing 'punishment' on the Hutu, the judiciary's impartiality is also called into question. (Similar accusations of the International Criminal Tribunal for Yugoslavia being a form of victors' justice ring true to the ears of an important proportion of Serb public opinion.)

This resentment of 'Tutsi impunity' is visible in, for example, the joke that the ICTR, whose French acronym is the TPIR, should be renamed the TPIH – le tribunal pénal international des Hutus. By leaving these allegations unresolved, the RPF leaves itself open to the possibility that political opponents will inflate the size and nature of RPF abuses.

Lastly, the unspoken assumption that all Hutu who opposed the genocide were killed in 1994, and thus that the Hutu who were in the country during those months and alive today are morally, if not legally, responsible also undermines justice and national reconciliation: can such a project succeed on the basis of such distrust?

Poverty

In 2002, Rwanda's GDP grew by 9.7 per cent, ranking it among the top three performers in sub-Saharan Africa for that year. Yet according to government figures, approximately 60 per cent of Rwandans live on less than US$1 per day and the United Nations Development Programme ranked Rwanda 162nd out of 173 countries in its 2002 Human Development Index.

It is difficult to overstate the magnitude of poverty in Rwanda. In a country where 94 per cent of the population live in rural areas, there is also a 'mental' distance between the urban elite in Kigali and the peasants 'on the hills'.

Rural Rwanda has not been actively engaged in justice and reconciliation debates – though this may change with the *gacaca* tribunals. As in South Africa, where victims of apartheid are calling for reparations for the legacy of 'economic apartheid', the most destitute genocide widows and orphans – for whom the legacy of 1994 is also, in a very immediate sense, socio-economic – have been benefiting from the Fond National pour l'Assistance aux Rescapés du Génocide (the FARG) created in 1998.

Importantly, this assistance goes only to Tutsi, as the genocide was against the Tutsi and so they are the only ones to qualify as survivors (rescapés). This helps reinforce the perception of victors' justice, mentioned earlier, among Hutu families that may have also lost family members or had property confiscated or destroyed.

A direct economic consequence of *gacaca* , if it is successful in alleviating the burden on the penal system, will be that thousands of (Hutu) families will no longer have to struggle to feed potentially productive members of their family that have been in jail for up to ten years, with an unknown proportion of them having been falsely accused to begin with.

If grinding poverty contributed to the ease with which the peasant masses where mobilised for the genocidal project, then ensuring that rural Rwanda is not excluded from the benefits of economic growth will not only serve the obvious purpose of improving the quality of life of millions, it will also help prevent the despair, humiliation and feelings of exclusion that contribute to the cycles of violence in the Great Lakes region and to the dynamics of genocide in Rwanda in 1994.

Debating Rwanda's Histories

A telling indicator for how much Rwanda has moved towards national reconciliation is the fact that since 1994, no history lessons have been taught in Rwandan schools. There has thus been no debate in the public domain about why the 1994 genocide happened. This is important because one cannot say much about the prospects of reconciliation without first reflecting on exactly what it is that gives rise to demands for it. What motivated such large parts of the population to participate? If some were coerced into killing, why were some others such zealous, innovative and cruel killers?

The Government of National Unity's project of creating an all-inclusive Rwandan nationalism around the 'Banyarwanda' label relies on achieving a broad-based consensus among Rwandans that justice has been served. Can this be achieved without a reconciliation with history?

Conclusion

Rwandans have come a long way since 1994. Above and beyond their individual struggles with their very personal experiences of genocide, Rwandans have had to contend with periods of renewed insecurity in the north-west of the country, worrying escalations of violence in Burundi (the Rwandan 'Siamese twin'), a war in neighbouring DRC, severe deterioration of relations with Uganda, the repatriation of some two million refugees since 1994, and a general loss of interest in the international media and the international community.

Perhaps of more immediate relevance for the 94 per cent of Rwandans who live in rural areas, pockets of droughts and food insecurity have been periodic and the very real daily struggle for survival continues unabated. In this context of grinding poverty, 'justice and reconciliation' perversely become a luxury. Projects to foster unity need to become more relevant to rural Rwandans in order to become more effective. Only then can Rwandans afford to start thinking about justice and reconciliation. The government also needs to recognise that a vibrant and independent civil society and media is not a potential threat but a sustainable, countervailing force should there be attempts to foment a new cycle of violence, for which the Great Lakes region is tragically infamous.

Safe Sanctuary?
The Role of the Church in Genocide

Camille Karangwa
Pambazuka News 150, 1 April 2004

1994 WAS THE MOST tragic year in the history of Rwanda as the country experienced a genocide that swept away more than a million Tutsi. This was a carefully conceived, planned and carried out genocide, as proven by its record death toll. The world was shocked.

To this day, people still wonder what the causes of this slaughter were. Some even point at the church of Rwanda, in this instance the Catholic Church, which was then the most representative and the most influential in the country. Indeed, it represents more than 60 per cent of the population and had for a long time boasted the moral high ground, which could have been used to curb this disaster.

The question is then to know whether the church tried to make use of its influence or if, rather, it failed to fulfil its duties, as several analyses seem to confirm. As we commemorate the tenth anniversary of those tragic events, it is important to sort the events out and draw out the responsibilities of the parties. This contribution is based on personal experience as well as various investigations in this field.

As soon as they arrived in Rwanda in the 1900s, the first settlers and white missionaries found a well-structured country ruled by the Mwami. Even though the power was concentrated in the hands of the Tutsi minority, the missionaries did not deign to protest against this situation.

They even found it natural and went as far as asserting that the Tutsi were intellectually superior to the Hutus and were the only ones able to rule the country. They invented the Hamite myth that said the Tutsi were actually white men with a black skin. They developed typologies that were probably influenced by the evolutionist theories that were fashionable in those days.

The schools they opened were almost exclusively reserved for Tutsi children. They also made an obvious effort to convert to their religion numerous children from the aristocracy.

For decades, the Belgian colonial power therefore relied on the Tutsi, stockbreeders more akin to a cast than to an ethnic group, to rule the country and dominate the Hutu farmers, by far the largest group in the country.

But in the late 1950s, when the Tutsi elite started to wave claims of independence and the Mwami contemplated appealing to the United Nations, both Belgium and the church decided to defend the democratic rights of the Hutu majority, embodied by Grégoire Kayibanda, former secretary of the bishop of

Kabgayi and founder of the Party for the Promotion of the Hutu People (ParmeHutu).

The Catholic Church actively involved itself with the first Hutu revolutionaries, often former pupils of its schools, and denounced the social injustice it had once promoted. A letter from Mgr André Perraudin, then bishop of Kabgayi, which was published to mark Lent 1959, agrees in many ways with the broad outlines of the Hutu manifesto launched on 24 March 1959.

In this pastoral letter entitled 'Super Omnia Caritas', the prelate declared that the country's resources as well as its political and judicial powers were largely in the hands of people of one race only. He predicted imminent bloodshed if the situation remained unchanged.

After a referendum – carefully guided by the Belgian colonial power and the church – had installed a republic, thus exiling the last king, the Tutsi were stripped of their power, evicted from their lands and physically threatened. Hundred of thousands of them sought refuge in neighbouring countries, notably Uganda.

Throughout the next three decades, the church was perfectly aware of human rights violations but did not lift a finger. It gave its blessing to the abuses of power of the young republic and got further involved in social activities. This conniving silence was indubitably interpreted by the rulers as a sign of support.

Grégoire Kayibanda, the first president, was close to catholic circles and had clergymen among his counsellors, specifically his grace André Perraudin, who was seen as his spiritual father. The first republic displayed notorious intransigence towards the exiles and exercised undisputed power under cover of majority democracy. Instead of grasping this opportunity to reassure the royalists and the Tutsi in general, the government was driven by feelings of revenge.

Every time an attack was launched by the exiles, the Tutsi paid for it with their blood. This was the case in the years 1961–62. The president himself said that such action by the exiles endangered the lives of their brothers who remained in the country. The Catholic Church, present across the country, did nothing to stop the mass killings and went on working hand in hand with the government until it collapsed.

Major-General Juvénal Habyarimana, then an army staff officer, seized power in 1973. The church, ignoring this illegal seizure of power, gave full support to the new regime. Indeed, when the MRND, the party of the president and future grassroots of the infamous Interahamwe , was founded in 1975, some religious leaders became active members. A system of ethnically based quotas introduced by the government was also applied in some religious schools. The same racial discrimination was applied in the choice of bishops.

At no point did the church raise its voice to denounce the dictatorship of the

MRND and its policy of exclusion. Those who dared to criticise it, such as Mrs Félicula Nyiramutarambirwa and father Silvio Sindambiwe, have paid dearly for their views.

The church also took an active part in party propaganda. Certain homilies often sounded like popular meetings. After the attack of the FPR rebels in 1990, the government did a mock attack on Kigali and arbitrarily arrested thousands of Tutsi. The church again missed the opportunity to distance itself from the government.

Mass killings like those in Bugesera and Bigogwe, which were aimed at Tutsi, did not change anything. When it was time to contribute to the war effort, the church was more than eager. This connivance between the church and the state continued until the genocide and even its eruption in April 1994 did not change the position of the church. The first massacres on the morning of 7 April took place in Kigali at Remera Christus Centre where priests, seminarians on holiday and other visitors were killed.

The behaviour of these men of God in those crucial moments is revolting to say the least; some of them even handed over their own colleagues to the executioners; others refused to shelter in their parishes the refugees flocking there; and others offered to hide them – and then brought in the Interahamwe.

This was the case of the two Benedictine nuns, Consolate Mukangango and Julienne Mukabutera, who used to run the convent in Sovu and collaborated with the killers to the point where they provided them with the petrol that was to set ablaze the building where 500 Tutsi were hiding. They have recently been sentenced by a Brussels court to 15 and 12 years respectively.

The case of minister Elizaphan Ntakirutimana should not be ignored either. At more than 70 years of age, he was the minister of the Adventist Church of the Seventh Day in Mugonero, Kibuye. The International Criminal Tribunal for Rwanda recently sentenced him to 10 years in jail. Instead of answering the cries for help of his Tutsi colleagues, who relied on his influence in the area and begged him to intervene, he sent in the militia men while he himself drove killers to different massacre sites in his own vehicle.

These are only a few examples among thousands. Indeed, other religious people are still held prisoners or are wanted by justice. Churches, once seen as sanctuaries, were turned into slaughterhouses. The churches of Nyarubuye, Cyahinda, Karama, and Kibeho have become remnants of this sad episode. Men of God, who once were seen as role models and enjoyed an indisputable moral authority, did not know how to use it to save the lives of innocents. Their silence and their participation in those fatal moments brought, in the eyes of the killers, a kind of 'acknowledgement and legitimacy' to the ignoble acts.

Priests and ministers have always been considered upright, wise and even saintly. Their attitudes clearly had an enormous influence on their congregations. The highest hierarchy, doubtlessly closer to the government, did not use its influence to bring political officials to their senses. Five weeks after the genocide had started, four Catholic bishops and a few ministers of the Protestant Church published a document, which was, to say the least, half-hearted, in which they called on both parties, the then government and the RPF troops, to stop the massacres. The word genocide was not even suggested.

When the government fled the fights and settled in the centre of the country, the bishops abandoned their dioceses to follow it. They later did the same thing when, after the defeat, they scattered into Zaire, Tanzania, Cameroon ad elsewhere.

The attitude of the church at the end of the genocide was not one of great courage. Some of its members went into revisionism, others tried to cover up the crimes of their colleagues. To this day, the church as an institution has never apologised for this very serious failure.

The church at all levels, from the Vatican to the episcopal council of Rwanda, is content with saying that the crimes of some of their people have nothing to do with the church as a whole, thus seeming to ignore that these people were educated, ordained and appointed by the church.

Furthermore, those who ran towards them did so because they saw them as representatives of the church. This is not to deny the church's social and economic contribution, but here it failed seriously. Whether one admits it or not, it played an active part in the misery that has befallen Rwanda and has lost some of its credibility. Not to acknowledge this would be foolish.

Children of Rwanda:
Legacy of the Genocide,
the Future of Rwanda

Sara Rakita
Pambazuka News 150, 1 April 2004

RWANDA'S CHILDREN have seen the worst of humanity. Ten years after a group of politicians set in motion a genocide in an attempt to retain power, the devastating consequences for those who were left behind are unmistakable.

Traditional protective structures for children including family networks, the judicial system, and the education system were decimated. As a result, children – many of whom survived unspeakable atrocities – are still the victims of systematic human rights violations day in and day out.

Thousands have been arbitrarily arrested and denied prompt access to justice. Hundreds of thousands more living around the country have been abused, exploited for their labour, exploited for their property, or denied the right to education. Thousands have migrated to city streets in an effort to escape these abuses only to find themselves in even more precarious conditions. In the face of the daunting challenge of rebuilding a society devastated by war, poverty, and AIDS, protecting their rights has been sidelined. But this does not do Rwanda's children justice.

Those who planned and executed the genocide of 1994 violated children's rights on an unprecedented scale. Children were raped, tortured, and slaughtered along with adults in massacre after massacre around the country. Carrying their genocidal logic to its absurd conclusion, they even targeted children for killing – to exterminate the 'big rats', they said, one must also kill the 'little rats'.

Countless thousands of children were murdered in the genocide and war. Many of those who managed to escape death had feared for their own lives; they survived rape or torture, witnessed the killing of family members, hid under corpses, or saw children killing other children. Some of these children – now adolescents – say they do not care whether they live or die.

Perhaps the most devastating legacy of the genocide and war is the sheer number of children left on their own, who live in precarious conditions and are extremely vulnerable to abuse and exploitation. On Rwanda's green hills, up to 400,000 children – 10 per cent of Rwandan children – struggle to survive without one or both parents.

Children who were orphaned in the genocide or in war, children orphaned by AIDS, and children whose parents are in prison on charges of genocide, alike, are in desperate need of protection. Many Rwandans have exhibited enormous generosity in caring for orphans or other needy children.

Yet, because so many Rwandans are living in extreme poverty themselves, to some, vulnerable children are worth only their labour and their property. Foster families have taken needy children in, but some have also exploited them as domestic servants, denied them education, and unscrupulously taken over their family's land.

These children, often suffering the effects of trauma, have nowhere to turn and they know no other fate. Traditional societal networks – severely eroded by poverty, the HIV/AIDS epidemic, and, not least, the consequences of the genocide and war – have failed them.

Thousands of children have migrated to city streets to fend for themselves. There, they live in abysmal conditions, suffer poor health and hygiene, and face a near constant risk of harassment by law enforcement officials and arbitrary arrest.

As recently as February 2004, municipal authorities continued to brutally round children up by force in an effort to 'clean the streets' before heads of state came to attend the historic New Partnership for Africa's Development (NEPAD) summit. It seems the presence of unkempt street children is inconsistent with the image of the city with the newest Intercontinental Hotel. Girls living on the streets are frequently raped, sometimes even by law enforcement officials, yet few of those responsible have been prosecuted.

Although they garner less sympathy, children who took part in the genocide are also victims. Some 5,000 people were arrested on charges that they committed crimes of genocide before they reached the age of 18. Their rights were first violated when adults recruited, manipulated, or incited them to participate in atrocities, and have been violated again by the Rwandan justice system.

One boy who confessed and was convicted of genocide said he had been given a choice of killing his sister's children or being killed himself. He was 16 years old at the time. Large numbers of these children were in fact arrested unjustly.

Another boy, arrested at age 13 after the genocide, confessed to having killed in order to escape torture, although he now maintains that his confession was false. He had just witnessed other detainees being tortured at the hands of Rwandan government soldiers. His father, among others, had died as a result of torture the night before. He and a thousand others who were younger than 14 in 1994, and thus too young to be held criminally responsible under Rwandan law, were freed after being transferred from detention facilities to re-education camps in 2000 and 2001. The government had been promising to release them since 1995.

As many as 4,000 children who were between 14 and 18 years old during the genocide continued to languish in overcrowded prisons until last year, and some may still be detained. Their adolescence is gone. Despite repeated, hollow promises that their cases would be given priority within the over-burdened justice system, they have been subjected to the worst of a bad situation.

Juvenile defendants have been tried at an even slower rate than adults. Few have enjoyed the right to adequate legal counsel and other due process protections guaranteed under Rwandan and international law. A few hundred, for whom prosecutors had not conducted investigations or made case files during their years of imprisonment, were provisionally released in 2001 after their neighbours cleared them of wrongdoing in public meetings.

Ironically, now that the government has finally made some progress in dealing with the massive failures of the justice system – including organising *gacaca* courts to deal with the bulk of genocide cases and releasing most of those who had been below the age of criminal responsibility and those who confessed – it has become even harder to draw attention to the plight of young adults who remain in detention for crimes they allegedly committed as children, especially those who proclaim their innocence. 'We feel that justice has left us,' one of them said.

The international community has provided billions of dollars to assist in the reconstruction and rehabilitation of Rwanda and continues to donate tens of millions of dollars each year. Yet inadequate resources have been devoted to address the desperate needs of child protection. And there have been insufficient efforts to ensure that money earmarked for the protection of children is actually used for that purpose.

The majority of Rwandan children have been victims of armed conflict. Thousands have been arbitrarily arrested and denied prompt access to justice. Hundreds of thousands more living around the country have been abused, exploited for their labour, exploited for their property, or denied the right to education. Thousands have migrated to city streets in an effort to escape these abuses only to find themselves even worse off.

Rwanda can and must do more to protect their rights. The government has embraced international standards on children's rights and has passed a strong law on child protection. But words are not enough. Ten years of promises to protect their rights has meant little in practice for vulnerable children. We must not remain complacent while so many children continue to suffer. The future of Rwanda depends on it.

Why? How?
Searching for Answers
in the Diaspora

Vincent Gasana
Pambazuka News 150, 1 April 2004

APRIL MARKS THE TENTH year since the genocide that left a million dead in Rwanda. There will be many acts of remembrance, public and private. Many will be intensely personal. There will be those who wish that we would all forget, that the whole thing would just go away. Many of these will be in prisons in Rwanda, Tanzania or hiding out in capitals around the world. The feelings and reactions about the date will be as varied as the individuals who dared not look away.

Much more complex is the reaction of Africans in the diaspora. For them as for many others around the world, it was difficult to know what to make of the scarcely believable horror that forced itself on their lives through television sets. The shock of what was taking place before the world's eyes froze most people's analytical faculties. In some sense, the whole world participated in the genocide in Rwanda. Thanks to the miracle of television, we all went along as spectators. Unwilling, reluctant spectators, horrified and yet gripped by the terrifying depths to which human souls could sink. As people watched help-lessly, representative governments, chiefly Great Britain, the United States and of course France, worked overtime to ensure that what was happening in Rwanda was not called genocide, because then they would have been obliged to intervene. For them this technicality was all-important.

And so a more convenient, comforting description gained currency in news-rooms. The world was informed that what was taking place in Rwanda was 'tribal killings'. It was an Old Faithful that never fails to satisfy the questions what and why whenever a conflict in Africa degenerates to such an appalling extent that it forces itself on the attention of a wider world that would rather focus its attentions elsewhere. For most people watching, this line provided some comfort in that it at least provided a context into which they could put the abominable crimes they were being forced to witness.

The line provided a way in which they could distance themselves from what was being done. Such savagery could have nothing to do with them. It could only be done by that 'other', the 'other' that did not have their sensibilities.

The irony is almost chilling; this is how the organisers of the genocide spoke of their eventual victims. The Batutsi were 'snakes' (Rwandans' horror of snakes should be understood in a biblical sense: an insidious and perfidious killer) that not only could but should be mercilessly destroyed. They were not to be thought of like other people, they were different, they were the other. Upwards of 300,000 children were killed in the genocide, although 'kill' is too kind and innocuous a word for how their young lives were ended before they had hardly begun. The leaders of the genocide simply put the rhetorical question to the Bahutu population, 'When you hunt for a snake, do you spare its young?' Such reasoning was designed to make even infanticide acceptable.

For Africans in the diaspora, there could be no such easy comforts. The people committing such unspeakable crimes were no aliens that could be disowned, they were just like them. Diaspora Africans could not distance themselves from the perpetrators of the genocide by seeing them as the other – the other that were not like them, the other that were capable of such inhumanity that they themselves found so abhorrent. They had to endure that terrible unease that must come with witnessing a human being just like you descend into such depths of inhumanity that could not be imagined.

The dictionary description of the word 'empathy' is the power to enter into the feeling and spirit of others. The trouble with empathy is that while it leads one to identify and wish to protect and comfort the victim, it cannot protect itself from the horror of the knowledge that the perpetrator is a human being just like oneself. How could the minds and hearts that could just as easily be theirs, not only perpetrate, or even contemplate such an abomination? How could the eyes that could easily be theirs bear to look upon such evil?

As it should have done, the Rwandan genocide challenged the assumptions for the basis of our own humanity. If a general observation can be made about how Africans in the diaspora responded to this most profound and personal of challenges, it is that above and beyond the abhorrence that gripped every decent human being, they felt it incumbent upon them to help in some way. And many did. In Britain, a number of organisations both large and small collected money and material for Rwanda, long before the call to respond to the crisis begun to be heard commonly in the mainstream.

A number of individuals organised fund-raising events. This was particularly true of those in the media. A number of well-known professionals exploited their celebrity status and managed to bring together a number of pop stars and other entertainers for fundraising events. The speed with which this was done was surprisingly impressive and for the few Rwandans then living in the United Kingdom (UK) profoundly touching.

The diaspora community in the UK is relatively small, powerless and lacks any real organised unity. It was for instance notable that while they were organising events for Rwanda, holding meetings, talks and seminars about Rwanda, neither the individuals nor the organisations involved had any awareness that there existed a Rwandan community in their midst.

While they talked of the need to show support and solidarity with their Rwandan brethren, they had no idea that they could share these feelings and deliver these messages face to face in the same city. Conversely, the tiny Rwandan community in the UK stoically continued to plough a lonely furrow, doing all it could to support people back home. The community never realised that less than three-quarters of an hour's drive away, people who thought of them as brothers and sisters were almost desperate for an opportunity to help. With this state of affairs it was therefore most impressive that so many were galvanised into action so quickly and so effectively.

There was, however, another side to this general picture. In Britain, after the initial shock of the first images from Rwanda, one of the determining factors in black people's response to the harrowing events in Rwanda was the extent of their identification with Africans in Africa and Africa itself. This identification or lack of it is in turn influenced by their respective backgrounds. The majority of people of African descent in the West are descendants of Africans that were forcibly removed from Africa during the slave trade.

From the moment of capture, these Africans were no longer treated as human beings. Once in the Americas or the Caribbean, those that survived the slave ships were soon deprived of everything that any human being takes for granted. They were stripped of their identity, even their names were take away and replaced with those of the slave owners. 'Forget you are African, remember you are black' was drummed into their beings, often with whips. To be African was to be a person with a heritage, a family, a name. It was to belong. To be black was to be a subspecies, a beast of burden. For good measure, the idea of Africa was depicted as a dark primitive place from which the slaves should be grateful to have been delivered.

Over centuries, this notion has been burned into the psyche of many people of African descent. It has lain dormant ready to be triggered by any occurrence or happening that might lead to self-awareness or self-analysis. It is an enduring intellectual and psychological war in which many diaspora African scholars and activists have been engaged for centuries. For many black people whose view of Africa and Africans have been shaped by this outlook, the Rwandan genocide, like other conflicts in Africa, are no more than the expected atavistic struggles in a modern age. This was a view held by a large minority within the African diaspora.

It is a view that has been termed 'the internalisation of racism' by informed opinion within the African diaspora. Such thinking, or perhaps more accurately, such feelings were by no means restricted to diaspora Africans whose ancestors had gone through the slave trade. While they are burdened by what has been called a 'slave mentality', many Africans still on the continent or who have relatively recently become part of the African diaspora, can be said to be burdened with a similar mentality, which we may term a 'colonial mentality'.

And this too came to the fore during the genocide. A veteran journalist of Cameroonian origin, whom it might be unfair to name, was interviewed by one of the major television news networks and his responses were revealing. He was offended by events in Rwanda and Burundi, he said, because they were responsible for perpetuating Africa's image in the West as savage and uncivilised. He irritably opined that these countries should refrain from making the rest of the continent look bad.

A million people had been killed in ways that would defy the most depraved imagination and yet for this senior African journalist, the deepest injury was to the image of Africa, the deepest worry, withdrawal of approval from the West. His was by no means a minority view. The former Secretary General to the United Nations Boutros Ghali was clearly of the same mind, when he visited Rwanda and complained of the smell from the dead. It is a view shared by Africans of a certain generation for whom the West's view of itself as the arbiter of civilisation has become a deeply ingrained belief. For them Africa is indeed the 'Dark Continent'.

Small Pan-African groups on the fringe in London had anticipated these feelings and had begun to rail against them long before they had been expressed in response to the genocide. For them the genocide was just another battleground against the colonial and slave mentalities. They automatically spoke of the Rwandan conflict as a colonial legacy, anxious to pre-empt and counter feelings of African insecurity and inferiority. They were more right than they imagined. Ethnic divide in Rwanda is a recent political construction, which grew from the seeds sown by German and later Belgian authorities. True as this may be, however, one is still faced with the fact that it was Rwandans who first accepted alien views of themselves, abandoned their own civilisations and massacred over a million of their compatriots.

When the first European arrivals from Germany arrived in Rwanda and espoused such fantasist ideas that the Batutsi were a different, finer race from the Bahutu, many from the two main ethnic groups did not challenge this view. Instead a number of earlier Batutsi and Bahutu intellectuals took up these ideas. It was these ideas that were repeated in the first massacres against the Batutsi in the 1950s and 1960s, during which hundreds of thousands died. It is these same ideas that were heard again in 1994.

There can be no rational explanation for the Rwandan genocide or any other genocide for that matter. None the less, when human beings are visited by such overwhelming disasters, they try to seek comfort in asking why and how. From within the African diaspora, there was and continues to be a collective chorus of why and how. They need, want and demand an explanation.

However there is no explanation for genocide. Why did the Nazis murder six million Jewish souls? Could even the Nazis say why? The best that can be done for Africans in the diaspora, who ask why, is to explain the circumstances and conditions surrounding the genocide. As for why they were committed, it is for every human being to answer that. Information may help and much needs to be done to provide it. A black American acquaintance asked me where I came from and when I said Rwanda, he asked me whether it was in South America. Most people know more about Rwanda now of course, but not much more.

Many diaspora Africans have done and are doing much to increase under-standing: programme makers, journalists and writers like Jack Mapanji from Malawi – who offered a poem in response to what he witnessed – and many others. Rwandan communities in the diaspora can offer information but none of us can answer the question why.

Why Does Genocide 'Happen'?

Rotimi Sankore
Pambazuka News 150, 1 April 2004

THE GENOCIDE IN Rwanda in April 1994 must not distract from the fact that genocide is a global phenomenon that knows no racial or geographical boundaries. In its modern form, genocide was perfected by the fascist Nazi regime led by Adolph Hitler in Germany from 1933 to 1945. The Khmer Rouge also demonstrated in the killing fields of Cambodia from 1975 to 1979 that genocide could be carried out as efficiently in a different social and political context.

In more recent times the world watched live on satellite television in the 1990s while genocide was perpetuated in the heart of Europe as Serbia, Croatia and Kosovo became household names for the grimmest reasons known to history. Going back even further, the transatlantic slave trade has been described as genocidal, though the mass murder of millions of Africans over 400 years was more a by-product of plunder, exploitation and repression rather than the specific goal of slave dealers and the states that backed the slave trade.

But why does genocide happen? Why do human beings, the so-called most civilised and intelligent of the species that inhabit the planet, turn to mass murder?

In answering this question, the most important point to make is that genocide does not just happen. It is prepared for, consciously executed and is based on reasonably identifiable social, political and economic conditions. What differs is the extent to which these conditions apply or exist, and the degree of preparation by the perpetrators.

The second most important point to make is that genocide is not 'triggered' by a single event that pushes the perpetrators over the brink. On the contrary, the so-called 'trigger events' are excuses for setting in motion the logical end to a process prepared for well in advance.

Only when the world acknowledges the existence of these processes can we collectively identify the signs or beginnings of what is likely to end in genocide and douse the fire before it becomes an all-consuming flame.

In the case of Rwanda, it is a popularly held myth that the shooting down of the plane carrying the then Head of State Juvénal Habyarimana and the Burundian President Cyprien Ntayamira on 6h April 1994 triggered the genocide that followed over the next 12 weeks and left well over 700,000 dead (nearly 10 per cent of the country's population of over eight million). Nothing can be further from the truth.

Before the shooting down of the airplane by yet unidentified persons, the social and political conditions had been prepared by various factors. One key factor was the dictatorship established following the seizure of power by General Juvénal Habyarimana in 1973.

Habyarimana ruled in the name of the 'majority' and imposed a dictatorship on the entire country. In addition, the official discrimination against the Tutsi minority was so much that within two decades, half a million had fled the country.

The government estimated Tutsis at 9 per cent of the population and restricted them to 9 per cent of jobs and educational opportunities. (Many of the exiles later joined the rebel Rwandan Patriotic Front, RPF). In order to consolidate the government's hold on power, Tutsis were painted as the enemy within (and without), and anyone that did not treat them as such was a sympathiser of the enemy, deemed to be 'no better than them' and likely to face the same fate.

This is a classic manoeuvre used by a variety of regimes throughout history to divide society, promote a climate of fear and insecurity, encourage racism, xenophobia or ethnic hatred and mobilise their supporters to systematically suppress and eradicate the so-called enemy. The Nazis in Germany used this strategy to near perfection over the period of their rule.

Official discrimination on its own is not enough to involve a significant percentage of the population in mass murder. Hate speech (using crude or sophisticated propaganda) must be deployed on a mass scale, and organised armed bodies of men infused into society to provide the 'back bone' and direction for mass murder. Where the prerequisite social conditions do not exist, or hate speech does not have the desired effect of involving significant numbers of everyday citizens in mass murder, it still facilitates their acquiescence to genocide carried out by smaller organised units of killers.

But even hate speech must have a clearly identifiable target to lead to genocide. This means that the 'targets' must be isolated and identified as systematically as possible. This is achieved by obvious means such as clearly marked or distinct clothing, less obvious means such as identity cards, or crude social stereotyping using race, ethnicity, language or physical appearance.

In the case of Rwanda, this had already been pre-facilitated by the Belgian colonialists through the issuing of identity cards based on ethnicity and the classic colonial strategy of creating an artificial elite through which colonial powers rule in countries where colonialists are vastly outnumbered.

During colonial rule, the artificial classification and imposition of a minority elite created the basis for a long-lasting resentment which was seized upon after independence by Hutu extremists to build a power base. The similar creation of artificial borders, the cynical divisions of ethnic nationalities, the imposition of artificial elites and so forth by colonial powers have provided the basis for many conflicts in Africa.

Simply put, genocide has become the method though which organised groups within society, whether based on ideology, race, nationality, ethnicity, religion or language, consciously pursue a strategy of achieving or consolidating power, through manipulating economic, social or political conditions and insecurities, to unite significant sections of society behind them and against a real or artificially created enemy whose extermination or repression is promoted as vital to the 'survival of the species.'

The main tools are: hate speech, the use of mass propaganda to spread lies, insecurity and create myths promoting a climate of simultaneous fear and dehumanisation of the intended targets; and the organisation of armed bodies of men in preparation for, or to actually direct, instigate or carry out violence and mass murder. All of these factors and those mentioned earlier are clearly identifiable and if left unchallenged build up to make genocide almost inevitable.

But how can genocide be tackled?

General education and enlightenment, an understanding of social, political and economic issues and of individual and mass psychology will all help to make people less susceptible to manipulation of their fears and insecurities.

However, while sharp economic, social and political inequalities remain a characteristic of human society there will always be a possibility that people will be open to manipulation by those that see such cynical manipulation as their path to power and the trappings that go with it. Interventions by United Nations forces or others may stop specific cases of genocide from playing out, but this cannot be a permanent solution.

In Africa, the legacy of colonialism, serious economic problems, deepening inequalities and ongoing conflicts mean that there is a possibility that an increasing number of incumbent governments or powerful groups could promote religious, racial, ethnic or social differences and conflict as a way of acquiring or consolidating their hold on power rather than addressing the root causes of desperation. History shows that once set in motion conflicts are difficult to stop. How civil society and pro-democratic forces tackle the issues is crucial to the future of Africa.

Overall, there is no doubt that the central challenge facing humanity today on all continents is to resolve the inequalities and injustices on which genocide can be built.

Mirroring Rwanda's Challenges:
the Refugee Story

Sarah Erlichman
Pambazuka News 150, 1 April 2004

THE RWANDAN GENOCIDE sparked massive population shifts in the country and across the Great Lakes region. Millions of uprooted people scattered and regrouped. In the wake of devastating death and displacement, the landscape of human settlement was completely altered.

The return of diverse groups of Rwandan refugees over the course of ten years since the genocide has shaped the country's current political, physical, social, and economic environments. Rwandan refugees' experiences in exile and on return differ according to their histories, their ethnicity and class. They are rural and urban, well educated and illiterate. Many were raised in Rwanda, others in neighbouring African countries, in Europe, and beyond.

Some, having been born in exile, have come to Rwanda for the first time after 1994. Yet all have returned in the hope of rebuilding lives and livelihoods in the country they have always called home. The refugees have returned with a vast wealth of knowledge, experience, assets and skills to the most densely populated country in Africa, where the struggling economy is dominated by agriculture.

The socio-economic integration of returnees remains a massive challenge to Rwanda. Productive agricultural land, and even basic shelter, healthcare, and education, remain inaccessible to many. Sharing community resources is perhaps the greatest challenge to peaceful resettlement and reintegration of returned Rwandan refugees.

A Brief History of Rwandan Refugees

Beginning in 1959, as Belgian colonists began to withdraw from power, the politicisation of ethnicity lead to the transfer of power to the majority ethnic Hutu in Rwanda. Targeted attacks on ethnic Tutsi began. Estimates indicate that during the period between 1959 and 1967, 20,000 Tutsi died, and another 300,000 fled Rwanda as refugees with a small number of elite Hutus and Twa into neighbouring countries.

In 1964, estimates of Rwandan refugees in asylum countries were 40,000 in Burundi, 60,000 in Zaire (now DRC), 35,000 in Uganda, and 15,000 in Tanzania. Political crises and refugee flows from neighbouring countries have contributed to the complexities of Rwanda's refugees. In Burundi in 1972, anti-Hutu violence and killings by the Tutsi government forced thousands of Burundian Hutu refugees to flee into Rwanda. These refugees contributed to further anti-

Tutsi attacks in Rwanda in 1973 and thousands more Tutsi fled Rwanda. Refugees who fled Rwanda between 1959 and1973 are generally referred to as 'old-caseload refugees'.

Land and property left behind by refugees from Rwanda was subsequently occupied by others who remained or entered the country. This became a political issue. By the 1980s, the Habyarimana regime claimed that repatriation of Rwandan refugees was impossible due to land scarcity. Throughout the 1970s and 1980s, Rwandan refugee communities created secret political and military alliances in exile. The RPF was formed from such groups.

New directions of displacement began with the RPF invasion of Rwanda from Uganda in October 1990. Internally displaced people (IDPs) within Rwanda, mainly Hutu fleeing RPF attacks, regrouped into camps of hundreds of thousands surviving in miserable conditions throughout the ensuing war.

As the genocide began in April 1994, RPF soldiers began to advance from the northern border area. Behind the troops over 600,000 'old caseload refugees' followed, some of them entering Rwanda after more than 30 years of exile in Uganda. Ahead of the advancing RPF fled the mainly Hutu 'new caseload refugees'.

In April, an estimated 500,000 fled to Tanzania. In 24 hours alone, 250,000 crossed the Rusumo bridge between Rwanda and Tanzania over 28–29 April. By May, about 200,000 mainly ethnic Hutus from Butare, Kibungo, and Kigali-Rural had fled to northern Burundi. As the RPF took control of Kigali in July, the French military launched Operation Turquoise, creating a safe zone beyond RPF control in southwest Rwanda to protect fleeing Hutu, including leaders of the military and government responsible for the genocide as well as ordinary civilians.

Three hundred thousand fled to Bukavu, Zaire in July and August, as the French Operation Turquoise pulled out. Another 300,000 were grouped into IDP camps in the region. In northwest Rwanda, the home of the elite of the Habyarimana regime, one million refugees fled to Goma, Zaire during four days in mid-July.

The refugee crisis in eastern Zaire attracted the assistance of the international community on a scale leagues beyond what had been provided in Rwanda during the genocide, or even after. Among the refugee population, Hutu Power extremists controlled the camps and the aid. They continued to mobilise and arm themselves against the new RPF regime. Political violence was pervasive in the camps.

Despite the relief aid that sustained the refugees, a deadly cholera epidemic killed 50,000 refugees in Goma. During late July and August, 200,000 refugees returned from Goma to Rwanda. By the end of 1994, two million Rwandans had fled the RPF advance, being forced to run by Hutu extremist leaders, or fearing retribution for the genocide. Over 500,000 of these were in Tanzania,

250,000 in Burundi, and more than 1.2 million in Zaire. Among the refugees were Burundians who had fled to Rwanda in 1972. By the end of 1995, 225,778 Rwandan refugees (80,000 new caseload) had returned to Rwanda. Another 1,707,032 Rwandans remained in 50 refugee camps.

Return and Reintegration of Refugee Returnees

Between 1994 and 1996, approximately 800,000 (mainly old-case refugees) had followed the call of the new Government of National Unity to return home to Rwanda. Still, massive forced population shifts continued throughout the region during the second half of the 1990s.

The Rwandan camps in Zaire continued to threaten the RPF regime and Tutsi of Rwandan origin living in the Kivus of Zaire. In October and November 1996, Rwandan- and Ugandan-supported Alliance de Forces Democratique de Liberation attacked all of the camps in eastern Zaire and pursued ex-FAR and Interhamwe deeper into Zaire's interior.

An estimated 600,000 refugees repatriated to Rwanda over six days, forming a line 260km long. By early 1997, the number had risen to 720,000. Other refugees fled in the direction of the militias towards the interior of Zaire, Angola, and Zambia. Concurrently, conflict has forced 15,000 Congolese and 5,000 Burundians to seek refuge in Rwanda. In December, 500,000 Rwandans were forcibly repatriated by Tanzanian authorities.

Internal displacement remained a serious concern within Rwanda, especially as ex-FAR and Interhamwe launched attacks on northwest Rwanda from their bases in Zaire in mid-1997. In 1998, following the fall of Mobutu and the rise of Laurent Kabila, the second Congo war forced tens of thousands of Congolese refugees into western Rwanda. These were eventually accommodated in refugee camps which remain today.

As the old-caseload refugees returned, the only available properties were those that had been abandoned by the new-caseload refugees. As the new-caseload refugees began to return, the pressure for new housing became considerable.

The solution that had been foreseen in the 1993 Arusha Accords to accommodate refugee return and prevent conflicts over land was a villagisation scheme where services would be centralised and modern agricultural technology accessible. According to the Arusha Accords, refugees returning after more than ten years were not to seek to reclaim previous properties that had been occupied by others, but were to be resettled on unoccupied land with government assistance.

In the aftermath of the genocide, new caseload refugees were entitled to reclaim the land and property they had recently abandoned. The villagisation or *imidugudu* scheme was adopted as a means to create shelter for old and new caseload refugees, and others in need of shelter, such as displaced genocide survivors, and young people seeking new homes.

The *imidugudu* scheme was criticised by the international community for forcing resettlement to villages in poor sites, for inadequate provision of services, and insufficient compensation to the previous occupants of resettlement land.

Still, the government's scheme received sufficient support from the international community for massive construction of shelter and social infrastructure such as schools and health centres. UNHCR alone supported the construction of nearly 100,000 houses for 500,000 people between 1995 and1999.

Despite the political and financial support which fuelled *imidugudu* development, the reality is that meeting the land and housing needs of returned refugees has been an enormous challenge and is not yet resolved. As the flow of returns has slowed in recent years, so has donor support to resettlement. In 1999, the Brookings Initiative estimated that 370,000 households were living in inadequate shelter. Donor support and the initiatives of private individuals to construct their own homes reduced this figure to 192,000 in November 2001.

Another estimate by the US Committee for Refugees, found 150,000 IDPs were living without permanent shelter or basic social services in 2001. More recently, the Norwegian Refugee Council estimated there were nearly 200,000 IDPs in need of shelter and social services in July 2003.

UNHCR studies have found that a large number of returnees have never received any land. Moreover, many returnees are among the poorest in their communities, without access to healthcare, education for their children, or basic shelter needs. Among returnees are many individuals and families in need of special psychosocial support: children orphaned or separated from their parents; spouses separated from their partners by death or war; survivors of physical and sexual violence.

The needs of such returnees are in large part provided for by local government structures, which tend to keep registers of returnees and 'vulnerable' families. Returnees themselves resist being regarded as a separate category in their communities. The support they request, such as healthcare 'mutuelle' associations, school supply packages, shelter construction supplies, and agricultural tools are linked to community development and poverty alleviation plans. Still, as more returnees return with few resources, pressure on their Rwandan communities increases.

The majority of both old caseload and new caseload refugees planning to return to Rwanda have already done so. Between 60,000 and 80,000 Rwandan refugees are estimated to be still living in Uganda, DRC, Malawi, Zimbabwe, Zambia, and elsewhere.

The majority are expected to repatriate through state-sponsored, UN-assisted programmes over the next two years. As the stable political situation in Rwanda continues, those who choose not to return will be considered to have integrated into the countries where they are and will no longer be considered refugees requiring international protection. In addition to civilian refugees, demobilised soldiers are also returning to Rwanda and undergoing re-education, resettlement, and reintegration. It is expected that 81,462 combatants of ex-FAR, Interahamwe, and other militia groups, will have demobilised and returned to Rwanda from DRC by the end of the period 2001–05. In November 2003, the Rwandan government welcomed the return of ex-military leader of the Forces Démocratiques de la Libération du Rwanda followed by approximately 100 ex-rebel soldiers.

The Future of Rwanda's Refugees

Rwandan refugees are as diverse as Rwanda's population and play an integral role in reconciliation and development efforts in the post-genocide context. Many who gained higher education and skills in exile returned to strengthen the urban middle and upper classes. Rural returnees contribute to the agricultural sector, which remains the backbone of the Rwandan economy. Returned refugees face the economic realities that make livelihoods a struggle for most Rwandans.

Distinctions remain between communities of returnees accustomed to the culture of their country of exile, and in the nature of their exile – some suffered in dismal refugee camps, others survived comfortably in cities. Not least of the distinctions between returned refugees are their ethnicity and the reasons for their flight. Political consciousness developed during exile fuel Rwandan politics. Refugees are a crucial element of Rwandan reconciliation and socio-economic development. The challenges ahead for Rwandan refugees mirror those for the country as a whole.

Neutralising the Voices of Hate: Broadcasting and Genocide

Richard Carver
Pambazuka News 150, 1 April 2004

RADIO TÉLÉVISION LIBRE des Mille Collines (RTLM) was almost the first thing that outside observers noticed about the Rwanda genocide:

> Hutus could be seen listening attentively to every broadcast.... They held their cheap radios in one hand and machetes in the other, ready to start killing once the order had been given.

Or this:

> Much of the responsibility for the genocide in Rwanda can be blamed on the media. Many people have heard of Radio des Mille Collines, which began broadcasting a steady stream of racist, anti-Tutsi invective in September 1993.

Hence it was hardly surprising (if rather belated) when, in 2003, three Rwandan journalists, two of them from RTLM, were found guilty by the International Criminal Tribunal on Rwanda of participating in the genocide through their broadcasts.

The verdict of the Arusha tribunal seemed to close that chapter and it would be easy to accept that those found guilty deserved their fate and leave it at that. But what, in reality, was the role of RTLM in the genocide? And what lessons can usefully be learned from it?

The prominence of RTLM in Western media accounts of the genocide can be easily explained. Journalists and editors always love media stories for essentially narcissistic reasons. They are taken with the idea that they have an enormous influence on public behaviour – for good or bad. Here was an example of the immense power of the media.

Yet many of the accounts of RTLM's role do not stand up to a moment's scrutiny. Take the example already quoted: did Hutu really stand clutching radios in one hand and machetes in the other, waiting to be 'incited'? Which Hutu do we mean (presumably not those who fell victim to the genocidaires)? And if they were so disposed towards genocide, why did they need to wait for the radio to tell them to carry it out?

This version of events rested upon a particular interpretation of why the genocide took place. It assumes that primitive and primordial 'tribal' hatreds only had to be unlocked for Hutu to begin slaughtering Tutsi. Yet every serious account of the genocide stresses its highly planned and organised nature. That RTLM and its owners were part of the plot to commit genocide cannot be disputed. However, the assumption that RTLM was a necessary precondition for genocide is unproven and unprovable.

The influence of media content on public behaviour has been a subject for endless and inconclusive academic study over decades. We cannot say with any certainty whether, for example, violent television programmes will predispose children to behave violently. Yet many serious commentators have concluded with certainty that the RTLM broadcasts incited genocide. There were indeed contemporary accounts in the Western media of genocidaires 'confessing' that they had committed their crimes because the radio had told them to. Such testimony was plainly self-serving yet was usually taken at face value.

The point here is not to exonerate RTLM from responsibility. However, without examining precisely the nature of RTLM's crimes we cannot hope to draw any useful lessons.

Even ten years on, the weakness of most accounts of RTLM's role remains a lack of concrete analysis of either the content of the RTLM broadcasts or their impact on their audience. The latter is more excusable than the former: it remains almost impossible to conduct any scientific study of how RTLM affected people's behaviour.

Yet it is possible to analyse RTLM's output. To some extent this work has been done, although the findings are still often ignored. (In 1996, Linda Kirschke wrote a detailed account of RTLM's broadcasts based upon tapes and transcripts. I base my observations on RTLM's output on her research.) The generally accepted understanding of RTLM remains that cited above: that it broadcast 'a steady stream of racist, anti-Tutsi invective'. In fact, the story is more complicated.

RTLM's role in the genocide can only be understood in terms of a strict distinction between what was broadcast before and after 6 April 1994. After that date it would be an understatement to accuse RTLM of incitement. The radio station did not try to persuade people towards genocide; it organised them to carry it out. RTLM broadcast the names and vehicle registration numbers of the targeted victims. This was purely a way of communicating intelligence to the militias carrying out the killing, giving them the information they needed to stop the victims at roadblocks.

RTLM's role during this phase was only secondarily one of propaganda. Under the 1948 Genocide Convention, any external power with the means to do so had not only the right to jam RTLM broadcasts, but the obligation to do so.

RTLM's output before 6 April 1994 poses questions that are more complex. The ethnic propaganda that RTLM broadcast was much more subtle than most accounts would suggest. RTLM was a slick and youthful station playing popular music. It was apparently the favoured listening of the rebels of the Rwanda Patriotic Front – the very targets of its 'anti-Tutsi invective'. The meaning of RTLM's often elliptical ethnic references would have been well

understood by a Rwandan audience. But it was conveyed with a sophistica-
tion and wit that contrasted with earlier broadcasts from radio Rwanda,
which, unlike, RTLM, was under direct and formal government control.

Retrospectively it is clear that RTLM's broadcasts between its launch in
September 1993 and 6 April 1994 provided evidence of its owners' complicity
in planning the genocide. They may also have helped to create a popular
mood more favourable to genocide.

So far, this article has focused on what was exceptional and unique about the
Rwandan situation, as most discussions of RTLM tend to. Yet it is also important to note how RTLM emerged in a way that was completely typical of failed
democratic transitions in Africa.

In 1989 President Juvénal Habyarimana was edged into a reluctant transition
to a multi-party system. Yet this was accompanied by no thorough reform of
public institutions in Rwanda, including the broadcasting system. The publicly
funded broadcaster, Radio Rwanda, remained under strict government control.
There was no transparent and accountable system to licence private broadcasters. Indeed, the only private station eventually to be licensed was RTLM, owned
by a group of extremist Hutu allied to a faction within the government.

This scenario – lack of democratic control over broadcasting in a period of
political transition – has been played out in countless countries in Africa and
elsewhere. While the consequences have seldom been as disastrous as in
Rwanda, the practical lessons should by now be well understood. There needs
to be an institutional reform of broadcasting that involves mechanisms for
genuine public control over public broadcasting, an open and accountable
system for issuing private broadcasting licences and space for the emergence
of community media.

Rwanda was neither the first nor last time that the media have participated
in massive human rights violations or crimes against humanity. The role of
Nazi anti-semitic media in the European genocide in the 1940s was addressed
in the Nuremberg trials (which provided some precedents for the Arusha tribunal on Rwanda). In the years immediately before the Rwanda genocide,
sections of the media in former Yugoslavia had been actively fomenting ethnic
crimes. Since 1994, media have tried to incite violence in Burundi, Congo/
Zaire and Zimbabwe, among others.

The last of these examples is instructive. The Media Monitoring Project
Zimbabwe (MMPZ) has drawn explicit parallels between RTLM and the role
of the state media in inciting violence against the Zimbabwean opposition.
Although the scale of the violence is much less, the institutional framework is
very reminiscent of Rwanda. The propaganda and misinformation of the
Zimbabwe Broadcasting Corporation is so potent precisely because there is no
alternative. As in Rwanda, the public broadcaster is under tight government
control and there is no space for independent private radio.

The Zimbabwe example is also relevant because MMPZ has tried to explain what is the significance and impact of the hate messages in the government media. They have concluded – unlike the simplistic initial analyses of the Rwanda genocide – that the extreme language and baroque, fictitious conspiracies in the official media are not aimed at convincing the general public that the opposition are a tool of Zimbabwe's imperialist enemies. Rather they are intended to fire up the relatively small numbers of members of ruling party militias and security forces actually engaged in carrying out human rights violations. Most ordinary Zimbabweans know from their own experience that the ZBC talks lies; a small band of ruling party loyalists uses these propaganda messages to reinforce them in the correctness of their own brutal measures.

Such a thesis is very difficult to prove without conducting a type of sociological research that would be impossible in present-day Zimbabwe (or Rwanda). But it may also provide a useful understanding of how RTLM functioned in preparing the genocide. On this hypothesis, RTLM was not primarily concerned with convincing ordinary people to participate in genocide; it reinforced the conviction of those who were already part of the conspiracy to commit genocide.

Aside from the conclusion that a proper political transition should include democratisation of the media, the practical conclusions to be drawn from the RTLM experience are equally tentative. The criminal prosecution and conviction of the RTLM journalists was immensely important. It establishes the principle of the accountability of journalists for the consequences of what they broadcast. It does not, however, show what steps should be taken to prevent such material from being broadcast in the first place.

Freedom of expression advocates have always been rightly wary of any suggestion of prohibiting 'hate speech', however obnoxious it might be. They argue that violent and intolerant views should be combated by allowing tolerant and pacific opinions to compete. In practical terms that is saying that a plural media environment is the best way of neutralising RTLM and its kin.

Any call to prohibit 'hate speech' must be treated with the utmost care. To whom is such a call addressed? In the case of Rwanda it might have been directed to the very government that was promoting and encouraging 'hate speech'. Anti-hate speech laws notoriously have the opposite effect from that intended. The African state with the most extensive battery of laws prohibiting 'incitement to racial hatred' was none other than apartheid South Africa. The laws were used, of course, against opponents of the apartheid system.

Or perhaps the call was directed to the 'international community'. I have already suggested that RTLM's broadcasts after 6 April should have been jammed. At that stage the radio station was being used to organise the genocide. The fact that these orders were being issued over public airwaves gave them no privilege. This was not, by then, a freedom of expression issue.

But we should be very careful not to predate such a call to cover RTLM before 6 April. Giving powerful governments a general mandate to shut down broadcasting stations is an extremely dangerous precedent. An outcry over the role of Serb broadcasting in the former Yugoslavia effectively legitimised NATO's bombing of the official Belgrade broadcasting station in 1999. This was done to further NATO war aims in Kosovo. It was a war crime. We should beware of what we wish for in case the wish is granted.

Neither 'hate speech' laws nor international military action are the answer. The practical lessons from the RTLM experience are more prosaic. Pluralistic and accountable broadcasting is an indispensable part of building democracy and the voices of hate can only be neutralised if they are confronted with a variety of alternative points of view.

The Genocide Problem:
'Never Again' All Over Again

Part I

Gerald Caplan
Pambazuka News 177, 7 October 2004

TEN YEARS AGO, the international community stood by as the horror of the Rwandan genocide unfolded. This summer, Western political will could have stopped the mass killings in Sudan. Why do we not act?

On a quiet Sunday in the early summer of 1999, I was recruited into the tiny but growing army of enigmatic characters who devote their lives to studying genocide. It was a phone call that did it. Stephen Lewis, my lifelong comrade-in-arms and now UN Envoy for HIV/AIDS in Africa, was offering a chance for us to work together again, but on a subject of unprecedented gravity: unravelling the truth about the 1994 genocide in Rwanda. Rwanda became my obsession from that moment to this. Stephen was a member of a special seven-member International Panel of Eminent Personalities (IPEP), which had been appointed by the Organisation of African Unity (OAU) to investigate the genocide. Despite their genuine eminence – two were former African presidents, one a potential future president, another the former Chief Justice of the Supreme Court of India – the panel members just did not know what to do with the information they had been accumulating. After travelling to half a dozen nations interviewing people with links to the genocide, they did not know what they wanted to say. They decided they needed a writer post-haste. Appropriately enough, they sought an African writer, but for various reasons none of their choices was available. Stephen mentioned me. Though I knew little of Rwanda, I had a doctorate in African history; I had lived in several African countries; I had co-chaired two public policy commissions in Canada; I was a writer; and I had been involved in the struggle against white rule in Southern Africa. I suppose a combination of sheer desperation plus these credentials led to a near total stranger being brought on to take over the panel's task.

As it happens, Stephen and I had already discussed the panel at length. He was thrilled and honoured to have been appointed to it and I was wildly envious. I had gone to live in Africa for the first time as a doctoral student way back in 1964 and had kept renewing my connections over the years. So when the call came, I was willing and able, yet seriously anxious. Carol, my wife, very wise about many things (not least the secrets of my soul), proved so once again. We could cope as a family, she was confident, even if it meant I had be absent a fair bit. But she was not as sanguine about me. Could I deal with the subject emotionally? Could my already dark, lugubrious, pessimistic,

Hobbesian view of the world handle such intimacy with one of the most hellish events of our time? After a lifetime dedicated to various crusades for social justice, I had become the stereotypical glass-is-half-empty guy, always able to find an ominous cloud in a deep blue sky. My gag: being a pessimist may not be fun but at least I'm rarely disappointed. Now, this new assignment raised real fears of me being traumatised into utter depression and immobilising hopelessness. These were serious questions, but both Carol and I knew immediately they could only be answered after the event. There was no way I could resist this offer. This was history in the making. This was Africa, my life's preoccupation. This was another Holocaust, a subject that had tormented me forever. This was about the very nature of our species. I began getting my shots the next day and reported to the panel's headquarters in Addis Ababa, Ethiopia, the home of the OAU, nine days later.

I signed up on the assumption that the panel members would tell me what they wanted to say, and that I had be their pen. This was hardly my usual or favourite role but, under the circumstances, I was prepared to play it. I needed their guidance about how forthright they were prepared to be. Although no expert on Rwanda, I did know how controversial and sensitive the issues were. Since this was an OAU mission, presumably dedicated to offering an African perspective on the genocide, was the panel ready to say that there would have been no genocide at all if some Africans had not chosen to exterminate other Africans? How far were they prepared to go in describing the OAU's own failure to intervene effectively? Beyond Africa, were they willing to tell the truth and accuse the French government of virtual complicity in the genocide? Would they agree to condemn Rwanda's churches, above all the Roman Catholic Church, for their shameful betrayal of their flock before, during, and since the genocide? Were they prepared to say that American politicians (both Democrats and Republicans), fearful of losing votes if US soldiers were killed for such a remote cause, had knowingly allowed hundreds of thousands of Rwandans to die terrible deaths? Were they going to tell the truth about the serious human rights abuses that had been committed by the largely Tutsi Rwandan Patriotic Front – the 'good guys' in the genocide and now the government of the country?

To my astonishment, when the panel flew in to meet me in Addis Ababa, they offered no guidance at all. To this day I am still not sure I understand it. Maybe they were paralysed by the enormity of the topic and their responsibility. All I know is that after my very first meeting with the members, I was left to produce the report on my own, sending them drafts for approval. I was distraught. How was I to deal with all the vexing issues I had fruitlessly raised?

Waiting for the flight back to Toronto, where I would do all my reading and writing, I went for a long and dusty walk with Dr Berharnou Abebe, the panel's research officer, a remarkable Ethiopian intellectual with whom I had immediately bonded. Berharnou grasped the situation completely. Like other non-Rwandan Africans I was to meet, he felt personally ashamed of the geno-cide and approached his role on the tiny panel professional staff with the utmost gravity. We walked and walked, going over the problem again and again, getting grimier and more hoarse with each polluted block. Finally, he stopped, looked at me, and said: 'It is simple, Gerry. You must write not for the seven, but for the 700,000. It is their story that you must tell.'

Ignoring the murky politics of both the OAU and some of the seven panel-lists, I accepted Berharnou's advice with a vengeance. I would give them a draft based on wherever the evidence led me.

For almost a year, I immersed myself in the topic totally. I thought of nothing else. Weekends and evenings disappeared. Somehow, I absorbed a wealth of knowledge as if by osmosis. In the end, however, the work was done and approved – even though some panel members were rather less enthusiastic than others in accepting some of my harsh, unforgiving, and thoroughly docu-mented assessments of the French and US governments, the Catholic Church, the UN Secretariat, the OAU itself, the post-genocide government in Rwanda, and just about everyone else involved in this terrible tragedy except Canadian General Romeo Dallaire. Dallaire, almost alone, emerged with his honour intact. Howard Adelman, a Rwandan expert at York University in Toronto, once wrote that Rwanda's was 'the most easily preventable genocide imagina-ble,' and the panel unhesitatingly accepted my suggestion that we call the 300-page report 'Rwanda: The Preventable Genocide.' What can never be for-given is that none of those with the capacity to prevent it cared enough to try.

The report was released in mid-2000. I do not mind saying the OAU had never seen anything like it – independent, outspoken, undiplomatic, and easily read, it was the very antithesis of the turgid bureaucratic documents the OAU normally spewed out. It was also largely ignored. Not because it pulled no punches, I am afraid, but out of plain lack of interest. Africa's heads of state, who had authorised the report two years earlier, never bothered to discuss it at all. I was deeply disappointed by the unceremonious burial of the report, suf-fering from the inevitable anticlimax after such an intense experience, and finding it hard to come to grips with what I had learned. Not only was the assignment over, so, it appeared, was my time with Rwanda. Wrong again.

About a year later, it dawned on me that outside Rwanda itself, the genocide was already being forgotten. I became extremely agitated. The survivors were living as traumatised, maimed paupers. Most of the perpetrators were getting away with murder, often mass murder. The sins of commission of the French government and the Catholic Church, and the sins of omission of the American and British governments, were being completely ignored: the 'globalisation of impunity' I had called it in the report. Carol, once again seeing things far more clearly than I could, suggested that the tenth anniversary of the genocide in

2004, two-and-a-half years away, could be a natural occasion to renew interest in the tragedy. The result was 'Remembering Rwanda,' an international voluntary movement organised with no funding, largely on my Mac, with the assistance of Louise Mushikiwabo in Washington and Carole Ann Reed in Toronto, with adherents around the globe, all dedicated to ensuring that the memory of the genocide and its victims would not be buried, and that those responsible for it would not escape accountability.

I had already befriended some diaspora Rwandans who signed up immediately. They included a group of remarkable widows, particularly Esther Mujawayo in Germany and Chantal Kayetisi in New Hampshire, who had lost their husbands, among dozens of other relatives, to the genocide while they and their children miraculously survived, and who are dedicated to making sure the genocide would not be swept under history's table. Leo Kabalisa, one of life's natural gentlemen, was another; Leo, who now teaches French in a Toronto high school, counts by name 15 members of his immediate family and 82 of his extended family who were murdered during the 100 days.

Other Rwandans, though, were inevitably suspicious. In Johannesburg one night, I met with a group of Rwandan expatriates attached to the Rwandan Diaspora Global Network. I knew them through e-mail correspondence and, finding I had to be in Johannesburg on other UN business, I had asked to meet them. We had a good couple of hours, got along well, and agreed to work together. But it was obvious they could not quite figure out why I was doing this. What did I want? What could I get out of this? Rwandans, who have been betrayed by the outside world as much as any people on earth, are entitled to their suspicions of all outsiders.

In trying to explain my interest, I found myself, to my own surprise, telling them that I was Jewish. My family had fled Poland before the Hitler era, I said, and, probably as a result, I had great empathy with their own genocide. It was all true. Although I'm a convinced atheist, deeply at odds with those who represent themselves as the voice of Canadian Jewry, and a passionate foe of Israel's occupation of Palestine, I have always felt my Jewishness deeply. I have been fascinated with the Nazis and the Holocaust since my teen years. For decades now I have read, almost as a matter of principle, at least one book related to the Holocaust every year. Although many Jews disagree, for me the self-evident lesson of the Holocaust is a universal, not a particular, one: it is not merely that anti-Semitism must be opposed with all of our might, but that all injustice, racism, and discrimination is unacceptable and has to be combated. The Rwandans loved this answer. Many Tutsi regard themselves, with considerable pride, as the Jews of Africa. Most know about, and identify with, the Holocaust. Some have been to Auschwitz, others to Yad Vashem. Many are far more supportive of Israeli policies than I am. Yet my core Jewishness and our shared genocides is a bond between us.

Sometimes I learn from experience. During a visit to Kigali in 2002, I had the opportunity to address nearly 1,000 Rwandans at a major assembly dedicated to reconciliation. I described the Remembering Rwanda movement and asked, before they could: Why was a white outsider, a *muzungu*, in the widely used Swahili term, leading this initiative? The moment I said that as a Jew I instinctively felt a close bond with Rwanda, the mood in the huge parliamentary chamber palpably changed. Suddenly, trust emerged; we understood each other. The solidarity of victims prevailed. Certainly some suspicion still existed; I could hardly blame them. But after the speech I was confronted by a handsome, dynamic woman I did not recognise, who abruptly embraced me. Yolande Mukagasana, a genocide survivor, had made it clear in a brief e-mail that she did not know why I was involved in this issue, did not trust me, and could continue the fight for the memory of the genocide's victims without me, thanks anyway. Now, she said, she knew we would be in the struggle together. Yolande, a poet and storyteller and a passionate keeper of the survivors' flame, invited me to dinner later at her small house in Kigali, now home to 13 adopted children who were kibitzing in a room nearby. As I tried politely to continue eating, she pointed to the photos on the wall of her husband and three young children and explained in graphic detail how, ten years earlier, they had all been hunted down and murdered not far from where we sat.

This is the first of a two-part series entitled 'The Genocide Problem: "Never Again" All Over Again'. This article was first published in the October issue of The Walrus, *a new Canadian general interest magazine. It is reproduced here with the permission.* The Walrus *magazine is available on newsstands and book stores in Canada. For more information about* The Walrus: *www.walrusmagazine.com*

The Genocide Problem: 'Never Again' All Over Again

Part II

Gerald Caplan
Pambazuka News 178, 14 October 2004

The Genocide Specialists

FROM THE FIRST, I had thought my report should put the Rwandan geno-cide into some historical context, and I began reading in the field of genocide generally. Before long, I had come face to face with the burgeoning world of genocide studies. This subculture, I soon discovered, is quite separate from that of high-profile Holocaust studies. While some specialists in 'other' geno-cides are also students of the Holocaust, for a long time only a handful of Holocaust specialists were prepared to accept experts in comparative geno-cides as their kin. According to New York City College Professor Henry Huttenbach, a Jewish refugee from Hitler's Germany, most Holocaust special-ists still demand that the genocide of the Jews be treated as qualitatively dif-ferent from – really a greater catastrophe than – the genocide of others. And 'any whiff of comparison was automatically condemned as a form of denial, revisionism, trivialisation, etc.' This is an enormously emotional and divisive issue, but the evidence surely corroborates Huttenbach's assertion. In his intel-lectually thrilling and morally courageous study, *The Holocaust in American Life*, University of Chicago historian Peter Novick introduces the concept of 'the Olympics of victimisation,' a fierce competition for primacy among the world's victims that the Jews are determined to win. Largely, they have suc-ceeded. Even a good number, though not all, of my newly discovered geno-cide studies family share the view that the Holocaust – always with a capital 'H' – is at the farthest point of the genocide continuum.

In 1999, when I began working on Rwanda, the world of non-Holocaust genocide studies was just beginning to flourish. Frank Chalk and Kurt Jonassohn's *The History and Sociology of Genocide: Analyses and Case Studies* in 1990 was way ahead of the curve. It was Rwanda and Srebrenica that really set things off. The International Association of Genocide Scholars (IAGS) had been organised in 1994. In 1999, Huttenbach founded the *Journal of Genocide Studies*, the first of its kind not exclusively dedicated to the Holocaust. The same year, a two-volume *Encyclopedia of Genocide* appeared. In 2002, a thick and engrossing collection of essays appeared called *Pioneers of Genocide Studies* – imagine: pioneers already! – and Samantha Power won the Pulitzer Prize for her exceptional study *A Problem from Hell: America and the Age of Genocide*. Imagine: humanity had inflicted on itself an entire era of genocide, and we were living through it.

The field was taking off. In June, 2003, I was among 200 people attending the IAGS conference in Galway, Ireland. There were 44 intriguing panels to choose from, so many I could not even attend all the Rwanda sessions let alone those on Burundi, Srebrenica, Armenia, the Third World and the Holocaust, the Herero of southwestern Africa, Ethiopia, Guatemala, Korea, Bangladesh, Assyria, the indigenous peoples of the Americas and Australia, Cambodia, genocide prevention, genocide denial, comparative genocide, genocide art, genocide and children, survivors, truth commissions, the problem of reconciliation, the problem of reparations, the International Criminal Court, the International Criminal Tribunals of Yugoslavia and Rwanda, and even more.

Size is relative, of course. This small, tight world of genocide experts is something of a movable feast really: I keep meeting them at other conferences, in London, northern England, Stockholm, Lund, Washington, Toronto, and Rwanda itself. Their hero is Raphael Lemkin, the Polish Jewish lawyer who coined the word 'genocide' and was the driving force behind the 1948 UN Genocide Convention. They know by rote the convention's key clauses and even its wildly optimistic title: 'The Convention on the Prevention and Punishment of the Crime of Genocide.' And they know the politics. After long, acrimonious negotiations that included early intimations of Cold War hostilities, the General Assembly agreed soon after the Second World War that genocide would be defined as 'acts committed with intent to destroy, in whole or part, a national, ethnic, racial or religious group'.

From these few words spill a host of complications. How do you prove intent? Exactly how many victims are necessary to constitute a 'part'? What about 'politicide,' the word invented to describe attempts to eliminate political opponents, the stock-in-trade of both governments proudly promising to introduce 'socialism' – Stalin's USSR, Mao's China, Pol Pot's Cambodia – and those defending the 'free world' against 'socialism' – US-backed military dictatorships in Argentina, Brazil, Guatemala, Chile, Indonesia, the apartheid government in South Africa. What is the difference between mass murder, pogroms, or large-scale massacres and genocide, and why does it matter? And – the central conundrum – how can we know whether a conflict will escalate into a genocide until it actually does?

Then there are the bedevilling practical issues. What are the consequences of a determination that genocide is being carried out? Countries that ratify the convention 'undertake to prevent and to punish' genocide perpetrators, and are entitled to call on the UN 'to take such action under the Charter of the UN as they consider appropriate for the prevention and suppression of acts of genocide.' That's all. There's no call for direct military intervention. So, de-spite the apparent angst by the Clinton administration in 1994 that if it recognised Rwanda as a genocide it would be obliged to dispatch US troops, many authorities agree that a strongly worded resolution at the Security Council would fulfil the obligations of the convention – even if the genocide continued.

These issues have been debated at interminable length by the cognoscenti, who mostly agree about the flaws of the 1948 convention and disagree about attempts to amend it. As a result, like it or not, it will remain unamended, unsatisfactory as it clearly is, while the new International Criminal Court and the rest of us make do as best we can. And we will continue to disagree on what is and what is not a genocide. Some well-regarded scholars argue there have been as many as 50 such calamities since the world vowed 'Never Again' after Hitler's defeat in 1945. Others say that only four really meet the criteria set out in the UN Convention: the extermination of the Hereros, the Armenians, the Jews, and the Tutsi. It is more than a merely pedantic academic debate. But it will never be resolved. Genocide specialists seem to hold, simultaneously, two quite separate big ideas: that under certain circumstances all humans are capable of perpetrating unspeakable crimes against humanity; and that the only sound motive for being a 'genocide freak' – as one of them wryly calls the group – is to figure out how to prevent its recurrence. Intuitively, the two may seem to be in conflict. After all, the record indisputably shows that humans have used violent means to resolve disputes ever since our species first evolved. How can we prevent genocide – or violence between humans of any kind – since humans are clearly hardwired to resort to force under any number of circumstances? To activists, however, the resolution of this dialectic is obvious: we must learn to predict the onslaught of genocide and have the capacity to nip it in the bud.

It came as no surprise to me that so many well-known, highly reputable genocide scholars subscribe to the old insight memorably articulated by Walt Kelly's sweet comic book character, Pogo Possum: 'We have met the enemy and he is us.' You can not study this subject without wondering about yourself. And we all do. Most of the two dozen men and women who are the 'pioneers of genocide studies' explicitly believe that they themselves are potentially capable of the most atrocious behaviour imaginable. In the words of scholar and author Eric Markusen, 'the vast majority of perpetrators, accomplices and bystanders to genocidal violence are not sadists or psychopaths, but are psychologically normal according to standard means of assessing mental health and illness.' Yehuda Bauer, an Israeli and one of the Holocaust scholars, told me that genocidal attitudes now exist among both Palestinians and Israelis. This is not a man to use such language loosely. As for Rwanda, hundreds of thousands of Hutu were actively involved in the genocide. Most of them were ordinary Rwandans. What possible reason is there to believe they were fundamentally different from me? Or you?

But genocide scholars believe – hope? pray? – that our capacity for evil can be constrained. Perhaps the driving passion of genocide scholarship is to learn from the past to prevent recurrences in the future. As the presentations at the Galway conference amply demonstrated, these are scholar/activists who make no pretence to scholarly detachment. It is not that they eschew solid academic research; on the contrary, most take it very seriously and some are very good at it. But many openly pursue their academic work for activist ends. Virtually all of them are committed either to the prevention of future genocides or to having the world offer appropriate recognition to their own special genocide. A good number are committed to both. Indeed, there is now a Genocide Watch and a full-blown International Campaign to End Genocide supported by 24 active member organisations.

Why should this be? After all, you will not find all of the innumerable students of war marching with the peace movement, and no one expects them to. They are scholars for the sake of scholarship – or, perhaps, for publication. But I can confidently say that all experts in the Armenian genocide have as their overriding purpose getting the world to recognise the 1915 genocide inflicted by the Turks. What drives them mad is the continuing success of Ankara in pressuring the governments of Germany, Britain, the US, and – in an unnerving triumph of realpolitik over the solidarity of victims – Israel, to refuse to officially recognise the genocide of the Armenians.

The personal is political in genocide studies. Most authorities on the Armenian genocide are Armenians, descendants of the genocide's victims or survivors. Here, of course, is the key to their militancy and activism. Similarly, most of the pioneers of Holocaust and genocide studies, and the founders of the International Association of Genocide Scholars, and the *Journal of Genocide Studies*, have been Jewish – survivors, relatives of survivors, or child refugees. Another perceptible group, small but influential, focus on genocide scholarship from a Christian perspective; that is, genocide as the ultimate violation of the laws of God. This, needless to say, is not the bellicose Christianity that so many Americans now seem to embrace.

So Galway was not just another academic conference, a talk shop where the arcane and obscure so often reign. This was a coming together of people who had consciously steeped themselves in the most terrible calamities humans have wrought on each other. Many had been touched directly by a genocide. All had a cause, most of them worthy ones. Just about every imaginable horror show of the past century was flagged in those few days.

Yet every single person at that conference was aware that 'Never Again' had proved to be one of the greatest broken promises in history; as any genocide maven will aggressively tell you, 'Again and Again' is the more accurate phrase. The very reason the genocide prevention movement is thriving is because the phenomenon itself is thriving. Look at the last decade alone. Bosnia and

Rwanda. Serbs and Kosovars. Chechnya and East Timor. Nuclear threats, inherently genocidal, between Pakistan and India. Sierra Leone, with its child militias and child amputees. Potential genocide in the Ivory Coast. Burundi on a knife's edge. Rwanda enigmatic and unpredictable. The ongoing calamity in the eastern DRC. And the latest test case: the disaster in Darfur in western Sudan.

If crimes against humanity continue – and they do, as I write – it is not because specialists in genocide are not trying to prevent them. The question is how to do so. Most of these 'preventionists' argue for an early warning system that would allow experts to predict when a genocide is likely, so that the world can be informed and take appropriate action. For the last couple of years, some advocated for a 'genocide prevention focal point' to be set up permanently at the UN, and as his contribution to the tenth anniversary of the Rwandan genocide, UN Secretary-General Kofi Annan announced something very much like that. The premise is straightforward: through empirical and scientific observation of conflicts, we can isolate the variables and causal mechanisms at work and predict future genocides before they occur. With this information, we can then intervene and prevent the tragedy.

Once again, complications arise. There is no more reason for genocide scholars to agree on everything than for genocide victims to do so. Not everyone agrees on which conflicts in the past have been 'real' genocides. Not everyone agrees on the variables and stages that lead to genocide. In practice, it is usually more credible and accurate to speak of large-scale massacres and atrocities than of genocide. The Nazi genocide against the Jews did not begin until 1941. Until it was actually launched in Rwanda, no one could be sure there would be a genocide; but there had been anti-Tutsi pogroms galore. Already there is a heated dispute as to whether Darfur constitutes a genocide or 'ethnic cleansing.' Surely there is no need to resolve this semantic dispute before intervening?

Two intertwined dilemmas remain. Without meaning to sound pretentious, I had say that preventionists must address the question of human nature. In spite of endless 'Never Again' rhetoric and unprecedented efforts to prevent genocide in the past decade or so, and in the face of the rapid growth of what has been dubbed the 'genocide prevention industry,' before our very eyes the phenomenon of genocide has continued and even intensified. In this sense, the work of the preventionists is a Sisyphean labour of hope and faith over reason and evidence.

Even more problematic is the premise that if we are able to forecast an imminent genocide, policymakers will then naturally jump in and end the crisis before it escalates. I do not see it: I regard it as the genocide specialists' equivalent of 'the truth shall make you free' – one of life's great fallacies. Foreknowledge of genocide might just as easily have the opposite effect. Given the track record to date, it is at least as plausible to argue that early warnings of potential genocide are most likely to help politicians distance themselves from any obligation to intervene in the conflict. In the words of

Samuel Totten, a highly respected genocide scholar, developing potential early warning signals 'is easy – and this is a vast understatement – compared to mobilising the political will of the international community to act when such signals appear on the horizon'. Two factors are at work here. Human nature, for politicians, is to avoid entanglements they cannot control and which have little political payoff. Beyond that, the interests of the preventionists' world and the powers-that-be seem largely antithetical. Almost all of us oppose the major interventions initiated by the US and Britain, while they in turn are largely indifferent to the interventions we plead for.

As I write, Darfur stands as the test. Despite a flurry of activity, at the moment the world is failing badly, the penalty, as always, being paid by those under siege. Darfur is routinely called 'the new Rwanda,' but I am more taken with the differences. The massive attacks by Arab Muslim militias on African Muslim peasants and farmers, supported by the terrorist government in Khartoum, began in early 2003. Since then, the usual suspects among humanitarian and human rights agencies, joined by the International Campaign to End Genocide, have been demanding that action be taken. Early in 2004, with the death, rape, and refugee counts mounting, the calls for action intensified. Mainstream media coverage became widespread around April with the tenth anniversary of the Rwandan genocide. An unprecedented informal coalition emerged, including the Bush administration. Maybe it is a genocide, almost certainly it is severe ethnic cleansing, and it is without question a world-class atrocity. Everybody now agrees the situation is intolerable. This makes the situation almost more terrible than Rwanda's a decade ago. Despite everything we know, despite all the demands made on the terrorist Sudanese government by the most powerful forces on earth, nothing has changed. Verbal threats are backed by mealy-mouthed resolutions promising serious consideration of future action if the militias are not suppressed immediately. Meanwhile, the arrival of the rainy season in May blocked supplies to the hundreds of thousands of displaced African refugees, and the raids continued. How many more will be added to the 50,000 dead and the hundreds of thousands of pathetic refugees, while the world attacks with a torrent of words?

The real comparison with 1994, then, is simply inaction in the face of gross provocation. At the end of the day, no Geneva Convention on genocide, whatever its language, and no early warnings, however unmistakable, can substitute for political will among the powers-that-can. The extent of recent coverage of the Darfur tragedy suggests that media and public interest can indeed influence governments to appear to care. But garnering such interest, as Darfur plainly shows, is a long, drawn-out process, and the move from concern to action can take forever. Pessimists will not be disappointed.

For the record, none of those who betrayed Rwanda has ever faced the consequences. Not a single government has lost an election for allowing hundreds of thousands of Africans to be murdered. Not a single French politician has been held accountable for allowing the genocidaires to escape from Rwanda to Zaire/Congo, thereby setting in motion the catastrophic wars that have since plagued the African Great Lakes region. No one has been called on to resign for their actions or advice. Bill Clinton's 957-page memoir, *My Life*, calls Rwanda 'one of my greatest regrets,' and spends exactly two pages in total on the subject. This is truly the globalisation of impunity.

Nor did those guilty of sins against Rwanda deign to atone by commemorating the tenth anniversary of the genocide in Kigali in April. Kofi Annan went to Geneva instead. The US sent a mid-level diplomat who offered a derisory handout of a $1 million (US) for orphans, widows, and aids victims. Canada's delegation consisted of a former junior cabinet minister and the ambassador to Rome who advises on things African. Among all Western nations, only the Belgians sent their prime minister to apologise and repent. The Rwandans were disappointed but philosophical; their expectations were low.

None of this can give the preventionists a single reason for optimism. It is true that the Remembering Rwanda movement achieved some success. Commemorations of the tenth anniversary occurred around the world and Rwanda got more media coverage in those ten days than during the past ten years. But even if this attention proves to be sustainable, even if the victims and the survivors and the perpetrators and the 'bystanders' are all remembered, what then? We will not have changed. Darfur reminds us that, once more, 'Never Again' seems beyond human nature. Too many of us like to cause harm and too few of us care enough to prevent it.

Yet we go on. Why? Maybe because if we refuse to give up, we will stumble across an answer. Maybe because it matters that the victims gain some posthumous dignity. That the survivors will know someone cares. That the perpetrators are reminded that they can run but they can't hide. That those guilty of crimes of commission or omission – the French, the Americans, the Catholics, the Brits – will remember that there is no statute of limitations on accountability, and that we will keep naming and shaming them as long as is necessary. For myself, maybe it is because Carol will be reassured that I emerged from my encounter with genocide gloomier than ever but not ready to surrender. Not yet immobilised. And no less willing than before to throw myself – with the usual modest expectations, of course – into the eternal struggle that the pursuit of social justice and equality has always demanded.

This article was first published in the October issue of The Walrus, *a new Canadian general interest magazine. It is reproduced here with their permission.* The Walrus *magazine is available on newsstands and book stores in the US as well as Canada, with subscribers from all over the world. For more information about* The Walrus: *www. walrusmagazine.com.*

CHAPTER 3

JOINING HANDS: REGIONAL INTEGRATION IN SOUTHERN AFRICA

Regional Cooperation: What Future for SADC?

Henning Melber
Pambazuka 180, 28 October 2004

RECENT TRENDS seem to suggest a shift away from strengthening of regional cooperation in southern Africa. But such regionalism has been hitherto a declared priority on development agendas. Hampering factors currently include political differences such as the controversy over Zimbabwe. This escalated into a sharp division of views among the member countries of the Southern African Development Community (SADC). It is hardly an exaggeration to state that the inability to agree on a common approach has an almost paralysing effect. The following analysis is, however, concentrated on socio-economic factors of concern, which divide the region further instead of bringing it closer together.

Strategic Shift Towards NEPAD

The New Partnership for Africa's Development (NEPAD) seems to emerge increasingly as a type of mega-NGO to channel aid-funds into developmental projects, which at best claim, but in reality fail, to be driven by a desire towards enhanced regional collaboration. The programmes and policies funded under NEPAD are implemented mainly by countries and not by regional bodies. Hence NEPAD in effect undermines rather than strengthens an agency such as SADC (or any other regional institution).

This is a trend despite the fact that NEPAD attributes substantial relevance to regional bodies when identifying ways and means to achieve the defined socio-economic goals. NEPAD claims that its agenda is 'based on national and regional priorities and development plans', which ought to be prepared 'through participatory processes involving the people'. So far, however, no visible signs would indicate that the collective (multilateral) efforts aim at a united regional approach in SADC's relations with the outside world.

Nor does NEPAD so far translate its noble aims into practical steps for implementation. The blue print emphasises sub-regional and regional approaches even under a separate sub-heading. It stresses 'the need for African countries to pool their resources and enhance regional development and economic integration ... to improve international competitiveness'. But the crux of the matter lies there: the emphasis on international competitiveness comes at the expenses of strengthening the local economy and the local people. Instead, integration in Africa should as a priority meet the socio-economic and environmental needs of its citizenries and not seek to turn even more into an export platform.

NEPAD claims further to enhance the provision of essential regional goods as well as the promotion of intra-African trade and investments, with another focus on 'rationalising the institutional framework for economic integration'. But again, such an approach neglects the local/internal in favour of the global/external orientation. The implementation of NEPAD will hence most likely have an adverse effect and assist in an increased outward orientation of a regional bloc at the expenses of internal consolidation. It is interesting to note in this context, that notwithstanding the decisive role of South Africa within NEPAD, SADC has so far hardly acknowledged and certainly not embraced the initiative.

Divisive Free Trade Agreements

The Free Trade Agreement between the European Union and South Africa (EU-SA FTA) negotiated since the mid-1990s, had a similarly divisive effect on the southern African region by entering into a preferential trade relation with one country and thereby enhancing differences within the region resulting from existing conflicts of interest among the national economies.

South Africa herself, the monetary zone, the South African Customs Union (SACU) and SADC are already not in harmony at any time and less so given the effects of the FTA on regional economic matters. Hence the EU intervention adds more friction. The new economic partnership agreements (EPAs) negotiated between the countries in Africa, the Caribbean and the Pacific Islands (ACP states) on the one hand and the EU on the other not only seek to replace the previous Cotonou Agreement by means of sub-regional separate negotiations but also aim towards compatibility between EU-ACP trade relations and the World Trade Organisation (WTO). They are hence dependent upon the settlement of the Doha Development Agenda's controversial and yet unresolved issues.

Interestingly enough, the draft European Constitution makes no reference to cooperation with ACP states. It is only fair to assume that the EU enlargement shifts interest even further away from the neighbouring continent towards more collaboration closer to Brussels. In addition, the negotiations by the EU aim at separate accords with each region, and no country may negotiate in more than one bloc. As such, SADC is reduced to seven member countries (half of the 14 SADC states) under the EPA negotiations.

It is not far fetched to see that there is an inbuilt conflict between regionalism as it exists and the negotiation of new multilateral processes. Countries might differ over the advantages between benefits from the continued protection of regional arrangements or the creation of individual preferential access within other trade agreements. But if regionalism is considered as a problem or obstacle towards further global harmonisation under the WTO, it stands little chances of being a viable point of departure for strengthening in particular the least developed countries (LDCs) in the South within the global trade arrangements.

Instead, the predictable outcome of the current negotiations under the WTO related agreements will be a shrinking of 'development space'. To avoid such inegalitarian pseudo-partnerships, a shift in balance from the drive to homogenise trading commitments to other states towards granting states reasonable scope to choose appropriate levels of national protection is required. A development strategy would therefore have to operate in a zone where both internal as well as external integration reinforce rather than undermine each other. Instead, issues of internal integration (including issues of regional integration) have largely dropped off the development agenda as the gospel of the free trade paradigm dominates the discourse.

EU and US as partners?

The same limiting effects can be expected from the free trade agreement between SACU and the USA. The SACU-US FTA seems to promise nothing different from the US-American African Growth and Opportunity Act (AGOA), which tends to separate and divide instead of bringing African economies and interests closer. The benefits from AGOA differ among African countries according to their resources.

Ironically, in those countries which have been allocated LDC status under AGOA (receiving additional preferential treatment), external capital (from mainly East Asian countries) has managed to exploit the opportunities so created to supply the US market with cheap textiles from these countries under preferential tax regimes. The by and large unqualified and underpaid workforce in the local sweatshops is reaping negligible benefits from the super exploitation. Neither does the treasury in these states benefit, as initial investments and running costs for operations are substantially subsidised with public revenue instead of providing tax income from the profits generated.

Such recent trends point towards less rather than more regional cooperation and integration. The political and security interests might lead to increased support from the G8 (the group of eight most industrialised countries of the Northern hemisphere) and the strengthening of initiatives towards closer regional collaboration in reducing armed conflicts and securing more stability. Such stability continues, however, to be perceived as regime security, in contrast to a concept of human security. The latter would give primacy to human rights in favour of the citizens and not preference to the governments in power.

Even if there would be achievements in this direction, the multidimensionality and heterogeneity of a region like southern Africa is likely to persist and may eventually increase. This does not prevent external support from providing further positive regional interdependence. But this requires more than merely opening up to the global economy. More so, it would have to revisit matters of regional economic collaboration and seek the involvement of the majority of the African population in these countries. The current initiatives by the EU and the US under the WTO offer little to no promise that they will contribute to such a desirable tendency, either in SADC or elsewhere.

SADC's Regional Security Arrangements

Laurie Nathan
Pambazuka News 154, 29 April 2004

IN 1992 THE SOUTHERN African Development Community (SADC) was established as a regional organisation with a mandate to promote economic integration, poverty alleviation, peace, security and the evolution of common political values and institutions.

There were great expectations that the demise of apartheid and the Cold War would usher in a period of sustained stability and development at national and regional levels. Yet over the following decade the SADC region remained wracked by a high level of conflict that included civil wars in the Democratic Republic of Congo (DRC) and Angola, as well as violence and state repression in other countries.

SADC was largely ineffectual in these situations, distinguished less by its peacemaking efforts than by its fractious internal quarrels. The formation of the SADC Organ on Politics, Defence and Security – a common security forum whose stipulated functions include the prevention and resolution of conflict – was itself bedevilled by acrimonious disputes among member states over a ten-year period. In this commentary I address three questions: what accounts for the difficulty in establishing the organ? What are the reasons for SADC's poor record of peacemaking? And why was the analysis and prognosis of many academics and activists so flawed in the early 1990s?

Many analysts attribute the difficulty in establishing the organ to disagreements over its status and structure or to competition and animosity between South Africa and Zimbabwe. These diagnoses are superficial and incomplete.

Three more substantial problems have prevented SADC from creating an effective security forum. First and most importantly, there is an absence of common values among member states. There are two key lines of division: between democratic and authoritarian tendencies in the domestic policies of states, and between pacific and militarist orientations in their foreign policies.

As in the case of Europe, a viable regional organisation with a political and security mandate can institutionalise the common values of its members, develop common policies and contribute to peace and stability. However, the viability of such organisations depends in the first instance on the existence of common values.

In the absence of sufficient normative congruence, states are unable to resolve or transcend their major disputes, achieve cohesion and act with common purpose in crisis situations. In the realm of political governance, there are many de jure democracies whose executives are intolerant of dissent, hardly accountable to parliament and insufficiently committed to respect for human rights and the rule of law.

According to Jonathan Moyo prior to becoming Zimbabwe's Minister of Information:

> the assertion that the majority of African governments are now democratic ... has no empirical basis. It is true that multiparty elections are now common in Africa but this truth does not describe a fundamental development. The change is strategic, not substantive ... Just look at Zambia and Malawi since the fall of Kenneth Kaunda and the late Kamuzu Banda. Zimbabwe is following suit with reckless abandon.

In 1993 SADC's framework and strategy document, prepared by the SADC Secretariat, called for the forging of common political values based on democratic norms, the creation of a 'non-militaristic security order' and the establishment of mechanisms for conflict avoidance, management and resolution.

The document highlighted the need to address non-military sources of conflict and threats to human security, such as underdevelopment and abuse of human rights. The proposed strategies and mechanisms included a forum for mediation and arbitration; the ratification by states of key principles of international law; a non-aggression treaty and non-offensive defence doctrines; democratic civil-military relations; and reductions in military force levels and spending.

Many states did not support this anti-militarist agenda, however. Progress towards establishing a security forum was delayed over the next seven years by antagonistic and recriminatory debates around the organ's status and structure as manifestations of underlying political and strategic differences among member states.

The second reason for the difficulty in operationalising the organ lies in the reluctance of SADC states to surrender a measure of sovereignty to a security body that encompasses binding rules and decision-making in the sphere of high politics and the possibility of interference in domestic affairs. This reluctance derives from the political weakness of states and the absence of common values, mutual trust and a shared vision of the security body.

Third, southern Africa is characterised by small economies, underdevelopment and weak administrative capacity, which undermine the efficiency and effectiveness of all of SADC's multilateral forums and programmes. Ten years after its formation, SADC estimated that only 20 per cent of its 470 projects met the criteria for properly integrated regional projects, the rest being essentially national projects.

In addition to its inability to prevent violent conflict, SADC does not have a record of successful peacemaking. In many intra-state conflicts it has refrained from critical comment and diplomatic engagement, treating violence and crises in governance as purely domestic affairs.

In the case of state repression and abrogation of the rule of law in Zimbabwe, on the other hand, SADC has repeatedly expressed solidarity with the government.

There are several reasons for these responses. First, SADC states are keen to avoid adversarial relations that might jeopardise regional trade and functional cooperation. Second, governments that are not fully democratic are naturally unwilling to speak out against neighbouring countries that engage in undemocratic practices. Third, southern African states are determined to maintain a posture of unity and solidarity.

Forged in the heat of the struggles against colonialism and apartheid, this posture militates against public criticism of each other. The imperative of solidarity is greatest when foreign powers raise concerns that are perceived or can be portrayed as reflecting a 'neo-colonial' agenda. Solidarity of this kind enhances regime security at the expense of human security, masks rather than transcends the substantive disputes between states, and does not constitute a foundation for a common security forum.

Fourth, SADC's poor record of peacemaking is due to the impasse around the organ. The absence of an agreed set of norms, strategies and procedures for addressing high-intensity conflict has contributed to collective inertia, divergent and parochial approaches by individual states, ill-conceived interventions of doubtful legality, and a confused mixture of peacemaking and peace enforcement.

Most of these problems were evident in SADC's response to the crises in Lesotho and the DRC in 1998. The dispute between member states around the DRC crisis crippled the organ and gave rise to the notion of 'two SADCs', with two camps pursuing contradictory pacific and militarist strategies.

In the early and mid-1990s a number of academics and activists were involved in efforts to establish a common security forum and were optimistic about its prospects. What mistakes did we make? The reasons behind them might offer insights into future activities and policy recommendations.

First, we based our models of common security on the European experience without analysing adequately the nature of our own region and of its states in particular. We were strong on ideas and norms but weak on analysis. Second, we relied too much on the compelling need for a common security body and paid too little attention to the requirements for its success. Third, we overestimated the durability of the political bonds forged during the liberation struggles and underestimated the significance of the political differences between states.

Many analysts continue to make this mistake, arguing that the organ breakdown can be overcome by states forging a political consensus on human security, democracy and respect for human rights. If states do not support these norms and values at the national level, however, they will not support them at the regional level. Regional policy on security is a product of national policies on security.

Fourth, we were preoccupied (as many analysts still are) with the architecture of security arrangements when the critical issues in fact lie elsewhere:

structure follows strategy; strategy follows objectives; objectives are shaped as much by values as by interests; and the organ breakdown has occurred at the level of foundational values.

In general, we overstated what was possible at the regional level and understated what was required at the national level. Where democracy and human security do not exist, they are most likely to be attained through broad-based popular struggles.

CHAPTER 4

NOT YET A FORCE FOR FREEDOM: THE PROTOCOL ON THE RIGHTS OF WOMEN IN AFRICA

Rights of Women in Africa: Launch of a Petition to the African Union

Mary Wandia
Pambazuka News 162, 24 June 2004

THE AFRICAN CHARTER on Human and Peoples' Rights recognises the importance of women's rights through three main provisions. Article 18(3), covering the protection of the family, promises to ensure the elimination of all discrimination against women and also ensure protection of the rights of women. Article 2, the non-discrimination clause, provides that the rights and freedoms enshrined in the charter shall be enjoyed by all irrespective of race, ethnic group, colour, sex, language, religion, political or any other opinion, national and social origin, fortune, birth or other status. And Article 3, the equal protection clause, states that every individual shall be equal before the law and shall be entitled to the equal protection of the law.

However, the above provisions are not adequate to address the rights of women. For example, while Article 18 prohibits discrimination against women, it does so only in the context of the family. In addition, explicit provisions guaranteeing the right of consent to marriage and equality of spouses during and after marriage are absent. These omissions are compounded by the fact that the charter emphasises traditional African values and customs without addressing concerns that many customary practices, such as female genital mutilation, forced marriage, and wife inheritance, can be harmful or life threatening to women. By ignoring critical issues such as custom and marriage, the charter inadequately defends women's human rights.

The World Conference on Human Rights held in Vienna, Austria in 1993 made advances to human rights theory and practice with respect to women's human rights. The Declaration and Programme of Action of the World Conference on Human Rights at Vienna emphasised: 'The human rights of women and of the girl child are an inalienable, integral and indivisible part of universal human rights.'

It also emphasised that the elimination of violence against women is a human-rights obligation for states. This was the first attempt to address the marginalisation of women's human rights from the work of mainstream human rights. Thus the slogan that emerged from Vienna was: 'Women's rights are human rights'. Following almost directly on from Vienna, it was imperative for the African Commission on Human and People's Rights (ACHPR) to expose the specific inequalities that impact negatively on the lives of women and thereby acknowledge that 'women's rights as human rights must be respected and observed'.

Developing the Protocol

Article 66 of the charter that provides for the establishment of protocols and agreements to supplement its provisions gave impetus to the consideration and subsequent formulation of the Protocol to the African Charter on Human and Peoples' Rights on the Rights of Women in Africa.

The process started with a meeting organised by Women in Law and Development in Africa (WiLDAF) on the theme 'The African Charter on Human and People's Rights and the Human Rights of Women in Africa' in March 1995 in Lome, Togo. The meeting called for the development of a protocol to the charter on women's rights. The meeting also called on the ACHPR to appoint a Special Rapporteur on Women's Rights in Africa. The assembly of heads of states and government of the Organisation of Africa Unity (OAU) at its 31st Ordinary Session in June 1995, in Addis Ababa, mandated the ACHPR to elaborate a Protocol on the Rights of Women in Africa.

The first draft was prepared by the experts group meeting organised by the ACHPR and the International Commission of Jurist (ICJ) in Nouakchott, Mauritania, April 1997. The experts comprising of members of the ACHPR, representatives of African NGOs and international observers prepared the first Draft Protocol that was submitted to the ACHPR during its 22nd Session held in October 1997 for consideration and comments. The draft was also circulated to NGOs for comments.

The 12th ICJ workshop on 'Participation in the African Commission on Human and People's Rights', October 30 to November 1, 1997, in The Gambia, provided the opportunity for NGOs to make input into the Draft Protocol and pass a resolution calling upon the ACHPR to ensure the completion of the Draft Protocol in time for presentation to the next session of the ACHPR.

The First Meeting of the Working Group on Women's Rights that brought together members of the ACHPR, the ICJ, WiLDAF and the African Centre for Democracy and Human Rights Studies (ACDHRS) was held in Banjul, the Gambia on 26-28 January 1998. The meeting amended the draft protocol and developed the terms of reference for the appointment of a Special Rapporteur on the Rights of Women in Africa.

During its 23rd session, held in April 1998, the ACHPR endorsed the appointment of the first Special Rapporteur on Women Rights in Africa with a mandate that included working towards the adoption of the draft protocol on women's rights. The ACHPR forwarded the draft protocol to the OAU Secretariat in 1999. The Inter Africa Committee (IAC) and ACHPR met to merge the Draft Convention on Traditional Practices with the draft protocol in 2000, in Addis Ababa, Ethiopia.

The first OAU Government Experts Meeting on the draft protocol was held in November 2001, in Addis Ababa, Ethiopia. The experts amended the draft protocol developed by the ACHPR and called on the OAU to schedule a second AU experts meeting in 2002 to consider the draft again before the hosting of an OAU ministerial meeting on the same issue. African women's organisations participated in the meeting as observers. The OAU scheduled the second experts meeting and ministerial meeting twice in 2002 but had to postpone them due to the lack of a quorum. Thus the draft was not presented for adoption by the inaugural summit of the African Union (AU) held in Durban, South Africa in July 2002 and it seemed that there was little political will among African governments to move this process forward.

In January 2003, African women's organisations from across the continent met in Addis Ababa, Ethiopia at a meeting convened by Equality Now, FEMNET and the Ethiopian Women Lawyers Association (EWLA) to come up with strategies to lobby the AU and individual governments to schedule and attend the expert and ministerial meetings on the draft protocol. Represented at the meeting were ACDHRS, Akina Mama Wa Africa, the Association of Malian Women Lawyers (AJM), the Association of Senegalese lawyers (AJS), Equality Now, EWLA, Femmes Afrique Solidarite (FAS), FEMNET, WILDAF, and WRAPA. These organisations pooled comments in a collective mark-up to strengthen the document and bring it into line with international standards. Following the meeting they met with officials of the AU, including the then Acting Commissioner for Peace and Security, who was in charge of the protocol, and urged him to call for the second experts and ministerial meetings on the protocol in March 2003 in an effort to ensure that the draft protocol was adopted by the AU summit in July 2003. The organisations further lobbied ministries of justice and gender at national level through their networks to confirm that they would be there ensure the AU obtained the required quorum.

The Second AU Experts Meeting followed by the Ministerial Meeting on the Draft Protocol was held in March 2003, in Addis Ababa, Ethiopia. The meetings amended and adopted the draft protocol and recommended it for adoption by the Executive Council and Assembly of the AU. African women's organisations attended the meetings as observers and lobbied the experts and ministers to strengthen the draft protocol to the level of regional and international human rights agreements on women.

The Second Ordinary Summit of the AU adopted the Protocol to the African Charter on Human and Peoples' Rights on the Rights of Women in Africa on 11 July 2003 in Maputo, Mozambique. The assembly appealed to all member states to sign and ratify the protocol in order to ensure its speedy entry into force. The protocol will enter into force after 15 countries have ratified it. The protocol will complement the African charter in ensuring the promotion and protection of the human rights of women in Africa.

Content and Meaning for Women in Africa

Mainstream international human rights standards are defined in relation to men's experience, and stated in terms of discrete violations of rights in the public realm whereas most violations of women's human rights occur in private. The private/public dichotomy that is detrimental to women continues to exist. In most African countries, the same constitutional provisions that guarantee gender equality allow exceptions in the so-called 'private law' areas of customary law, personal law and family law. Serious violations of women's human rights such as violence against women and provisions that discriminate against them are found in that private sphere.

Human rights guarantees in the legally binding human rights conventions such as the right to life, to bodily integrity, and to be free from torture, cruel and degrading treatment, have not been interpreted to include such acts as domestic violence, rape, female genital mutilation, forced sterilisation, forced childbirth, and numerous other forms in which violence against women and girls is manifested in Africa.

Provisions on women's human rights in the UN Convention on the Elimination of all Forms of Discrimination Against Women (CEDAW), and the Beijing Declaration and Platform for Action have not involved a conceptual shift or effected structural changes needed to implement their resolutions. The protocol primarily complements the African charter and international human rights conventions by focusing on concrete actions and goals to grant women rights. It further domesticates CEDAW and the Beijing Declaration and Platform for Action in the African context.

The protocol is in three sections. The first section covers the rationale behind its elaboration, making reference to both regional and international commitments on women's human rights. The second section outlines the rights to be upheld by the protocol. And the third and final section covers implementation by addressing the manner in which it is to be adopted and monitored, as well as the process through which it may be amended. The protocol affirms four broad categories of rights: civil and political rights; economic, social and cultural rights; the rights to development and peace; and reproductive and sexual rights.

Status of Ratification

Almost a year after its adoption, only one member state of the AU, the Comoros, has signed and ratified it. Twenty-eight member states have signed but are yet to ratify it as of 12 May 2004. This calls for 14 more countries to ratify in order for it to come into force. Its entry into force is critical because it will commit governments to:
■ Submit periodic reports to the ACHPR on legislative and other measures they have undertaken to ensure the full realisation of rights recognised under the protocol
■ Integrate a gender perspective in their policy decisions, legislation, development plans and activities and ensure the overall well-being of women
■ Include in their national constitutions and other legislative instruments fundamental principles of the protocol and ensure their effective implementation
■ Eliminate all forms of violence and discrimination against women in Africa and promote equality between men and women.

Advocacy Needs and Initiatives

Given the time and effort necessary to persuade governments to adopt this protocol compared with the desperate urgency to promote, protect and safe-guard women's human rights in Africa, African civil society organisations have to campaign and lobby governments to sign and ratify the protocol as soon as possible and in any event, as a gesture of commitment, before the next AU Summit to be held in Addis Ababa, Ethiopia in July 2004.

Oxfam GB, Equality Now, FEMNET, CREDO for Freedom of Expression and Associated Rights and Fahamu have started a campaign targeting 14 countries that have already signed with the aim of lobbying them to ratify the protocol. They have drafted a petition to be presented to the AU Summit in July 2004. Please sign up at http://www.pambazuka.org/petition/petition.php?id=1

To supplement their efforts you could as an individual or organisation:
■ Contact relevant government officials in ministries of foreign affairs, women's affairs, and justice and urge them to ratify the protocol
■ Urge governments to be fully involved in the full realisation of the human rights of women, if they have not done so
■ Encourage government officials to include the issue of the protocol in contacts with other governments and to state their positions publicly in the media or other events
■ Inform and increase public awareness about the protocol by putting women's issues on the human rights agenda at various fora
■ Mobilise national and local support for the protocol among academics, parliamentarians, and the media

■ Work on creating a better and common understanding of issues as provided for in the protocol;

■ Support the organisation of local focal points on the protocol to lobby and monitor government positions. The focal points will later be effective in the monitoring of implementation of the protocol by governments.

Conclusion

The protocol, once it comes into force, will usher in a new and significant era in the promotion and protection of the rights of women in Africa and end impunity for all forms of violations of the human rights of women in Africa. As Dr Angela Melo, Special Rapporteur on the Rights of Women, ACHPR notes:

> The women of Africa who have suffered for long, their efforts at building our beloved continent have gone on for long without acknowledgement, and the men of Africa should be equally committed to the task. The urgent need to work towards the ratification and effective implementation of the protocol urgently is a great challenge, yet a duty we all owe to posterity and to Africa.

Unfinished Business –
African Leaders Must Act Now to Ratify
the Protocol on the Rights of Women

Faiza Jama Mohamed
Pambazuka News 162, 24 June 2004

IT TOOK ALMOST a decade (eight years to be precise) for African leaders to finally agree on a text and adopt the Protocol on the Rights of Women in Africa at the Second Ordinary Summit of the African Union held in Maputo in July 2003. The protocol is a legal framework for African women to use in exercising their rights. It is comprehensive in that it addresses various concerns of women of different ages and conditions based on the realities of their lives. For that reason it is welcomed and celebrated by all African women.

Before it finally came onto the agenda of the heads of states meeting last year, several obstacles had to be overcome. The first experts meeting convened by the OAU (now the African Union) in November 2001 brought together officials who in the majority regrettably had little legal or gender expertise. As a result, the draft document that came out of that meeting had serious gaps and was of a lower standard than other comparable international law instruments such as the Convention on Elimination of all Forms of Discrimination Against Women (CEDAW) and the International Covenant on Civil and Political Rights (ICCPR), which most African states had already ratified.

The experts meeting also failed to reach agreement on some aspects of the draft. A future date was set to finalise the outstanding provisions, but this and other meetings called by the OAU/African Union had to be cancelled for lack of a quorum. Activists around Africa saw two problems: the document was weak and did not adequately address the specific issues relating to African women, and progress was slow because of the repeated lack of a quorum. This illustrated the low priority accorded to women – although they make up over 50 per cent of Africa's population – by the very governments they have voted into office.

Activists then decided it was time to refocus their efforts. Various consultations were held around Africa among civil society organisations. Equality Now, an international human rights organisation, joined the process in July 2002 at a meeting convened by the United Nations Fund for Women (UNIFEM) in Nairobi. Equality Now also consulted with the African Women's Development and Communications Network (FEMNET), the African Centre for Democracy and Human Rights Studies (ACDHRS), Women in Law and Development in Africa (WiLDAF), and other regional and national groups that were most actively engaged in working toward the passage of a strong protocol for the protection and promotion of women's rights.

In January 2003, Equality Now convened a strategy meeting of activists in Addis Ababa, proceeding with the meeting although the governmental meeting it was scheduled to coincide with was again cancelled for lack of a quorum. The meeting discussed, reviewed and strengthened the text of the draft protocol with the help of women's rights organisations from across Africa. The collective mark-up thus produced was widely distributed across the continent for promotion with national governments. The coalition of activists also lobbied African governments to send delegates with legal and human rights expertise to the scheduled meeting of the African Union.

Equality Now was nominated to take on a coordinating role and to work closely with the Secretariat of the African Union to encourage a successful meeting. In response to the campaign several countries held national consultation meetings with civil society organisations to review the mark-up. Several countries also brought members from civil society as part of their delegation to the experts meeting.

All in all, countries were much better prepared when they came to the experts meeting in March 2003 and many were also open to improving the existing document. Immediately prior to the meeting of experts and the African Union Ministerial Meeting in Addis Ababa, Equality Now's Africa office convened another meeting of women's rights activists and organisations, in order to coordinate a strategic plan for advocacy and to ensure that the substantive provisions of the draft protocol were strengthened during the course of the experts' and ministerial meetings. These advocacy efforts had a dramatic impact on the draft protocol, which was significantly improved during the course of the meeting. Subsequently, on 11 July 2003, the African Union adopted the Protocol on the Rights of Women in Africa.

The campaign by activists for the Protocol on the Rights of African Women represents a successful model of cooperation among national, regional and international women's NGOs that led to concrete results. The African Union's Commissioner Djinnit Said also saw the campaign around the protocol as an excellent model for collaboration between the African Union and civil society organisations and said as much in a meeting the African Union hosted earlier in the year to consult with African civil society organisations.

One year after its adoption, however, only 30 countries have signed the protocol and only one (the Comoros) has ratified it. It needs 15 ratifications to enter into force. Until then these rights remain hypothetical! All the past efforts by civil society will have been wasted if the protocol is not ratified. And the majority of women in Africa will continue to be deprived of protection under international law of many of their basic rights. For this reason, activists have once again pooled their resources, energy and focus to urge governments to honour their commitments to uphold women's rights by ratifying the protocol as soon as possible, ideally by the heads of state summit in July 2004.

Women around Africa are daily monitoring the website of the African Union taking note of which of their leaders are true to their commitments. Women's organisations and human rights organisations in Africa have launched national campaigns to lobby their respective governments, engaging in dialogue with the relevant ministries of justice, foreign affairs, gender and in some cases even the heads of states offices to impress upon them the importance of ratifying the protocol without delay.

With a concerted effort, together we can achieve ratification. That is why activists in Guinea-Conakry are working hard to sensitise parliamentarians and decision-makers through workshops and meetings in an effort to win support for the ratification of the protocol. Groups in Kenya are engaging in dialogue with several ministries (Ministry of Gender, Sports and Culture; Ministry of Home Affairs and the Ministry of Foreign Affairs) to sensitise them and discuss the process of ratification and the need to speed up the ratification process. In Mali women are planning to hold information and sensitisation forums with parliamentarians as well as mobilising women's organisations to make a declaration urging the government to ratify the protocol. In South Africa plans are underway to inform the Office of the President and the Department of Foreign Affairs and the State Law advisors as well as the Parliamentary Commissions on Justice, Quality of Life and the Status of Women about the protocol and discuss the obstacles to its early ratification. And these are just some of the activities planned around the continent to press for ratification. It is imperative that governments heed our urgent call for women to be guaranteed equal status to men and equal protection of their rights.

The Protocol for the Rights of Women in Africa as it stands now is a piece of paper without any force. By ratifying it, governments will be taking the first step towards recognising the equal worth of women. Implementation will then be critical. The protocol makes many equality advances for women under international law, including affording special protection to vulnerable groups such as widows, the disabled and those from marginalised groups. It is only by protecting and promoting the rights of all its peoples that Africa will be able to access its full resources and lead the continent to prosperity. The Beijing +10 review process offers African governments an opportunity to demonstrate their determination to lead their peoples along the path to development. One concrete benchmark is the seriousness that they give to the Protocol on the Rights of Women in Africa. If they ratify it now they will have a concrete achievement to bring to the table later this year when the continent comes together for the Beijing +10 conference, as a gesture of recognition for the human rights of women as a priority agenda of the continent.

We call on African leaders to honour their commitments to women and act now to ratify the protocol!

A Plea for Ratification

Zeinab Kamil Ali
Pambazuka News 162, 24 June 2004

SOME BIG EVENTS in life pass by unnoticed by human intelligence. We must generally wait for the analysis of historians several decades later to see if the events classify as historic. It is often said quite mechanically that history is repeating itself, without thinking about the lessons to be drawn from such pronouncements. Must we wait for the end of the century to recognise the historical value of the Protocol on the Rights of Women?

With the Constitutive Act of the African Union, it seems that Africa has taken a step forward. In fact, with strong regional structures and decisions that have been redynamised and honoured by the visionary leadership of the heads of states, Africa is now adorned with an essential that it had lacked: she is now equipped with a common will, a real union to mobilise her energies and forge a common objective in the fight against underdevelopment and the numerous ills that this entails.

There is no doubt that the highlight is the recognition of women as equal partners with men and the need for women's involvement in the running of African affairs, state affairs and family or private affairs. The African woman is now on at the centre of the credo of all political discussions. The consecration of the concept of gender parity in the Constitutive Act of the African Union, in the recruitment of commissioners and all other technical personnel brilliantly marks the end of an era where action to promote women was only included under pressure from donors, and without any concern for the improvement in the condition of African women.

The adoption of an African instrument specific to the rights of women reveals in plain language the appropriation by the African states of the principles of equality and non-discrimination.

In all the big meetings in the history of Africa, Africans have known how to show their courage and mobilise their energies so that their people's cause is heard. Through this protocol, which solemnly reaffirms their rights, the protection of their dignity and their non-disputable role in the management of the affairs of the state and in the decision-making spheres, Africans are recovering their traditional values. What does the Protocol to the African Charter on Human and People's Rights on the Rights of Women in Africa say?

As a regional instrument, it flows from the African Charter on Human and People's Rights adopted in 1981. The provisions of the protocol protect the rights of African women such as they are recognised and guaranteed to all human beings and particularly by the international instruments on human rights, namely the Universal Declaration on Human Rights, the International Covenant on Civil and Political Rights, the International Covenant on Economic, Social and Cultural Rights, the Convention on the Elimination of all Forms of Discrimination against Women and its optional protocols, the African Charter on the Rights and Well Being of the Child and all other conventions and international treaties on women's rights as human rights, inalienable, interdependent and indivisible.

The 12th consideration in the preamble provides the framework for understanding the protocol.

The Rights Protected by the Protocol

The rights protected in the protocol are diverse and are not exhaustively discussed in this paper. However the principle of equality cuts across them all. With its corollary, the principle of non-discrimination, the principle of equality is recognised in all African constitutions.

The francophone countries recognise equality between men and women formally and in law. In the other countries, however, there are specific mechanisms for putting into effect these legal principles. The protocol goes beyond the abstract of laws protecting women's rights. There are specific provisions to ensure that the laws are implemented with specific actions given to guide such processes. These are found in the provisions on the right to life, to integrity, security, elimination of all harmful practices, access to justice and equal protection before the law. The need for concrete application reverberates through the whole document and economic rights of women as well as the right to social protection are recognised.

The protocol is worded to take account of the African experience. The right to food security, the encouragement of the creation of a system of social protection in favour of women working in the informal sector makes real sense to African women. The protocol takes women's rights from a universal setting to one where all are able to access them. This is why it must be ratified. The majority of African constitutions possess the necessary legislative mechanisms to protect the rights of women. The ratification of the protocol will stir the constitutional mechanisms into action. Where they are absent, ratification will allow them to be established.

Further by virtue of Article 26 the states have an obligation to include the level of implementation of the protocol in their periodic reports to the African Commission on Human Rights. Paragraph 2 of Article 26 makes an interesting provision in as far as the budgetary question goes and this is indeed a soft spot for African states: African states must allocate enough funds for the implementation of the protocol. Hitherto the budgetary allocations have been very weak for women's issues.

Innovation of the Protocol

The protocol takes into account elderly as well as handicapped and illiterate women. This indicates the evolution of African society and further offers special protection for women in situations of distress, women in prison, and pregnant and lactating mothers. The recognition of the rights of widows is a further indication of this evolution as widows suffer a lot from traditional practices and a blatant disregard for their rights upon the death of their husbands. The rights of women to political participation and decision making is recognised as well, even though these rights are recognised in the ICCPR and its predecessor, the 1952 convention.

Article 9 introduces the term parity for the first time and paves the way for affirmative action in legislation in the member states. A distinction is made in the article between equality of chances and equality in result. It is noted that women must be made equal partners with men in decision-making processes as well as in policy formulation.

Women must be able to offer themselves to the electorate in a democracy and this can only happen if the political parties make it possible for them to do so. Political participation and its constituent characteristics must be looked at from the perspective of the rights of women.

Peace and development are interdependent in the same way that democracy and respect for human rights are interdependent. Human rights cannot be dissociated from women's rights. The human genus is made up of men and women. Harmony can only be attained if the rights of both are respected.

The right to peace and the right to development are hardly ever recognised in international conventions. This protocol is a first as hitherto these rights have only been mentioned in the General Assembly of the UN without being given real protection.

The main advantage of the protocol is that it seeks to harmonise the different systems regulating the rights of the family and women. The contradictions of the African systems are evident in the plural judicial systems, which often lead to confusion. The family in many African states is managed by traditional laws and by sharia in the Muslim states. As such, substantial breaches to the principles of equality and non-discrimination are entrenched in the constitutions – the supreme laws of these states. Article 6 shows the will to reconcile these opposing and fundamental differences in legal systems. Article 7 gives the courts and the judicial systems the duty to arbitrate over personal law and laws of the family.

Article 6c addresses the issues of marriage and highlights the objective harmonisation of the conflicting laws. It also brings to the fore the search for a new Africa based on harmony and free of contradictions. The preservation of African values rests with women, the custodians of legends and traditions known in our time for their unending fight for peace, liberty, dignity, justice and solidarity. I believe that this is argument enough to encourage the heads of states to emulate the Comoros in ratifying the protocol to the African Charter on Human and People's Rights on the Rights of Women in Africa.

The Entry into Force of the Protocol on the Rights of Women in Africa: a Challenge for Africa and Women

Kafui Adjamagbo-Johnson
Pambazuka News 162, 24 June 2004

THE ADOPTION OF the Protocol to the African Charter on Human and People's Rights on the Rights of Women by the conference of the heads of state and government at the African Union meeting in Maputo in July 2003 was undeniably an important event in the history of African women's struggle for the recognition of their rights.

This protocol, the fruits of exemplary collaboration between the African Commission for Human and People's Rights and civil society organisations, was identified as a priority for the promotion and protection of the rights of African women during a workshop in March 1995 on women's rights, organised by the commission, in collaboration with Women in Law and Development in Africa/Femmes, Droit et Développement en Afrique (WiLDAF/FeDDAF) and the International Commission of Jurists, based in Geneva.

The workshop recommended that a protocol on women's rights should be established and a Special Rapporteur on the rights of women should be nominated. The conference of the former Organisation of African Unity (OAU) mandated the commission to initiate and coordinate the process of developing a preliminary draft of the protocol. A working group was put in place to propose a text. Since the beginning, the process has been very participatory.

Civil society organisations mobilised themselves to enrich the first version written by the working group. This mobilisation increased during the process, as more and more organisations became interested in all steps of the development of the protocol. The numerous ups and downs that punctuated the process sometimes worried civil society members. The long wait between the first and the second meetings, due to successive postponement of the second one, and in the absence of a quorum, was one of the most difficult moments.

However, the lobbying efforts of civil society and the determination of officers of the African Union resulted in the second meeting of experts. This was followed by a meeting of ministers implicated in the process, who succeeded in registering the protocol on the agenda of the council of ministers in July 2003. Eight years after the beginning of the process, the protocol was thus finally adopted by heads of state.

I relive the joy manifested by the lobby of women's organisations at the announcement of the protocol's adoption, and salute the cooperation that coalesced between certain commissioners and these women. But nobody was fooled! Once the protocol was adopted, there remained many equally important steps to take: to obtain the necessary signatures and ratifications for its entry into force and to respond to the challenge of its effective implementation.

One year on, where are we at in the process? Thirty signatures and one ratification had been registered by 15 June 2004, less than three weeks before the next AU heads of state and government conference. Twelve of the signatory countries are in West Africa, eight in East African and five in southern Africa. Lobbying work must continue in all the regions of Africa, particularly in Central and North Africa, where only three and two signatures, respectively, have been registered. It is important to note that we are still far, very far, from the 15 ratifications necessary for the entry into force of the protocol. And the question of its ratification must absolutely, in one way or another, be added to the agenda of the July 2004 summit in Addis Ababa, in the interests of women, African populations and the African Union.

But why is ratification of the protocol so important?

For African women, the entry into force of the protocol will be an essential step towards the recognition of their rights, the daily violations of which are the source of immense suffering. The protocol will offer, following the example of the Convention on the Elimination of all Forms of Discrimination against Women (CEDAW) a legal framework of reference, allowing diverse actors, as well as the population, to daily work towards the effective respect of women's rights. But, in addition to CEDAW, the legal framework of the protocol reflects specific violations to African women. Its preamble justifies the adoption of the protocol by citing the continued existence of discriminations against women and harmful traditional practices, despite commitments made by states at regional and international levels. It also expresses leaders' formal support to the principle of equality between men and women.

In addition to these declarations, the protocol contains provisions to respond to problems as crucial as the multiple violations of rights in marital relations, violence and grave risks to the life, physical and moral integrity, and security of women and girls, the pressing reality of which we cannot deny in our societies. The entry into force of the protocol offers an invaluable framework for ending violations against civilian, refugee and combatant women and children, particularly girls, in periods of conflict, and for upholding the challenge of peace in Africa, a condition sine qua non for development.

The fight against traditional practices harmful to the health of women and girls needs the protocol, which provides guidelines for eliminating them. Economic and social rights as vital as the right to health, including reproductive health, to education and to inheritance rights for widows and girls, which are daily transgressed out of ignorance or deliberately, would be better protected if actions taken could rely on adequate measures, such as those recommended in the protocol. Definitively, there is no doubt that, in the interests of hundreds of thousands of women and girls in Africa, the protocol on women's rights must be ratified as quickly as possible.

For African populations and societies, the absence of a legal framework of reference to fight against violations of women's rights currently constitutes a real handicap for the optimal participation of women in the development of their countries and of Africa, even though they constitute more than 50 per cent of the population of the continent.

Finally, the credibility of the African Union, which demonstrated its commitment to promoting women's participation and gender equality, notably through parity in the African Union Commission and in the equitable representation of judges of the African Court for Human and People's Rights, rests on proving its coherence and consistency by implementing the protocol without delay. By doing so, the AU and its member states will show the world that, for them also, women's rights are truly an integral part of human rights, and that they are determined to promote and protect them without any discrimination.

The imminent entry into force of the protocol will mark, in sum, a decisive step towards entrenching a culture of respect and exercising the human rights of women in African societies. For all these reasons, every human rights defender, man or woman, should feel concerned and lobby governmental and parliamentary authorities in order to convince them to ratify the protocol on women's rights and take steps for its effective implementation. Our mothers, our daughters and our sisters, including those who are rarely accustomed to demand their rights, cry for help in a meaningful silence, but are often too quickly assimilated into resignation. It depends on each person to ensure that the voice of the voiceless are finally heard by those who are responsible for the fate of African populations.

African States:
Equal to the Task?

Hannah Forster
Pambazuka News 162, 24 June 2004

Background

An important step to establish a legal framework for the promotion and protection of the rights of women throughout the African continent was taken
when the Protocol to the African Charter on Human and Peoples' Rights on
the Rights of Women in Africa was adopted on 11 July 2003 by the Assembly
of the African Union during its second summit in Maputo, Mozambique.

Scope

The new protocol will complement the African charter in advancing and
ensuring the human rights of the African woman. It covers a broad range of
human rights issues, including:

■ Access to justice and equal protection before the law
■ The right to life, integrity and security of person; the right to inheritance,
and calls for affirmative action to promote equal participation in the political
and decision making process; equal representation of women in the judiciary
and law enforcement agencies as an integral part of equal protection and
benefit of the law
■ The broad range of economic, social and cultural rights for women i.e. the
right to equal pay for equal work and the right to adequate and paid
maternity leave in both private and public sectors; the rights of particularly
vulnerable groups of women i.e. elderly women, disabled women, widows,
'women in distress' – pregnant or nursing women in detention, poor women,
women from marginalised population groups are all recognised; protection
against harmful traditional practice; for women in armed conflict; refugee
women; right to food security and adequate housing; and recognition of the
right of women to participate in the promotion and maintenance of peace.

Landmark Provisions

■ The reproductive right of women to medical abortion when pregnancy
results from rape or incest or when the continuation of pregnancy endangers
the health or life of the mother
■ The legal prohibition of female genital mutilation.
   The African Commission on Human and Peoples' Rights will supervise the
implementation of the protocol pending the establishment of the African
Court on Human and Peoples' Rights.

States parties to the protocol commit themselves among others things:
■ To indicate in their periodic reports to the African Commission the legislative and other measures undertaken to ensure the full realisation of the rights recognised in the protocol
■ To include in their national constitutions and other legislative instruments these fundamental principles and ensure their effective implementation
■ To integrate a gender perspective in their policy decisions, legislation, development plans, and activities and to ensure the overall well-being of women
■ To take effective measure to prevent the exploitation and abuse of women in advertising and pornography.

The protocol will enter into force 30 days after the deposit of the 15th instrument of ratification. The African Centre for Democracy and Human Rights Studies (ACDHRS) has followed the process of the protocol with keen interest since the beginning of the discourse in the early 1990s. The lobby for the protocol has mobilised a wide number of networks when the inadequacies of the African charter in providing for the rights of women was realised. ACDHRS served as a member of the working group set up by the African Commission to develop and formulate the first draft, which was forwarded to the AU (then the OAU). Over the years, the centre continued to work closely with other organisations and activists on the continent to maximise our collective collaborative resources to advance this giant step in the cause of human rights.

The adoption of the protocol ushers in a new and significant era in the promotion and protection of the rights of women in Africa. To date, only one country has ratified the protocol on the Rights of Women in Africa, while 30 have signed, thus indicating their intention to do so.

The Appeal

While the African Centre for Democracy and Human Rights Studies congratulates African governments for adopting the protocol, we would wish to urge member states to pursue the process of ratification of the protocol with much vigour and speed to ensure a prompt entry into force of the instrument and therefore its implementation. If the protocol is ratified and fully implemented, it has the potential to become an important framework to end impunity for all forms of violations of the human rights of women in Africa. Furthermore, the process of ratifying and ushering in implementation would reinforce sates' commitment to ending discrimination and violence against women. The women of Africa who have suffered for so long, whose efforts at building our beloved continent have gone on for too long without acknowledgement, and indeed the men of Africa, should be equal to the task. This is a challenge and a duty we all owe to posterity and to Africa.

We therefore add our voice to all those of our brothers and sisters calling on states to stand up to this challenge and perform the duty it requires. The momentum should not be lost less history judges us unequal to the responsibility.

Putting an End to Female Genital Mutilation: the African Protocol on the Rights of Women

Faiza Jama Mohamed
Pambazuka News 173, 9 September 2004

IN JULY 2003 African Heads of States adopted the Protocol on the Rights of Women in Africa at their summit in Maputo (full text of the protocol is available at http://www.africa-union.org/). A little over a year later only four countries (the Comoros, Libya, Rwanda and Namibia) have ratified it. This is far from the required 15 ratifications for the protocol to come into force.

One might ask why ratification of the protocol is so important and what value it brings to African women. The protocol offers women in Africa not only a bill of rights that addresses issues in the African context, but it also obligates states to take action and allocate resources to ensure that African women enjoy these rights. The protocol offers a concrete blueprint to go beyond lip service and make states' undertakings accountable. These rights will, however, remain fictitious until member states of the African Union ratify and implement the protocol into their domestic legislation.

Amongst the rights articulated in the protocol is the right in Article 5 'not to be subjected to harmful traditional practices including female genital mutilation (FGM)'. Female genital mutilation is a harmful traditional practice that afflicts an estimated 130 million girls and women. According to the World Health Organisation (WHO), 6,000 girls per day are subjected to FGM around the world but mostly in Africa.

It is a practice that translates into the partial or total removal of the clitoris (clitoridectomy), the removal of the entire clitoris and the cutting of the labia minora (excision), or in its most extreme form the removal of all external genitalia and the stitching together of the two sides of the vulva (infibulation). The cutting is done generally without anesthetic and those who survive it experience lifelong health consequences including chronic infection, severe pain during menstruation, sexual intercourse and childbirth, and psychological trauma.

Communities that practice FGM defend it as a rite of passage and a social prerequisite of marriage. But it is also used as a way to control women's sexuality by safeguarding virginity and suppressing sexual desire. We, at Equality Now (www.equalitynow.org), an international human rights organisation that works to promote and protect the human rights of women around the world, consider FGM a human rights violation and an extreme form of violence and discrimination against women and girls. We welcome the protocol as a new tool that has potential effectiveness in protecting the human rights of women in Africa.

What the Maputo protocol offers is a comprehensive set of provisions that creates a framework for putting an end to harmful practices. It goes beyond a call to ending harmful traditional practices such as FGM and directs member states to take concrete action by:

■ Criminalising the practice and bringing to justice those who perpetrate it
■ Providing counselling support and treatment to victims of FGM
■ Initiating public awareness-raising campaigns to end the practice
■ Intervening to prevent FGM cases thereby saving girls before it happens to them.

African states must indeed urgently take responsibility to follow through with these obligations. Burkina Faso offers a good case in point, and is leading the way in the fight against FGM. Burkina Faso criminalised FGM in 1996 and followed that with national campaigns to inform its people about the law and why FGM must be ended. It also offered helplines for potential victims and concerned citizens to contact the authorities in good time to prevent the crime, and has put in place harsh punishment to demotivate those still determined to carry on with it. Furthermore, arrests and prosecutions of those responsible for subjecting girls to FGM were and continue to be publicised through the media to discourage potential perpetrators. As a result, Burkina Faso has seen the prevalence rate of FGM fall considerably over the years.

In some other African countries, even though they have adopted legislation to ban FGM, they have not followed through with the full programme of rights set out in the protocol and so have not produced similar results to those in Burkina Faso.

To save the thousands of girls affected each day by this harmful practice (and 6,000 girls is an enormous number with which to contend), African governments have an affirmative duty not to delay any further the ratification of the Protocol on the Rights of Women.

During 16-18 September, Kenya is hosting an international conference on FGM titled 'Developing a Political, Legal and Social Environment to implement the Maputo Protocol'. Linah Kilimo, Kenyan Minister for Home Affairs, and a long time activist against FGM, is leading the meeting and has secured President Kibaki's support for it. At the end of the conference, it is anticipated that the president or his foreign minister will officially hand over Kenya's instrument of ratification to the chair of the African Union Commission, Alpha Oumar Konare. If this plan succeeds, Kenya will be the fifth country to ratify the protocol following Namibia, which ratified it last month, and thereby laying out a legal framework to fight the practice and preserve the human rights of Kenyan women and girls.

Kenya appears to be on track and other African states also need to follow the example of the Comoros, Libya, Rwanda and Namibia in formally expressing their commitment to the human rights of women in Africa. As the continent next month gathers at the Seventh Conference on Women's Rights in Addis Ababa to review progress made in honouring commitments undertaken in Beijing and Dakar 10 years ago, ratifying the Protocol on the Rights of Women could well serve as an achievement to bring to the table.

From Beijing to Addis Ababa: What Progress for African Women?

Kafui Adjamagbo-Johnson
Pambazuka News 157, 20 May 2004

THE FOURTH WORLD Conference on Women held in Beijing in September 1995 raised hopes of a substantial improvement in women's condition across the world and particularly in Africa. The Beijing Declaration and programme of action considered by the United Nations' Secretary General to be 'one of the most remarkable documents ever produced by an intergovernmental conference' commits states to taking concrete action in 12 priority areas in relation to women's autonomy. Ten years after Beijing and on the heels of the seventh regional conference at Addis Ababa, where are we now? Have African women and girls really made remarkable gains in such essential areas as education, fundamental human rights, violence against women, their participation in decision-making, health and the fight against poverty?

Progress and Challenges in Education

Education, a fundamental human right for women, is also a tool for transformation and an essential means of implementing egalitarian objectives, development and peace. In ten years of implementation of the Beijing platform, noticeable progress has been made in education and training for women and girls. Efforts to bring about universal primary education for all, positive discrimination in favour of women's and girls' education and training in areas apparently reserved for men, and awareness-raising campaigns have had encouraging results. However, there are still major constraints on equal access to education for men and women. Cultural practices and stereotypes have a negative influence on access, maintenance and development of girls across the whole school curriculum. Credits allocated are usually insufficient and girls continue to be the object of sexual harassment in educational institutions, as is evidenced by the concept of 'sexually transmitted marks', which persists under different appellations in several African countries. These are only a few of the challenges to be faced before women and girls enjoy full human rights in education and training.

For the complete article in English see: http://www.pambazuka.org/ index.php?id=24944

Women and Other Gender Concerns
in Post-Conflict Reconstruction

Eugenia Date-Bah
Pambazuka News 179, 21 October 2004

PEOPLE'S EXPERIENCES during conflict are not gender neutral. The impacts of armed conflict as well as the coping strategies adopted by people tend to differ between men and women. Gender as an important element in determining vulnerability becomes even more acute in the conflict-affected situation.

However, men and women cannot be defined as homogeneous categories whose conflict experiences can be crudely divided along their gender-prescribed roles. It has to be recognised that, besides numerous gender-sensitive constraints, conflict also accentuates resourcefulness in the adoption of coping and survival strategies. This can lead to progressive and empowering gender role changes and fluidity.

The post-conflict reintegration and reconstruction processes offer a window of opportunity for enhancing women's and men's socio-economic security rather than for re-establishing the status quo ante, including the gender stereotypes and traditional gender divisions of labour. Therefore, the promotion of a more equitable, just and inclusive society with women and other previously vulnerable and socially excluded groups becoming full players should be one of the overall goals of post-conflict interventions.

Nevertheless, the new post-conflict reconstruction, institutions, structures, policies and laws that are put in place tend to lack the special gender sensitivity required in this context, and therefore they reintroduce the pre-war gender-biased positions and emphasise women's reproductive roles, eroding the strategic gains that accrue to women during war. Women's associations and groups therefore have important advocacy and advisory roles to play to ensure serious consideration of gender concerns.

The importance of including gender concerns in all peace-building, post-conflict recovery and reconstruction has been recognised by a number of UN resolutions (such as UN Security Council Resolution 1325), meetings and other events in recent years. For example, both the 1995 Beijing Fourth World Conference on Women and the 2000 Beijing +5 Conference covered this subject among other issues.

Despite this trend, consideration of women's concerns and other gender issues in post-conflict contexts, as well as in the general reintegration, reconstruction and peace-building processes, continues to be inadequate in research, policies, action programmes and debates on current conflicts. Thus the gender differences in human security in post-conflict situations continue to require focus.

Although the consequences of armed conflicts affect all population groups, women appear to bear a disproportionate burden owing to the nature of today's conflicts. As far back as 1944, the International Labour Organisation drew attention to the situation of women post-conflict through the adoption of some standards on the issue. One of these standards is the International Labour Recommendation No. 71 concerning Employment Organisation, Transition from War to Peace, which covers some of the vulnerable groups in the conflict and post-conflict context, especially young people, women and disabled people. With specific reference to women and gender equality, the recommendation states that: 'The redistribution of the women workers in the economy should be organised on the principle of complete equality of opportunity for men and women on the basis of their individual merit, skill and experience, without prejudice to the provisions of the international labour conventions and recommendations concerning the employment of women.'

A resolution adopted at the International Labour Conference in 1944 on the conflict issue covered a number of concerns including the employment of women. This recognised that special action is necessary to ensure that women as well as men benefit from the training, retraining and other employment measures and that the principle of gender equality must be observed.

The consideration given to women's special employment needs can be used as one indicator of the general lack of gender perspective. An ILO Expert Meeting on the Design of Guidelines for Training and Employment of Ex-Combatants (July 1995), for example, observed that 'there has been inadequate planning for women' in post-conflict societies and, therefore, called for action in this area. The pursuit of peace, reintegration and reconstruction needs to go along with equality to avoid compounding old problems, such as discrimination against women, social exclusion and the feminisation of poverty.

The Platform for Action adopted by the Fourth World Conference on Women (September 1995) acknowledges this and, therefore, has as one of its critical areas of concern 'the effects of armed or other kinds of conflict on women, including those living under foreign occupation'. It recognises that a peaceful environment is vital for women's advancement. It notes the serious human rights violations against women in these circumstances (such as systematic rape, enforced prostitution, sexual slavery and other indecent assaults) as well as the large numbers of women and children among refugees, internally displaced persons and civilian casualties, who tend to outnumber the casualties among combatants. Additionally, it draws attention to the heavy increase in the burden of women stemming from the rapid escalation of female heads of households and from caring for the large numbers of injured people. It acknowledges the important role of women and their resourcefulness in such situations. It calls, among other things, for women's greater participation in decision-making, conflict resolution and peace-building; the protection of women in situations of armed conflict; a reduction in human rights abuses; the promotion of vocational and other skills training so that women can become self-reliant; and the promotion of the human rights of women who have been affected by conflict. Gender analysis and planning require serious integration in conflict and post-conflict programming, such as in the fields of skills training and employment promotion, to ensure that gender equality is promoted.

Armed conflicts have significant impacts on households and the community. As confirmed in ILO studies, household structures are characterised by a drastic decline in the male population and an increase in the number of female-headed households. As a result, more women may engage in income-generating work, while some may lose access to land and labour or more secure livelihoods. In addition, women's work in the household increases because of the increase in the size of households, which is often accompanied by a greater number of dependants, as well as because of the general deterioration of working and living conditions.

The drastic decline in the male population also means that there are large numbers of widows and single mothers in conflict-affected countries. Widowhood affects women's social status, physical safety, identity and mobility and their access to services as well as their rights to property, land and inheritance. Women whose husbands are declared missing face even more difficulties, since their status is not officially recognised. Furthermore, displacement and the increase of violence contribute to the overall feeling of insecurity, uncertainty, and isolation, thus breaking social structures and community support mechanisms. Rebuilding depleted trust and cohesion within the communities is an important part of post-conflict recovery.

The erosion of social capital has important gender implications during and after a conflict. Recent research shows that gender identities that play an important role in determining and restoring trust have significant implications for the roles of different organisations in rebuilding social capital. Institutions, organisations and informal networks that are major actors in shaping the conflict and the post-conflict recovery, and in which, consequently, the social capital often erodes, are more usually men dominated. On the other hand, experience shows that women and women-run organisations that often build on solidarity arising from fear, violence and traumas tend to gain more trust in the community and so can play a critical role in bringing about peace and rebuilding the trust and cohesion in communities.

As identified in the ILO and other studies, armed conflicts challenge the traditional gender roles, and men and women may be pressured to adhere to the traditionally imposed ideals of masculinity and femininity. Men are often portrayed as the defenders of their culture and are expected to be aggressive, dominating and violent. On the contrary, women are proclaimed 'mothers of the nation' and are expected to support their brothers, husbands and fathers.

The ability of men and women to adhere to these prescribed gender roles may cause frustration, loss of self-respect and trigger violence. For example, an ACORD study in Northern Uganda has found that the conflict crucially challenged the traditional norms of masculinity such as marriage, fatherhood, and material and security provision. Heavy militarisation and displacement limited the ability of many men to provide for their families and fulfil their duties as husbands and fathers. Due to the lack of opportunities to gain assets (cattle or cash) necessary to enter married life, many young men were prevented from starting their families and getting recognition from their community. The study also showed that, although many men were not able to behave according to the norms of masculinity, it was difficult for them not to try to conform to these norms. Men's inability to reach these gender-constructed norms often means disempowerment in the public sphere, to which some retaliate by exercising power in the domestic sphere over their children and wives.

On the other hand, ideals of femininity in many cultures often embody willingness to find non-confrontational solutions and to work for the good of the community. As such, women are often connected to the rejection of war and conflict. However, women are also active members of political movements and armed forces because they are committed to the political, religious or economic goals of those involved in conflict. While during the conflict their participation is often welcomed, their gender identity becomes problematic once the communities start to recover.

Women's personal experiences of increased participation in the political, social and economic sphere may challenge the existing gender relations and norms, because for many women entering into the public sphere represents an empowering experience. The traditional gender division of labour may break down as more women enter the labour market, often engaging in traditionally male occupations. However, the conflict and post-conflict recovery period may also revive traditional values, thus pressuring women to resume their traditional gender roles.

Since the nature of conflict and its impacts are likely to differ between and within communities of a conflict-affected country, it is best to undertake a community-based needs assessment utilising participatory methodologies in order to understand and thus address localised issues in an inclusive manner.

Particular attention needs to be paid to those who might be excluded from regular community structures, as social exclusion is likely to increase for some groups during and after conflict (e.g. female ex-combatants, women who are viewed by their communities to have adopted socially unacceptable practices, those who are known to have contracted STDs including HIV/AIDS, etc). This approach is more likely to increase the visibility of women and the gender differentiated needs and interests arising out of conflict.

With respect to demographic changes, the evidence presented illustrates that the number of women who become the sole providers for their families increases as a consequence of conflict. Therefore, this increases their need for women and other gender concerns in post-conflict reconstruction. At the same time, the burden of women within the home tends to intensify. In order for women to participate in employment and training programmes which will assist them in achieving economic self-sufficiency, consideration must be given to the timing and location of training programmes so that they take account of the extent and nature of women's obligations.

Experience shows that reintegration programmes for refugee and internally displaced populations tend to neglect 'remainee' populations, thus producing further conflicts and tensions. This situation therefore argues again for a more holistic approach to programming, with opportunities open to all community members rather than to specific beneficiary groups. Furthermore, it should be remembered that in Mozambique and Guatemala refugee women lost out because the skills they gained during their period of refuge were not sustained or followed up. Efforts should be made to utilise skills which have been acquired, such as training of trainers, etc. It should also be recognised that some refugees and displaced persons will not return to their places of origin and will construct a new life or continue in a new community. The line blurs between displacement and resettlement.

An opportunity emerges to correct gender stereotypes in educational materials and to increase the number of women trainers. In addition, there is an opportunity to draw women into non-traditional skill areas, given the shift in gender roles during conflict. The challenge is to identify skill areas into which women have moved and to support them (e.g. appropriate extension services in agriculture). Training in life skills is needed to assist people to adapt to the new environments in which they may find themselves (e.g. rural-urban migration).

Deterioration in the health of both the women themselves and their family members as a result of the conflict may be a prohibiting factor to their participation in employment and training programmes and may restrict the kinds of activities they are able to undertake. However, additional income is necessary to pay for medical care.

It is necessary to identify survival or coping strategies which have had a positive transformative role in gender relations at the household and community level and to work toward supporting them through the extension of appropriate employment and training opportunities. Additionally, it is essential to reduce women having to resort to sex work by providing them with alternatives and reaching out to those who may have become socially excluded and increasingly more vulnerable due to the coping mechanisms they have had to adopt.

The non-involvement of women in government and policy-making arenas and the frequent failure to cover gender issues in peace accords and other framework documents may indicate a lack of commitment to and possible hostility toward adopting gender-sensitive policies. Yet the fluid post-conflict situation can create a window of opportunity to promote gender equality in the employment field through national policy and commitment to international labour standards and the implementation of appropriate labour market interventions.

Failing to seize this opportunity may further marginalise women and allow gender inequality to persist. Hence, there is a need to build institutional partnerships in an effort to more systematically ensure that gender is taken into account at all levels and across all programme areas.

Finally, the collection and analysis of gender-sensitive labour data may be an important contribution to conflict prevention as part of essential early warning and response work. For example, recent studies suggest that a large percentage of unemployed young men are an indicator of potential instability, as they are prone to entering into the illegal drugs and arms trade or the ranks of militants and fighters. Consequently, the retraining or employment-creation response at the micro level may provide alternatives to participation in armed forces. Clearly there is a need for pre-conflict preparedness and mitigation strategies, with a special focus on the micro level, to ensure proactive and effective post-conflict responses.

This article is based on extracts from 'Women and other Gender Concerns in Post-Conflict Reconstruction and Job Creation Efforts'. The article is part of a collection of articles in a book entitled Jobs After War: A Critical Challenge in the Peace and Reconstruction Puzzle, *edited by Eugenia Date-Bah and published by the InFocus Programme on Crisis Response and Reconstruction of the ILO. The publication documents some of the ILO's experience in tackling the post-conflict job challenge. ILO publications can be purchased on line at http://www.ilo.org/publns or email pub-vente@ilo.org*

CHAPTER 5

RESOURCE EXPLOITATION IN NIGERIA

Shell Fights Fires Over Niger Delta Oil Spill

Tim Concannon
Pambazuka News 140, 22 January 2004

AN OIL SPILL and ongoing fire in the troubled Niger Delta region of Nigeria indicates how badly relations between international oil-companies like Shell and oil-producing communities have deteriorated.

Members of the Elikpokwuodu community in Rukpokwu in Obio/Akpor Local Government Area of Rivers State say a rupture in a high-pressure, 28-inch pipeline operated by SPDC (Shell's Nigeria affiliate) in December caused the initial oil spill. The problem with the pipe dates back to 1963, according to the community.

Rukpokwu is about a 5-10 minute drive from Port Harcourt airport. The oil spill is on the fringe of a swampy area, 2km along a dirt road, immediately off the airport road on the outer fringes of the oil city of Port Harcourt proper. Port Harcourt is Shell's operational base in Rivers State. In other words, the spill is on Shell's doorstep but the company has still to put out the fire and clean up the spill.

According to Nigeria's *Vanguard* newspaper, the Chairman of Elikpokwuodu's Community Development Committee Mr Clifford Walter said 'more than three streams from which we fish are affected. Fishing implements were destroyed and SPDC has not responded to this disaster.'

'Our only source of drinking water, fishing stream and farm-lands covering over 300 hectares of land with aquatic lives, fishing nets and traps, farm crops and animals,' Nigeria's THISDAY reported the Paramount ruler and Chairman of Mgbuchi Community – Chief Clifford E Enyinda and Azunda Aaron respectively – as saying. 'Trees worth several billions of naira are completely destroyed by the spillage and was made worst by the three separate fires that broke out of the spill site.'

At the time of Stakeholder Democracy Network's (SDN) visit to the site on 7 January, there was a fire at the centre of the spill that was still burning. This was despite several attempts by Shell staff to put it out. The fire was restricted to an area no larger than approximately 20 metres by 20 metres. Surrounding bush and vegetation was charred and destroyed. No visible measures were in place to prevent the further spread of oil downstream, despite obvious risks from rainfall.

There appears to be a continuing underground fire at the spill site that is periodically re-igniting on the surface, but the causes of this re-ignition are unclear: it could be that the underground fire is spreading back to the surface, but deliberate sabotage cannot be discounted. Shell has been unwilling – or has felt unable – to post someone at the site to monitor the fire, which would make sabotage less likely.

Shell and the affected community are giving conflicting accounts of what has happened. However, one uncontested fact is that – while the initial spill occurred on 3 December 2003, and was reported to Shell on 4 December – on 7 January Shell was still negotiating 'relief materials' with the Elikpokwuodu community, that is how many bags of rice and temporary water supplies to provide.

According to members of the community SDN spoke to, when Shell staff and contractors visited, they came with an armed mobile-police escort, firing shots into the air. Shell staff excavated the pipeline, acknowledged that the problem was due to corrosion and sought to place a covering clamp over the pipeline. However, Shell workers found the 'clamp' they had brought was not long enough, so they departed without taking further action.

According to Shell press statements, the community denied Shell access to the site of the spill. Shell alleges that 'miscreants' set fire to the spill initially, and have re-lit the fire on several subsequent occasions.

Members of the community seized a Shell vehicle that was being used to fight the fire last week. There are indications the vehicle may be released this week, following three-way discussions between the community, the local authorities and Shell.

Roseline Konya, the Rivers State commissioner for environment, had previously made public criticisms of Shell over the Rukpokwu spill. The government would insist on Shell paying adequate compensation to the community, she said. 'We also see negligence, delay and lack of good-will from Shell on this matter,' Konya told reporters in Port Harcourt according to Dow Jones on 9 January.

This incident is the latest indication that the 'system' for dealing with spill-response is broken. From the perspective of communities and local human rights groups, this is seen as further evidence of Shell's overall attitude to dealing with these incidents: at their own convenience. There is a perceived double standard. Would Shell respond this way to a spill in Scotland or in Texas?

The incident comes at a time when Nigeria is becoming an increasingly important test of the claims of oil companies like Shell to transparency and corporate social responsibility (or CSR, to give it the acronym favoured by policy wonks in Europe and America.) Shell's senior management is coming under pressure from its shareholders to sort out its Nigerian operations.

Shell announced in mid-January 2004 that 3.9 billion barrels of oil and gas, or one-fifth of its reserves, were no longer 'proved' – meaning they cannott be retrieved as quickly as thought – much of which are in Nigeria, which is crucial to Shell's overall operations. Shell's shares have dropped from 401p to 359p following the announcement.

Shell has so far failed to explain the sudden regrading of its reserves to angry shareholders, but shutdowns, spills and community conflicts are likely to be one major factor making it difficult for Shell to guarantee its supplies in the delta. Is this a failure of corporate governance generally, or of Shell's approach to 'CSR' and community-relations in places like the Niger Delta? Shell investors must wait for a presentation on 5 February for an explanation by chairman Sir Philip Watts, but they had earlier called for the resignation of the man who used to run Shell's Nigeria operations.

The debate on the merits of Shell's CSR claims rages on in developed countries, but in Nigeria the standard responses from all sides – oil companies like Shell, and oil producer communities – involved in a spill like Rukpokwu seems to be producing the perverse outcome of delaying spill containment.

There are also good reasons to question whether third-parties to spills, like clean-up operators – the main financial beneficiaries of oil spills in the short run outside of the affected communities – share an interest with community leaders and activists in minimising the impacts of a spill on the environment, and public health and safety.

For its part, Shell's knee-jerk response to 'sabotage' – which has the effect of delaying spill responses – is fuelling a lack of trust and sense of general grievance in oil-producing communities.

There is growing concern that the frustration felt by oil-producing communities at the failure of the oil-industry to deal with spills quickly and adequately is combining with general political instability in the region, with possibly calamitous results.

'Ethnic conflicts' rage over land in the oil-producing Warri region – to the north of Port Harcourt – which in reality are also part of a wider war between criminal groups and factions in the army, navy and government for control of black-market oil and a host of other related issues.

Following elections in 2003 that were criticised by international observers as unfair, resentment is simmering in the delta. The oil industry extracts billions of dollars-worth of oil from the impoverished region, but the Nigerian government returns a tiny fraction of this to the producer-communities. Much of this disappears through bribery of government officials. Groups like Transparency International routinely rate Nigeria as one of the world's most corrupt countries.

In the Niger Delta, local conflicts are combining with a general sense of political and economic disenfranchisement to make a highly combustible mixture. The oil companies must share part of the blame for creating this volatile situation, through their environmental management. The creeks and inlets of the Niger Delta are threaded with a network of pipelines, many of which pre-date Shell and other companies' operations in the 1970s. The age and general state of deterioration of pipelines will become a significant issue in the delta more widely, if oil-producing communities' frustration over continuing spills like Rukpokwu build up.

Oil and Corporate Recklessness in Nigeria's Niger Delta Region

Joel Bisina

Pambazuka News 167, 29 July 2004

NIGERIA IS AFRICA'S largest and most complex country, with a population of 120 million people from over 250 tribes. The vast, swampy terrain of the Niger Delta region supports almost 20 million people, many of them in isolated communities only accessible by boat. The Niger Delta serves as the economic nerve centre of the Nigeria Federation with its vast oil deposits. Presently, crude oil accounts for about 85 per cent of the nation's revenue. Oil from the Niger Delta accounts for 20 per cent of oil supply to the US, and has become increasingly important from a strategic perspective as conflicts continue in the Middle East.

However, this 'blessing' has become a curse for the people of the Niger Delta. They have suffered environmental devastation, economic poverty, and constant conflict. To make matters even worse, political considerations and greed on the part of a corrupt government have kept many of the earnings from these vast reserves from returning to the Niger Delta to help restore the region.

Since the discovery of oil and the production in commercial quantities in 1958, the people of the Niger Delta have known no peace. Today, violent intertribal and inter-communal conflicts, arms proliferation, ethnic militias and illegal bunkering (theft of crude oil directly from pipelines) have become synonymous with the region.

Economic activities related to oil and gas has placed the government's security emphasis on the need to produce oil and gas most effectively and efficiently. This type of security consideration ignores the impact on other environmental and human resources such as waters, forests, fish and the climate of the area. The youth of the region, a vibrant and energetic generation who should be supporting the productivity and the future of this area, are instead being continuously cut down by bullets from security operatives under the guise of the war on terrorism. Communities are razed and extra-judicial killings are the order of the day.

From the days of the hanging of playwright and prominent environmental rights activist Ken Saro Wiwa and nine other Ogoni individuals by the then military regime of General Sani Abacha, to the Odi holocaust and the burning and destruction of Awor and Fenegbene by the present Obasanjo administration, the story has been the same.

When oil production activities are intensified or activated in a very dedicated manner, riverbank erosion results, gas flares occur frequently, forests are cut down, rivers and streams are dredged, turned into canals or blocked and then polluted. Farms and sacred lands are not spared either; they may be acquired for oil and gas development or polluted, as production gets under way. Anything that is seen to obstruct or have the semblance of serving as obstruction to the free flow of oil is uprooted and destroyed, whether it is a human being, a community or a stream.

Compounding the plight of the people of the Niger Delta is the issue of environmental pollution. Oil production and dredging have caused acid rain, fouled the air and the water, and caused widespread and dramatic erosion. Whole communities have watched their lands erode away. Fishing and farming, the traditional occupations of these people, is no longer viable. This situation has caused poverty, hunger and desperation among these peoples, who are struggling to eke out a living.

The issue of ownership rights is key. Federal laws automatically transfer title to any land where oil is found to the federal government without adequate compensation to the landowners. This gives the federal government the right to enter into an unholy alliance with multi national oil companies in the name of joint venture operations at the exclusion of the people. The result is that the federal government and the multinational oil corporations share the resulting revenue on a ratio of 60:40 per cent with nothing left for the landowners. In addition, oil spills and other ongoing problems caused by the oil production are not attended to, so the area is left in much worse shape than before the oil reserves were found.

Underlying this complex and fraudulent economic arrangement is the issue of ethnicity and tribalism. There are 250 ethnic nationalities in Nigeria, with the Yorubas, Igbos and the Hausa/Fulani of the west, southeast and the north comprising the majority tribes. The minorities of the Ijaws, Itsekiris and other nationalities inhabit the oil rich Niger Delta region, which is swampy deltaic terrain, and is completely cut off from development, modern industries and social infrastructure. Educational opportunities are limited, and the closest healthcare facility is about three hours by speedboat.

Because the government tends to be populated by people who originated from the majority tribes which do not happen to be located in the delta, they have created a formula for sharing the revenues from oil production that favours other regions, further increasing the poverty in the delta and creating anger and conflict between the delta tribes themselves. Trust amongst the tribes has been eroded, while hatred and suspicion have grown, as they are made to believe that they are enemies to one and another by the divide and rule and divide and exploit attitude of an insincere national government and its dubious multinational collaborators.

The combination of these factors creates a potential powder keg. Because Nigeria is the largest nation in Africa and considered the leader in political and economic issues, any eruption could have a deeply destabilising effect on both the continent and the global community. By providing the world a more complete understanding of the real story behind the impact of the oil discovery and production during the last 45 years in Nigeria, perhaps we can find the resources to address these issues before a major eruption occurs.

Taking Control of Africa's Resources

Eno Anwana

Pambazuka News 167, 29 July 2004

FROM THE SLAVE TRADE era of the 15th century to the crude oil era of the 20th century, Nigeria's natural resource history has been fraught by a systemic cartel of merchants whose primary agenda was in the amount of natural resources they could garner from the country. In their exploitative ventures they raided whole communities, introduced internecine wars and conflicts, and ignited a raging fire of habitat degradation and fragmentation.

Historical records tell of the fact that the plundering of African natural resources fuelled the industrial revolution of Europe. Energy demands in the 20th century brought on the search for crude oil wells worldwide and Nigeria was not left out. From 1956, when the first oil well was successfully drilled in Nigeria, scrambling for Nigeria's resources by the Europeans took on a new dimension.

The oil boom era of the 1970s saw the downward plunge of the agricultural sector. There was a complete paradigm shift from the nation's then agrarian culture to an oil driven culture, moving ultimately from renewable natural resources to un-renewable resource trade. From the 1970s through to the early 1980s we witnessed a drastic drop in local food production. Importation rates of foods and finished products increased dramatically and our foreign debt escalated rapidly, bringing the economy to a crisis. During this period, from 1958 to 1983, we recorded $101 billion in estimated oil revenue earnings.

A plethora of environmental problems exist as a result of the oil trade. Communities where certain resources are harvested – in particular oil and gas – bear the impact of exploration and exploitation, while gains are shared to other areas that contribute next to nothing to national oil revenues.

In addition oil communities are impoverished and lack basic social infrastructures and amenities. One region in Nigeria which has borne the brunt of natural resource exploitation is the Niger Delta. This region played a key role in the country's economy in pre-colonial and colonial times and still maintains a primary position in present crude oil trade.

The Niger Delta: the Battlefield for Resource Control

The Niger Delta has featured in global discourse as a region plagued by non-violent demonstrations, violent protests and intra-communal wars over resource control. The source and underlying causes of agitation in this region must be clearly understood by the global community in evolving effective management strategies.

Agitations within this region take root from early colonial trade relations with the British incursion into the area. They made treaties with vulnerable

communities, plundered resource capital and introduced a subservient cultural pattern. Communities only benefited by giving up their farmlands in
exchange for ridiculous gifts. In those days, resistance came through such
visionary leaders as King Jaja of Opobo and Nana Olomu. These leaders, as
recorded by Nigerian historians, led their people in the struggle to rescue their
natural economy from the greedy control of the British who had devised a
'divide and rule' machinery of control over the people.

Control over the natural resource capital of the Niger Delta people is currently mirrored by the operations of the oil multinational companies, who
defraud whole communities of their livelihoods, paying ridiculous monetary
compensation in exchange for a devastated coastal ecosystem.

The oil companies make up the largest industry in the Niger Delta region.
Despite this, unemployment levels are still high, especially in the rural areas
where oil and gas reserves exist. In this region there are oil well reserves (17.9
billion barrels) and gas wells (3.4 trillion m3), contributing about 80 per cent
of federal government revenue.

Despite this vast coastal wealth, GNP per capita is below the national
average of US$280. Pollution of coastal corridors and wetlands is a recurrent
disaster. Gas flaring has become a notorious pollutant of the local communities of the Delta. Oil spills and gas flaring have destroyed whole fishing communities, reducing vital fishery resources and terrestrial vegetation and com-
promising the health of local people in and around oil installations.

Nigeria's resource base includes a vast network of rivers, floodplains and
rich rainforests, with vast deposits of minerals. However about 95 per cent of
natural forest cover has been lost to deforestation, leaving 5 per cent contained
in the southeast region. While dams upstream are a constant headache and
threat to the rich coastal biodiversity, deforestation ravages the teeming rain-
forest ecosystem.

The Nigerian Government and the Challenge of Sustainability

In a country where agriculture accounts for about 40 per cent of GDP and oil
production and exports (exporting over 2 million barrels/day) ranks sixth
worldwide, the government's management structure and environmental
action plan is essential to maintain balance and reduce abuse. The question
here is what has been the role of the Nigerian government in the management
of its natural resources?

To attempt an answer, one can say that even though the legal framework and
institutional structure for natural resource management is firmly established, it
still lacks the strength and drive which natural resource management
deserves.

Government response to environmental problems and the nagging problem of
unsustainable resource exploitation has been rather slow. Compromises in deals

with multinational companies have crippled the implementation of 'goodwill' national policies and laws. The management structure at best is fragmentary, and there are similar government agencies which carry out the same functions, often leading to conflict between government agencies and stakeholders.

For projects to be considered sustainable as contained in Agenda 21 of the Rio declaration three key aspects of development must be integrated into project planning and implementation: economic growth, social equity and ecological integrity.

Historical trends have shown that industrial activities in the delta have negated this all-embracing principle in the scramble for resources. Indigenous people, their laws and customs have often been sidetracked. Sustainability must therefore be redefined in this region and companies' licenses to operate must be revoked when found guilty. The country does not lack policies and laws, but the gap lies in the implementation and policing of resource utilisation.

Resource depletion has far-reaching multiplier effects and its importance is underscored by communal agitations and high national poverty statistics. It is instructive to evolve stringent measures to 'checkmate' the eclipse of our collapsing life support systems. We cannot afford to put new wine into old wine skin.

The issue of local content has to do with the active participation of the local indigenous people in decision-making processes. Local people are the best managers, they have over the years evolved methods and approaches in natural resource management that have preserved certain classes of biodiversity and we need to learn from them.

For sustainability, they must be integrated in all developmental issues, especially those that impact on their existence. The ideals of community based resource management (CBRM) can ensure the active participation of local stakeholders in project management and development. Promoting indigenous protected areas provides and example. In the southeast region there are several lakes and forests traditionally designated as sacred areas. Indigenous laws and customs have protected biodiversity in these areas over the years and we can start by integrating and institutionalising them into our system of protected parks or areas.

True federalism and sustainability can only be obtained by ensuring that the needs and aspirations of local communities are considered before any economic gains. Trade-offs are necessary to maintain equilibrium and rather than being overruled, social equity has to be sustained.

Africa and the Way Forward

The New Partnership for African Development (NEPAD) could through its review mechanism ensure that African countries strictly comply with the principle of active indigenous participation in the decision processes. But the question we must ask is: how sincere are participating African countries about moving the ideology of NEPAD forward? Can NEPAD be a panacea for our dependence on Western donors, who dictate the tune of our development? Or would we be strong enough as a people to wield the weapon of resource control and management by Africans against the hungry Western world?

We must evolve strategic alliances with other African nations to find long lasting solutions to the management of Africa's vast bank of natural resources. The question of capacity building then arises. Capacity building in natural resource management would mean a network of indigenous people who are able to exchange information and technology without barriers. An additional function would be resource tracking: we must insist on predetermined certification of forest and coastal land goods and services, which could serve as a monitoring device for products obtained from these ecosystems.

My concluding thought on sustainable natural resource utilisation and development in Nigeria, and Africa as a whole, is in our corporate realisation that for us as Africans, our greatest weapon against the incursion of the developed economics is our bank of natural resource capital.

It is time we as a race refused the lies of the Western world and shunned greed and mismanagement of both human and natural resources. We must encourage all Africans to imbibe the culture of proper management of our contested heritage. This must be clearly understood and articulated by the current crop of leaders as they promote the African Union through its NEPAD initiative.

CHAPTER 6

DISCUSSING THE DEMOCRATIC REPUBLIC OF CONGO, THE HEART OF AFRICA

DRC: Globalisation, War and the Struggle for Freedom

Ernest Wamba Dia Wamba
Pambazuka News 145, 26 February 2004

SINCE THE UNEXPECTED arrival of the Portuguese traveller Diego Cao at the mouth of the Congo river in 1482, the peoples of the area that became the Congo have had their lives determined more and more by processes which have started far away and over which they have had less and less control. At the time, they were hardly aware of the fact that in the world yonder, the need for peoples experienced in tropical agriculture would be forcefully satisfied by their best sisters and brothers being captured, kidnapped, shackled and shipped to America.

The resulting Atlantic slave trade, one of the cornerstones of globalisation, determined irreversibly the lives of the peoples of the area. Even their very survival depended on the evolution of remote processes assigning changing roles to the area. Suffering and modernisation would become almost two faces of the same coin marking their lives. The Atlantic slave trade was the first phase of globalisation, laying the foundations of the world market whose evolution would shape the adjustment and re-adjustment of parts of the world around an evolving centre.

Three processes are involved when looking at globalisation. The first is the historical process of effective transition to capitalism in each country. This involves the transformation of a double articulation of relations and forces of production. It is the long process of transforming or destroying the specific form of the African commune through the slave trade and colonialism to the present neo-liberalist structural adjustment programmes and poverty accumulation based epoch.

The second process is the historical formation and transformations of anti-colonial (in the broad sense including anti-Atlantic slavery struggles for life) 'mass' movements into more and more organised struggles for the recovering of land, bodies, psyches (selves) and cultures. This deals with the story about the changes of the agencies of struggles: their historical formation and transformations, their social character, their strategies, their programmes, their theories, prescriptions, dreams, ideologies of politico-social emancipation up to the conscious anti-globalisation civil society. In this process, we can only hail partial victories, mostly through accommodation rather than breaks from the commands from the centres.

Thirdly, the 'external domination' in Africa (or forced or willing incorporation of Africa in the outside originating processes) is what is often thought of as globalisation. It involves:

■ Obstacles to national liberation/independence and local/national self-determination, self-reliance, South-South initiatives and pro-people developments

■ Imperialist domination and regional expansionism

■ Forms taken by super-power struggles for world hegemony inside and around certain countries in relation to conditions of accession into and character of their independences

■ The transnationalisation process through multinational corporations and international economic organisations up to the ultra-liberalist destruction/reduction of the nation/state and the pursuit by the US of the politics of pure super-power, linking tightly politics to war and the US dream of becoming the Roman Empire of the present epoch

■ A world system of a political economy of crime (money laundering, drug and arms trafficking, new forms of labour/sex enslavement, private or super-power state terrorism, etc.) develops and comes along. High and low intensity warfare, through regional relationships of forces of super-powers' proxies, continues.

Thus we differentiate three phases of globalisation: the first phase is based on the Atlantic slave trade (sometimes viewed as a pre-globalisation phase), the second phase was the integration of Africa through colonisation and the third phase began in the late 1980s and still continues. The peoples who became known as the Congolese from the second phase miraculously survived the first two phases. While the population was being drastically reduced by the slave trade, people took sometimes self-defeating forms of resistance. Some preferred to commit suicide rather than be enslaved and for a long time women refused to bear children for the slave trade. Communal forms of resistance and more advanced forms of capitalist opposition to the slave trade helped people survive, only to be militarily conquered for domestic colonisation. The forgotten holocaust (Adam Hochschild, *King Leopold's Ghost*, 1998), during the so-called King Leopold's Congo Free State, the most brutal integration of the area into the world economy, reduced the population estimated at 20 million to a mere 8 million in less than 30 years. It has not been possible to completely heal the effects of the accumulated traumas, which strongly influence the forms, styles and sometimes content of the diverse cultures of our country. The continuing replay of those effects not only organise the submissive and docile character of public consciousness, but the regular violent outbursts that mark the bloody history of the Congo. Is the prevalence of the song a form of healing?

The international civilising agents of globalisation initially behaved in a way that made the country become what one of the most honest of them described as the Heart of Darkness. The colonialist attitude was more concerned about how much the Congo cost Belgium (Jean Stengers, 1957) rather than how much Belgian colonialism cost the Congo. Each attempt to recast the relationship between the Congolese and globalisation psychologically (radical prophetism as healing – Simon Kimbangu and others), politically (P.E. Lumumba and others), militarily (P. Mulele and others), etc, unleashed the most barbaric forms of violence to infinitely discourage the possible resumption of similar attempts. Kimbangu was condemned to death and then to a life sentence (he died in jail, 1921–1951), Lumumba and his companions' remains were dissolved in acid. Mulele's body, cut into pieces, was put in a bag and thrown into the Congo River joining in the ocean the bones of the rebelling slaves on the way to America. That was only the tip of the iceberg; how the less known ones were treated is not known.

Throughout its various phases since European contact, Africans have been forced into relationships imposed from outside, with catastrophic consequences for the majority. The transitions which took place – whether from slavery to abolition, from 'discovery' to occupation, from negation to acceptance of civil rights (1866–1966) (W.E.B. DuBois, Reconstruction), from colonial status to independence, from the Cold War to re-globalisation – have generally had a negative impact on the relations between people in the Congo and between the Congolese people and others (J. Depelchin, 2003). Globalisation involves relationships to diseases, to means of death (traffic of arms), to the ecology, to the economy of crime (money laundering, drugs, sexual slavery), to the economy dominated by the dynamic of extraction of natural resources whose market is outside the country and thus also of looting, to world hegemony, to sexuality, to God, to peoples' psychology and cultures generally.

Pan-Africanism, independence or freedom and (racial) equality have characterised the consciousness of the Black man facing the various phases of globalisation. From the anti-slave revolts up to the independence of Haiti in 1804. From the first Negritude calls (Brazil) to the US-initiated Pan-Africanist Congresses. From anti-colonial struggles to national liberationist movements and independences in crisis. The anti-slave question, the anti-racialist question, the Pan-Africanist or African Unity question, the national question, the democracy question, the social question, the question of the protracted demand for compensation for slavery and for the equality of humanity, etc: all are so many calls from the struggles against globalisation.

Pro-globalisation consciousness often opposes those calls and celebrates calls for submission to and docility vis-à-vis the grossest forms of denial of the right to reclaim history and above all, as Cabral said, to assert the right of African people to make history: 'The foundation of national liberation lies in the inalienable right of every people to have their own history.' (A.Cabral, *Unity and Struggles: Speeches and Writings*, 1980). To deny that right absolutely, the very existence of history is now being denied: history is globalisation made by everybody! Victims and victimisers are made equally responsible for the havoc that befalls humanity. The world is said to have become a village, never mind the fact that movement of people from some parts of that village to other parts is extremely selectively restricted. When the history of our people is allowed to be told, it is mostly done by historians acting as organic intellectuals of globalisation.

The Congo, without the willingness or consent of the Congolese, has been drawn into processes of mass destruction. In the 1940s the uranium which the USA used to execute its nuclear genocide of millions of Japanese at Hiroshima and Nagasaki, came from the Belgian Congo. The USA, responsible for 60 per cent of world pollution, is refusing to endorse the Convention on the Conservation of Nature; it sustains that irresponsible posture thanks to the deep and wild Congolese forest that minimises pollution's impact on the whole world. But does the West, responsible for most world pollution, care about helping the Congolese protect and reproduce the forest? Each time a major virus threatening humanity's health appears, the Congo is pointed out as a possible origin of the virus. What is done to equip the Congo to avoid those possibilities? Nothing of any importance has taken place in the Congo since its creation by Berliner powers (1884–5) without the involvement of external, generally Western, forces.

It is on this basis that the current situation of the Congo in the context of globalisation should be examined if we are going to be able to throw some light on this crucial and vital issue for the next generation of combatants for real freedom.

War and Impunity in the DRC:
Sowing the Seeds for Catastrophe

Innocent Balemba
Pambazuka News 163, 1 July 2004

MUTINY, REBELLION OR a new occupation by foreign forces of eastern Congo? This is the question that analysts of the Great Lakes region continuously ask themselves.

On 26 May 2004, the city of Bukavu did not sleep, but awoke to gunshots. Over the following two weeks the city and surrounding areas became the theatre of very violent fighting between regular armed forces and forces of the dissidents of the 10th military region commanded by Colonel Jules Mutebusi. Mutebusi was suspended in April by the Congolese military hierarchy and supported by three or four battalions led by another former officer of the Congolese Rally for Democracy (Rassemblement Congolais pour la Démocratie – RCD), General Lauraent Nkunda.

These events, which killed about 100 people and wounded many others, and led to the fall of Bukavu into rebel hands on 2 June, were reminiscent of the Kabila epic of October 1996, and that of the RCD in August 1998. This story resembles past events, but does it repeat them?

It resembles them because of the similarity of the context: several Congolese dissidents, the military and logistical support of Rwanda, followed by the rapid capture of Congolese cities without resistance and Rwanda denying its involvement.

The events in Bukavu and its surrounding areas were accompanied by a series of grave human rights abuses and war crimes. Besides the killings, there was systematic rape of women, children, even babies. The organisation Human Rights Watch documented dozens of cases of rape, including four three-year-old girls. The question that many people forget to ask themselves is why is history repeating itself? Why has the Congo seemingly not learnt its lessons from past events?

It was 2 August 1998 when an armed group called the RCD, supported by Rwanda, took the city of Bukavu. It started with the execution of dozens of military people loyal to Kinshasa at the Kavumu aerodrome. The group continued quickly on to Goma, then Kisangani, then Kindu, etc, while other columns attacked the Inga roadblock and occupied the Kitona military base, in Bas-Congo province. They created their headquarters in Goma.

The government of Laurent Kabila, which had not yet succeeded in setting up an army during its 13-month reign, was on the verge of falling and called upon Angola, then Namibia, Chad and Zimbabwe for assistance.

In the following months, Jean Pierre Bemba declared another rebellion in the north – the Movement for the Liberation of Congo (le Mouvement pour la libération du Congo – MLC) – with the support of Uganda.

Internal difficulties led the RCD president Ernest Wamba dia Wamba and the former president of the RCD 'assembly' Mbusa Nyamwisi to create the RCD-Kisangani (which later became the RCD-ML), based in Kisangani, also with Ugandan support.

The methods of the belligerents were simple: killings, destruction, torture and rape.

It was over the next four years that probably the most devastating war for humanity would continue. It involved government forces supported by Zimbabwe, Namibia, Angola and Chad; the RCD supported by Rwanda and Burundi; and the RCD-ML and the MLC supported by Uganda.

This long war, which some analysts called the 'African World War' caused more than three million deaths and more than two million refugees and internally displaced people. Systematic massacres were committed in villages such as Mkaobola, Kasika, Burhinyi, Shabunda and Kisangani. In some places, these massacres bordered on genocide. In Kasika, for example, RCD troops supported by Rwanda decimated approximately 1,500 civilians, that is almost 10 per cent of the members of the Banyindu ethnic group, at 18,000 people, one of the smallest of the 300 ethnic groups in Congo. The RCD's efforts eliminated customary chiefs, religious leaders, human rights activists, etc. The people responsible for some of these crimes are known and their abuses documented, but they have never been punished.

The MLC committed massive human rights violations and crimes against humanity, including cannibalism against the Mbuti (pygmy) groups in the Mambasa district of Eastern Province. The RCD-ML, the armed resistance Mai-Mai (or Mayi-Mayi) as well as other armed groups also all committed several human rights abuses, such as rape, killings, pillage, etc.

In addition to these violations, the belligerents engaged in economic exploitation of Congo's riches: wood and minerals. The fauna was also systematically destroyed. Forced labour was used to the profit of armed groups.

On 22 July 2002 in Pretoria, the parties to the conflict signed peace accords, which paved the way for the end of this devastating war. The agreement allowed for power sharing amongst the different factions, offering positions of responsibility in the new transitional institutions, curiously in relation to the level of involvement in crimes, implying that crimes can pay. When the transitional institutions were put in place in Kinshasa, the RCD, MLC, RCD-ML, Mayi-Mayi, non-armed political opposition and civil society shared power. Besides the civil society and the non-armed political opposition, it would be fair to talk of power sharing amongst criminals.

However, a group of largely Rwandophone officers in eastern Congo, as well as certain nominated parliamentarians and senators, refused to join the transitional institutions in Kinshasa, despite the efforts of the new government. They established themselves in the city of Goma, capital of the province of North Kivu bordering Rwanda, where the governor, Eugene Serufuli had already allegedly set up a militia under the cover of the organisation called 'All for Peace and Development' (Tous pour la paix et le dévéloppement – TPD). Neither the RCD nor the government seemed to have full control over the governor of Goma or the group of officers in question. These officers had something in common: blood on their hands and impunity.

The events of May and June 2004 benefited from disorder: an army not yet unified and consequently no unified command of the eastern region; the absence of a legitimate territorial administration; massive human rights violations; and generalised insecurity in the eastern part of the country.

These officers seemed to have profited from the situation to organise themselves. Significant stores of arms were found in the possession of the officers and security agents close to the RCD in February 2004. The next month, Colonel Mutebusi, then second commander of the 10th military region (South Kivu), led a mutiny against the head commander, General Prosper Nyabiolwa, for having arrested Major Kasongo for indiscipline and transferred him to Kinshasa. The general escaped and fled to Kinshasa, while three of his bodyguards were killed, allegedly by Mutebusi's men.

The RCD, which has always been supposed to administer this part of Congo while awaiting the establishment of a new territorial administration, came to the defence of the mutineers and threatened to leave the transitional government if Major Kasongo was not freed, thus forcing the government's hand. Investigation of the arms cache was never pursued. Mutebusi was suspended but never punished. Impunity!

Following this, Mutebsi started another mutiny on 26 May 2004. He attacked the positions of the regular army and the situation degenerated until the intervention of the United Nations Peacekeeping Mission (MONUC). The city of Bukavu was divided in two (Mutebusi controlled the part bordering Rwanda and the regular army controlled the rest of the city) for a week.

But, from Goma, General Laurent Nkunda headed towards Bukavu with his 2,000 men to reinforce Mutebsi. He is believed to have been supported by troops from the Rwandan army. He raised the spectre of genocide against the Banyamulenge in Bukavu, a thesis which he later rejected when retreating. This argument was also rejected by MONUC, human rights organisations based in the region, the Banyamulenge organisation Shikama, Commander Masunzu – a Munyamulenge leading an armed group in the high plains of Itombwe.

There were, however, serious human rights violations committed on all sides. Civilians were killed and rape appeared to be systematically used by the mutineers as a weapon of war. In the Idap, Muhungu, Ndendere and Bugabo areas, door-to-door rape was practised, leading some to believe it was a punitive action by the mutineers.

When, on 2 June, Laurent Nkunda took the city, two new groups appeared, who allied themselves with the two opposing parties. Mr Odilon Kurhengamuzinmu, commander of the militia called Mudundu 40 (M40), which during the last three years had changed alliance between Kinshasa and Rwanda on several occasions, this time associated himself with Mutebusi. A dissident faction of M40 led by Foka Mike allied itself with the regular army.

Under the occupation of the mutineers from 2 to 8 June 2004, the city of Bukavu was the scene of flagrant human rights violations. In addition to approximately 100 dead, the local organisation Justice for All (Justice pour tous) has compiled a non-exhaustive list of 617 women and girls raped, 18 stores pillaged, 254 people wounded by bullets, 60 vehicles stolen, 12 depots of manufactured goods and food stores pillaged and the Business People's Cooperative (Coopérative d'hommes d'affaires – COOPERA) burnt. The central bank and commercial bank were looted of all their reserves by the mutineers.

Rwanda's involvement in support of the mutineers in the form of soldiers and arms has been reported by the local organisation Heirs of Justice (Heritiers de la justice), the Congolese Transition Support Committee (Comite d'accompagnement de la transition congolaise – CIAT), largely composed of representatives of the G8 countries, and a coalition of Belgian NGOs.

The Rwandan government denies its involvement, reminiscent of its denials in 1996 and 1998 that Rwanda was not in Congo, even while its troops fought beside Kabila's Alliance of Democratic Forces (Alliances des forces democratiques – AFDL) and the RCD.

Following diplomatic pressure, Rwanda, which had hosted some 3,000 refugees in May and June, closed its border with Congo. Bukavu was retaken by the regular army on 9 June 2004, leaving Mutebusi and his ally M40 to occupy the town of Kamanyola and a part of Luvungi and Bwegere, close to the Rwandan border in the Ruzizi plains, some 60km south of Bukavu.

Fighting continues in various parts of the South Kivu region, boding ill for a possible stagnation or breakdown of the fragile peace process in the country.

The impunity of those responsible for crimes committed in eastern Congo over the past six years seem to be the determining factor in the continuation of abuses against civilian populations. Those who have never heard of war crimes include troops under the command of the infamous Major Bora Uzima in South Kivu; Gabrial Amisi, alias 'Tango Fort' (currently in the regular army) in Uvira, Kasika and Fizi; Laurent Nkaudna, who was behind the massacres in Kisangani; Jules Mutebusi who was responsible for the bombing of the Banyamulenge; Thierry Ilunga (currently in the regular army) in Mwenga, etc.

These officers are currently either peacefully reintegrated into the regular army (Amisi and Ilunga) or are currently in leadership positions in eastern

Congo and implicated in the current war in South Kivu. None of them have ever been sanctioned or punished for their responsibility in these crimes.

The system in place in Congo, the Truth and Reconciliation Commission, established on the South African model, seems to pave the way for the continuation of impunity.

The option to cover up and leave unpunished war crimes and crimes against humanity such as the systematic rape of three-year-old girls; the indiscriminate bombing of civilian Banyamulenge populations by Rwandan helicopters; the massacre of civilians in Kisangani, Kasika, Makobola, Burhinyi, etc; the cannibalism against Pygmy communities in the Eastern Province: Is this the way for the Congolese state to re-establish itself?

In my opinion, this will only sow the seeds of an even more catastrophic sociopolitical situation in eastern Congo.

A History of the DRC in One Line:
Leopold, Resources, Coups, Impunity

Interview with Joseph Yav Katshung
Pambazuka News 163, 1 July 2004

IN 1998 WHAT BECAME known as Africa's world war erupted in the Great Lakes region, with the DRC acting as the battlefield for a host of African countries. What followed was four years of extraordinary violence and a death toll that some put in the millions. Since 2002 a peace of sorts has prevailed, but the fall of Bukavu in eastern DRC in late May seemed to put this on shaky ground. Pambazuka News emailed questions to Joseph Yav Katshung, Executive Director of CERDH (Centre d`Etudes et de Recherche en Droits de l`Homme et Démocratie), to find out more about the situation in the DRC.

Pambazuka: What is the aftermath of the failed coup attempt in Kinshasa and the crisis in the east of the country? What did actually happen and is a clearer picture beginning to emerge as to the circumstances of events and the forces at play?

Joseph Yav Katshung: As may be recalled, the coup attempt took place in early June 2004. This, however, must be seen within a greater context. Before this, in late May, the city of Bukavu (east of DRC) fell to rebels, who are RCD dissidents, Laurent Kunda and Mutebusi, who are said to be supported by the Rwandan government. A few days later, they withdrew back into Rwanda taking with them property looted from the city. It is reported that the rebels committed extensive human rights violations, notably rape, torture and killings of innocent civilians.

The following week, Eric Lenge, a major serving within the special presidential guard (Garde Speciale de la Sécurité Présidentielle), appeared, at 2.30 that morning, on national television accompanied by about 20 soldiers and announced that the transition process was suspended forthwith. He also asked civilians to stay in their homes for their own safety.

They later went to the Tchatchi military camp where they were surrounded by security forces. About eight of Lenge's men were arrested. The rest, including Lenge himself, managed to escape arrest. Rumours had followed that Joseph Kabila, the transitional government president had been killed. Soon thereafter, Kabila appeared on national television as an attestation that he was alive and that the transitional mechanism was still in place. The security forces were tracking down Lenge and his men.

Azzarias Ruberwa, one of the four vice-presidents, who is considered to have links to Rwanda, was suspected of being behind the coup attempt. This has however not been confirmed. In all, the coup attempt has had a negative

impact on the fragile transitional mechanisms. The little trust that was building within and among the government officials who belong to former warring
parties has plummeted. The army has also seen far reaching changes within
its high ranks.

Pambazuka: What impact will these recent events have on the transitional
process and the build up to elections next year?

JYK: Despite the hope it has inspired in the DRC and elsewhere, the current
institutional framework, which is supposed to prepare the country for the
promised free and open elections to be held by summer 2005 at the latest,
remains very fragile. It is not easy to say exactly what the effect of these events
will be. But one thing is for sure; the trust between the various elements in
government has thinned.

In terms of the peace process, trust needs to be built and an environment
fostered in which democratic elections can be held. It appears that there are
certain elements who are keen to stall the process.

Cumulatively, the various incidents in the country such as the coup attempt,
though isolated, may have the effect of undermining the process. Clearly, elections cannot be held in the current situation.

One reason that may be behind the current reticence is that if elections are
held, it is unlikely that they will ensure that high office goes to the leaders of
the various factions. For instance, there cannot be four vice-presidents. What
then will happen? Will those who lose out stay in government? It is possible
that the fear of losing such lucrative positions in the transitional government
is behind efforts to slow or stall the march towards democratic elections.

Pambazuka: Much has been written about the tensions between the DRC and
Rwanda. Have the reasons for these tensions been dealt with and how much
of a factor does Rwanda – and Uganda for that matter – remain in the DRC,
especially in the east of the country?

JYK: It is evident that Rwanda is largely behind the instability in eastern DRC.
A number of reasons inform Rwanda's support for the rebellion in this region.
Initially, after the genocide, Rwandans justified their invasion by saying that
they were pursuing genocidaires from the Habyarimana government who
were said to have sought refuge in the DRC.

Afterwards, their continued stay, incursions and support to the rebels was
justified by a different, yet subtle set of reasons.

First, the RPF government sees its role in the region as that of a leader.
Rwanda aspires to be a regional powerbroker and leader. These hegemonic
aspirations necessarily presuppose a belligerent stance against its neighbours.

Secondly, and most importantly, is the question of territory. As a small
country, Rwanda sees a major problem if the Banyamulenge who live in

eastern DRC have to go back to Rwanda. It is therefore a question of territory. Before the genocide, Rwanda was, and still is, one of the most densely populated countries on the continent. Owing to displacements in the genocide, land is a major issue in Rwanda.

Thirdly, it is for economic reasons. Rwanda is involved in the plunder of resources in the DRC: diamonds, coltan (a metallic ore used in cell phones), gold and timber. This was partially the reason why, having come into the DRC with Uganda as allies, they later fell out and engaged in armed combat in Kisangani. Rwandan citizens are said to control vast economic interests in eastern Congo. Rwanda considers that it has an obligation to protect its citizens in the DRC.

Pambazuka: We read a lot in the press about the role and hard work of South Africa in brokering a peace deal in the DRC. But there has also been criticism from some quarters that the South Africans have papered over some issues, with the danger that the peace deal will not last. How do people in the DRC see South Africa's role and where have the South Africans gone wrong?

JYK: It is true that South Africa has been instrumental in putting in place the transitional government. Initially, people were very enthusiastic about its role in the DRC as the main engine driving the process.

Things have, however, changed. Firstly, there is a general feeling that it is not Congolese, or Rwandans who won the war (if the armed conflict can be considered as such), but South Africa. This is largely in economic terms. South African companies have since invested heavily in the DRC and are behind most explorations and other economic activities. Some even think that this could have been the driving force behind South Africa's fervent involvement in the process.

Secondly, South Africa, which should be concerned about the process they helped put in place, has not taken a stand on the incursions by Rwanda, and Rwanda's continued plunder of resources in the DRC and the commission of human rights violations against Congolese citizens. Congolese no longer understand the role of South Africa. South Africa seems to be eating from both tables: it gives the impression to Kinshasa that it is committed to the process yet maintains a cosy relationship with Rwanda. They have failed to condemn the activities of Rwanda in eastern DRC.

Pambazuka: What is the human rights situation like in the DRC at present?

JYK: There has been little change in the human rights situation in DRC even after the transition process started. There are still massive violations of human rights: killings, rape, torture. This is particularly prevalent in eastern DRC. In Kinshasa, the unrest resulting from the attempted coup also brought with it violations, involving government security forces and members of various former rebel groups. Socio-economic life has equally not improved. Salaries have gone unpaid, the health and education sectors are in bad shape.

Pambazuka: To what extent does the DRC still suffer from the legacy of history in terms of slavery, colonialism and the Cold War and to what extent are the DRC's richness in natural resources a contributing factor to the present situation of the country?

JYK: DRC's fate is linked to the Leopoldian legacy and imperialism of former colonial masters. The DRC is a victim of its own abundance. Looters, over the years, have come and gone, having enriched themselves: Leopold, who considered DRC his personal property, then the Belgians who plundered and left the country in a state in which it was unable to govern itself.

This opened the door for looters who have plied the country at their will. The effects of the Cold War are still reverberating. The American support of Mobutu entrenched a despotic leadership that has seen the deterioration of the country, so rich yet so poor and at war with itself. Kabila, though initially with good intentions to remove Mobutu, soon fell into the same grave of plunder and misrule, especially after those who supported him to remove Mobutu – Uganda and Rwanda – staked their claim to the riches of the DRC. This led to the war between Kabila and rebels supported by the two countries. Then they moved in themselves. Cornered, Kabila sought help from Zimbabwe, Angola and Namibia. The visitors on their part started to plunder to finance the war. Then came South Africa.

It appears that all who come to the DRC, ostensibly to help her with her troubles, have their own reasons for doing so: her riches! Those who come to mourn and to commiserate with the DRC are, in the process eying, through their 'tears' what to take home with them!

Pambazuka: How to end impunity in the DRC?

JYK: That is a question. The raging war that began in 1998 caused hundreds of thousands of deaths among the civilian population and led to scenes of extraordinary violence. The International Criminal Court has announced that it will formally take up the Congolese case, but it will be unable to prosecute more than a few of the key figures responsible for the crimes committed. The Truth and Reconciliation Commission, one of the civilian institutions that emerged from the peace talks, is a different kind of instrument that focuses on forgiveness rather than punishment. We are therefore looking for a mechanism to address this issue.

Peacekeepers and Gender: DRC and Sierra Leone

Paul Higate
Pambazuka News 164, 8 July 2004

IT WAS LATE AT NIGHT when the woman farmer came out of her house in the village of Joru in Sierra Leone to go to the lavatory. She saw a large white truck that had stopped about 50 metres from her home. It was an unusual sight, so she hid and watched what was going on. Inside were two white men and a black woman, who was yelling, 'leave me alone'. 'The door was open and one of them was on top of her', recalled the farmer, 'K', who is in her fifties. 'The lady was really struggling. I saw that one was holding her down while the other was raping her …I saw both of them have their turn on her. After they had finished, I saw one of them drag her out of the cabin and put her in the back of the big truck. They then drove off' (Stuart, 2003).

Currently, there are over 55,000 military personnel and police from 97 countries serving in 16 peace support operations (PSOs) around the world. These personnel have to confront a range of complex challenges involving mass movements of people, war crimes including torture, rape and ethnic cleansing, as well as confronting child soldiers – frequently within hostile environments. Overall these men (and considerably fewer women) contribute a great deal to the peace, stability and reconstruction of post-conflict states and their traumatised and displaced populations.

While it is clear that many peacekeepers carry out vital work in tough conditions to improve the security of host populations, in recent years, a significant number of male peacekeepers have been implicated in the sexual abuse of local women and children. These exploitative activities have included the manufacture of a pornographic video by an Irish peacekeeper involving a local woman in Eritrea, the exchange of sex for goods and services in refugee camps in Liberia, Guinea and Sierra Leone and the routine use of prostitutes (including girls under the age of 18) in many PSOs (Enloe, 2000; Fisher, 2003; Higate, 2004; Naik, 2002; Rehn and Sirleaf, 2002).

Anecdotally at least, activities of this kind appear to be widespread and almost always involve peacekeepers abusing their positions of trust, power and privilege to acquire sexual services from local women, and young girls and boys. These actions can have negative short and long-term impacts on the victims of such abuse and the wider host population.

First, it could be thought that the presence of peacekeepers might signal a break with the past for local women. Given that many of these vulnerable

women have already endured unimaginable experiences of gender-based violence during the conflict, the close proximity of aggressively heterosexual military men might serve as an unwelcome reminder of their trauma. Second,
many local women are made pregnant by peacekeepers who then leave the
PSO and in so doing renege on their responsibility for paternity. Third, the
stigma attached by the wider community and families to the involvement of
local women and girls in prostitution may further marginalise individuals who
are desperate for income. Fourth, local men may struggle to form relationships
with local women as some of their potential female partners are drawn to the
power and privilege of peacekeepers with large disposable incomes. In these
instances, peacekeepers activities with local women can undermine their
broader relations with the local community, in this example causing friction
between local men and peacekeepers. Fifth, military men remain a key vector
in the transmission of HIV/AIDS. Finally, militarised commercial sex industries can become institutionalised and, after the peacekeepers have gone,
become a magnet for sex-tourists disposed to the abuse of young boys and
girls. This has been the case for a number of the regions used for 'rest and rec-
reation' by US troops deployed in South East Asia over the last 40 years.

Clearly then, the idea that 'boys-will-be-boys' – signalled by male peacekeepers' fraternisation with members of the host population – may not be the
benign activity that it is often argued to be. The post-conflict setting is especially sensitive and requires a host of skills including cultural awareness and
self-discipline. These challenges need to be balanced with peacekeepers' very
real human needs for affection and intimacy. In the remaining discussions of
this article I present findings from exploratory fieldwork in the UN PSO in the
Democratic Republic of Congo (DRC) (MONUC) and Sierra Leone (UNAMSIL).
Here, I attempt to provide some insight into how male peacekeepers perceive
their activities with local women and girls. My aim is to illuminate the ways
in which the male peacekeepers in the study both enact and perceive their
masculine gender identities.

In the spring of 2003, with the support of the Institute for Security Studies
(ISS) in Pretoria, I spent time in the DRC and Sierra Leone interviewing male
and female peacekeepers, civilian UN personnel and representatives of NGOs.
I also accompanied peacekeepers on patrol, spent time chatting informally
with them and observed their leisure-time activities in local bars and hotels.
Throughout this period of fieldwork research, my aim was to learn more about
peacekeeper's perceptions of gender in its widest sense, their experiences of
gender awareness training and, as the work developed organically, the nature
of their relation with local women and girls. I wanted to understand how these
experiences helped to shape the peacekeeper's masculinities (Higate, 2004).

The operating conditions of the PSO in the DRC are particularly challenging
(Ginifer, 2002). Average annual income per capita in the DRC is US$100; life

expectancy for men is 47 years and for women 51 years. Sierra Leone has a history of trafficking and sexual exploitation of women. The violent war in the country has involved rape, gang rape and sexual slavery, and is argued to have affected between 215,000 and 257,000 women and girls (Ministry of Gender and Children's Affairs, Sierra Leone, 1996). The documenting of sexual exploitation in refugee camps is likely to represent one aspect of a much wider instance of gender-based violence. Both PSOs have, in common with post-conflict societies more generally, a severe dislocation of the civilian population. This first extract comes from a fieldwork diary kept throughout the course of the work:

> I am waiting to brief the sector commander as to the details of my research in his geographical area of responsibility; this is an anxious moment for me, given the sensitivities of my developing interests in peacekeepers and prostitution. Three North African peacekeepers (in support roles to the sector commander) ask me about the details of the work. I explain that it involves 'gender issues' and 'gender relations', linked to the gender-awareness lecture attended by military observers in Kinshasa. There is an awkward silence, broken by some nervous laughter and quizzical looks. They ask me what I 'mean' by 'gender'. I stall momentarily, and my colleague rescues me by providing an appropriate definition. I find myself surprised that such a question might be posed as I hadn't considered the terms' potential to be interpreted differently from the ways in which I unthinkingly used it.
>
> (Extract from fieldwork diary, 20 April)

Participants struggled to recall the gender-awareness strategies in both PSOs. Some remembered the involvement of a woman in the proceedings, with others speaking at length about responsibilities and tasks that chimed more centrally with their roles as soldiers. It was clear that concerns around personal and team safety, patrolling conventions, radio-communication protocols, vehicle maintenance, care of and familiarisation with equipment such as electricity generators and medical problems had been successfully assimilated. Pride is institutionalised through discipline and the structures of units to which individual soldiers can feel loyal; pride in the military context is also masculinised, circulating within discourses of the peacekeeper as 'saviours of the war-torn citizenry' – who inevitably are women who require 'protection' (Stiehm, 2000).

When these sentiments were combined with what might be described as the neo-colonial orientations towards the host population evident in the two battalions from the Indian sub-continent deployed to Sierra Leone, it was possible to make sense of peacekeepers' interventions into local culture. For example, one officer explained with great pride how local women in the villages no longer 'showed their breasts'. He explained how he had held discussions with paramount chiefs who had been asked that the women in the villages 'cover up'. Several women had replied that they did not have sufficient clothing to meet the demands of the peacekeeping hierarchy. Members of the battalion then set about distributing clothing so that the women could ensure their breasts were no longer exposed to peacekeepers on patrol.

In another incident, early one night, we were driven around the town by a local NGO worker who expressed concern at the level of prostitution and the apparent impunity of peacekeepers in these activities. The town was alive with activity, and adjacent to one peacekeeper barracks were a fleet of velo-taxis waiting to take peacekeepers to local bars, hotels and a bushy area in which sex was alleged to take place. We were told that members of the contingent had to scale their barrack fence in order to make these liaisons, as they were formally subject to a curfew. Local women and girls were seen dotted around the vicinity of the barracks, as was one young man; their demeanour and location indicated that they were touting for business with peacekeepers.

A UN civilian worker had stated that in one class at the local secondary school 'at least two-thirds of the girls are paying their fees with money made from sleeping with peacekeepers', even though some of these girls were said to have regular local boyfriends as well.

Battalion personnel from a northern region of Africa, deployed in one of the eastern sectors of the DRC, were routinely observed with local members of the female community in bars, hotels and clubs. An NGO participant suggested that they 'weren't strictly allowed to have anything to do with sex-workers' although 'a blind eye was turned' to their activities. However, some concern had been expressed in the local town at the outcomes of several of these sexual liaisons that had culminated in pregnancy, leading to controversial paternity issues and further damaging the reputation of the UN.

Commanders did, however, make some concessions to local opinion by declaring certain bars as 'out of bounds' to peacekeeping personnel. To this, several peacekeepers responded by parking their UN vehicles away from the bars and clubs in question, and spending only enough time on the premises to link up with a local woman. Thus, activities of this nature were known to be ongoing, but definitive action tended not to be in force. Peacekeepers in both PSOs also employed other strategies to make their liaisons less visible. These included providing women with mobile phones so that they could be contacted more discretely, and indicating that the women they accompanied in hotels and other public spaces were 'translators'.

By contrast, in Sierra Leone the legacy of the UNHCR/SCFUK report detailing the abuses of refugees appeared to have influenced the extent to which peacekeepers were open about their use of sex-workers. For example, at various bars and clubs renowned as pick-up sites with sex-workers visited during my brief period of fieldwork, peacekeeping personnel did not wear uniform (unlike in the DRC fieldwork site) and tended to be low-key in their activities. The sensitive political climate around the nexus linking peacekeepers, prostitution, sexual abuse and the UN code of conduct prohibiting sexual abuse of women under the age of 18 shaped masculine performances in Sierra Leone in ways that differed from those observed in the DRC.

> During an interview in Kinshasa, a peacekeeper openly discussed the issue of prostitution:
> Peacekeeper: These guys want to see what it is like
> Interviewer: What it is like?
> Peacekeeper: Sex with young girls ... to see if it is different.
> Interviewer: Erm ...right
> Peacekeeper: Some of them have daughters who are the same age, 14 or 15, and they want to know ... they can have more than one at a time, it's an adventure. The guys might turn them down ... but the girls are persistent and then it becomes a challenge for them [the girls] to get [sleep with] him.

A female civilian UN worker in the DRC spoke of peacekeepers and civilian UN personnel keeping a mental tally of how many women or girls they had had sex with and competing with colleagues. She mentioned how she had seen older men, 'fat and balding' with 'plenty of young girls around them'. She added that in fact she preferred to work with a man who had a sexual outlet of this kind, as he was more likely to be 'controlled' in the office. She considered that 'the girls must have had a smell or something about them' that peacekeepers from overseas found attractive.

Once again, there was no recognition of the women's lack of alternative opportunities to generate income: they were being blamed for their predicament and their response to it. A central theme emerging in accounts from across the sample was that of the local women being 'enthusiastic' in attracting peacekeepers. A female UN civilian reinforced this point by referring to the ways that local women who were 'after peacekeepers' would lift up their skirts to passing UN vehicles to 'show them what they had'. The following excerpt from a military police officer captures this reversal of feminine and masculine roles, exchanging women's passivity for their part in the traditional role of the male in initiating sex: 'We were in a bar one night in [the local town]. It was full of girls, dancing and drinking ... all over us. [The name of the peacekeeper] paid one of the women to keep the others away from him, they were hassling so much.'

Other accounts presented as 'vocabularies of motive' – again from both male and female civilian and military participants – drew on this discourse in which peacekeepers' masculinity was (re)presented as vulnerable to the advances of local women intent on 'getting to know them better'. The following account, relayed by a male participant working for an NGO in Sierra Leone, frames the women as 'doing all the running':

> Just as soon as the [nationality of peacekeepers] are rotated, the women are straight up to Lunghi [the international airport in Freetown] to meet the new ones [replacement troops]. You see, they're having relationships, and all in love, and crying and waving them off [the departing troops] ... next thing, they're picking out the ones they like, just after they've landed!

The participant went on to speak of the 'relationships' between the peace-keepers (who originated from a neighbouring African country) and some local women. He injected a degree of glamour into his account, painting the peace-keepers as 'playboys' who were real 'ladies' men', able to provide well for 'their women'. In these terms, any notions of prostitution and the profound inequalities in power and privilege were absent from his understanding, which spoke more of affluence and carefree sexual and romantic liaisons.

In this article I have argued that while many peacekeepers do a good job whilst deployed, a significant number of others abuse their positions of power and trust through their sexual abuse of local women and children. These peacekeepers live out a masculine identity that has negative consequences on a number of local women and children and that may further undermine already vulnerable groups.

Though women in these contexts should not be seen as bereft of human agency, nevertheless, the opportunities and possibilities available to them are extremely constrained. The UN, whilst having in place a range of policies intended to combat the sexually abusive activities of its peacekeepers, appears largely ineffective in its response to perpetrators. Many of them go unpunished and act with impunity. Reasons for this are complex and involve delicate politi-cal and cultural dynamics at a number of bureaucratic and international levels. However, a significant component of gendered exploitation is argued here to relate to the dominance of masculine world-views and masculine culture that continue to struggle to take seriously the plight of many women and children in the post-conflict context. If we decide – as we should – that there is nothing essential or fixed about masculinities (suggested in the 'boys-will-be-boys' rhetoric), then we should make greater efforts to help change what is considered to be acceptable and unacceptable behaviour for male peacekeepers.

I would like to acknowledge the help of Nadine Puechguirbal, Vanessa Kent (at the ISS), Dr Marsha Henry and the continued support of Katinka and Mo in this and ongoing work.

For details of the references, see http://www.pambazuka.org/index.php?id=23056

CHAPTER 7

AN 'UNHAPPY BIRTHDAY': THE WORLD BANK AND INTERNATIONAL MONETARY FUND TURN 60

Recalcitrant Reformers Require Tougher Tactics

Patrick Bond
Pambazuka News 170, 19 Aug 2004

CALL IT INSTITUTIONAL change-management fatigue. Or an unlimited spin-doctoring capacity by clever public relations officials. Or naivety on the part of those NGOs, environmentalists, trade unionists and Third World activists who cheered the appointment of Renaissance Man James Wolfensohn as World Bank president in 1995. Whatever the excuse, the bottom-line is obvious: no substantive changes at the bank and International Monetary Fund (IMF). And yet the need for a radical transformation could not be more obvious, in the wake of the late 1990s legitimacy crisis, itself a function of at least four managerial and economic factors that still have not been tackled properly:

■ The institutions' 'democratic deficit', which made them unsuitable for genuine global governance
■ The continued reliance upon the neo-liberal 'Washington Consensus' approach to public policy
■ The bank's ongoing orientation to controversial mega-projects
■ Both agencies' failure to cancel Third World debt and cool international financial speculation born of liberalised capital markets.

But we have to be frank about what drives these institutions, even when their credibility is at an all-time low: lubrication of private capital accumulation and stabilisation of geopolitical tensions through subsidised credits (often 'bail-outs' for earlier commercial lenders). So the four factors were not really failures – they were and are integral to the workings of the international economy.

Did reformers understand this problem, and did they adjust their plans accordingly? Confusingly, hopes were raised in part because of the 1997–99 tenure of Joseph Stiglitz as chief economist. Simultaneously, other catalysts for change included commissions on structural adjustment, dams and extractive industries.

However, the internal procedural changes, rhetorical shifts, research reports, individual initiatives, and multi-stakeholder forum exercises that emerged since the short-lived Stiglitzian glasnost did not fundamentally affect operations. The view from the inside is revealing, as staff in the Middle East and North Africa section complained in a leaked 1999 memo to Wolfensohn:

> The World Bank is increasingly being drawn into activities which are politically sensitive (participatory processes, involvement of civil society, corruption and so on). There is no doubt about the importance and relevance of these for development and success of World Bank assistance, but staff are not well prepared to handle these issues which creates more anxiety and stress.

Yet because the legitimacy crisis has continued growing, it has been rhetorically important for the bank and the fund to claim they are now 'post-Washington' in their ideology. In March 2002, midway through the United Nations Financing for Development (FFD) summit in Mexico, the bank, fund and German officials began promoting the idea of a new 'Monterrey Consensus', which would usher in an era of fair global finance. Even John Williamson has argued in the IMF's own magazine that his celebrated 1990 definition of the Washington Consensus was misunderstood and manipulated by leftist critics.

The institution's 60th birthday provides a chance to review the reform agenda, and to ask whether the late 1990s challenge from high-profile critics – Stiglitz and other enlightened economists, some Third World governments and protest movements – was as effective as it could have been. Were issues posed by reformers – debt relief, community and NGO participation in neoliberal programme design, democratic governance, global financial regulation, and commissions dealing with structural adjustment, dams and energy – the correct ones to tackle?

And if all these reforms were foiled by institutional lethargy or worse, is it appropriate to consider an entirely different strategy, based on Third World states removing themselves from influence by the bank and IMF? Is collective default feasible, and should Northern supporters assist the process by refusing to buy bonds issued by the World Bank?

Debt Relief Deferred

Within a year of Monterrey, the World Bank made an embarrassing concession, regarding its prize reform: the highly indebted poor countries (HIPC) debt relief initiative. The bank acknowledged longstanding criticisms that its staff 'had been too optimistic' about the ability of countries to repay under HIPC, and that projections of export earnings were extremely inaccurate, leading to failure by half the HIPC countries to reach their completion points. Paradoxically, the bank blamed failure upon 'political pressure' to cut debt further, as the key reason repayments were still not 'sustainable'.

HIPC was a mirage from the outset, as even the moderate London lobby group Jubilee Plus admitted in its September 2003 progress report:

> According to the original HIPC schedule, 21 countries should have fully passed through the HIPC initiative and received total debt cancellation of approximately $34.7 billion in net present value terms. In fact, only eight countries have passed Completion Point, between them receiving debt cancellation of $11.8 billion.

Add a few other countries' partial relief via the Paris Club ($14 billion) and it appears that the grand total of debt relief thanks to the 1996–2003 exercise was just $26.13 billion. There remained more than $2 trillion of Third World debt that should be cancelled, including not just HIPC countries but also Nigeria, Argentina, Brazil, Mexico, South Africa and other major debtors not considered highly-indebted or poor in the mainstream discourse.

Inadequate financial provision for HIPC in Western capitals probably reflects the merits of using debt as a means of maintaining control over Third World economies. An 'enhanced HIPC' was introduced to give the appearance of concern, and at the G8's Evian Summit in 2003, the world's leaders agreed with pleas by African representatives to relook at the programme. Yet no fundamental changes or substantial new funds were mooted. Proposals to write off further debt owed by Ethiopia and Niger in April were, at press time, likely to be vetoed by the US Treasury.

Poverty 'Reduction' Strategy Papers

In 1999, HIPC was accompanied by a renaming of the structural adjustment philosophy: Poverty Reduction Strategy Papers (PRSPs). More than two years later, at Monterrey, South Africa's finance minister Trevor Manuel – who joined former IMF managing director Michel Camdessus as special envoys of UN secretary general Kofi Annan – argued that PRSPs were 'an important tool for developing countries to reduce their debt burdens … a thorough and useful PRSP requires time, resources and technical capacity.' He suggested the Bretton Woods Institutions increase their role, to 'provide more technical assistance to meet those particular challenges'.

In contrast to Manuel's desire for PRSP expansion, civil society resistance to structural adjustment increased across the Third World, including Manuel's home continent, sometimes in the form of 'IMF riots'. A May 2001 Jubilee South conference of the main African social movements in Kampala concluded:

> In addition to the constraints placed on governments and civil society organisations in formulating PRSPs, the World Bank

and IMF retain the right to veto the final programs. This reflects the ultimate mockery of the threadbare claim that the PRSPs are based on 'national ownership'. An additional serious concern is the way in which PRSPs are being used by the World Bank and IMF, directly and indirectly, to co-opt NGOs to 'monitor' their own governments on behalf of these institutions.

The latter gambit had begun to fail by the time the FFD convened in Monterrey. Even the World Bank's best African case, Uganda, heard its National NGO Forum report: 'Among CSOs there is growing concern that perhaps their participation in the endeavour has amounted to little more than a way for the World Bank and IMF to co-opt the activist community and civil society in Uganda into supporting the same traditional policies.'

Democratic Governance?

Barely acknowledging the power imbalances in the global system, the Monterrey Consensus offered only timid suggestions for global governance reforms. The bank and IMF took nearly a full year to come forward with a plan, which, as it turned out, was an insult to the concept of democratic global governance.

The Bretton Woods Institutions' nearly 50 sub-Saharan African member countries are represented by just two directors, while eight rich countries enjoyed a director each and the US maintained veto power by holding more than 15 per cent of the votes. (There is no transparency as to which board members take what positions on key votes.) The leaders of the bank and IMF are chosen from, respectively, the US and EU, with the US treasury secretary holding the power of hiring or firing.

In this context, some reformist gestures were needed for the sake of appearance. Nevertheless, the *Financial Times* reported that the 2003 bank/fund strategy emanating from the IMF/bank important development committee (chaired by Manuel) offered only 'narrow technocratic changes,' such as adding one additional representative from the South to the 24-member board. For the US, even those mild-mannered reforms were too much, and the Bush regime's executive director to the bank, Carol Brooking, opposed reforms and instead suggested merely a new fund for extra research capacity aimed at the two institutions' Third World directors. Asked about the democracy deficit at the September 2003 annual meeting in Dubai, Manuel merely remarked, 'I don't think that you can ripen this tomato by squeezing it'.

Fanning Financial Fires

A final example of Monterrey's amplification of the self-destructive tendencies of international finance was the conference's call for 'liberalising capital flows in an orderly and well sequenced process'. The Asian financial crisis had earlier stalled the persistent arm twisting efforts of US treasury secretary Larry Summers to force through an amendment to the IMF articles of agreement which would end all exchange controls everywhere.

When Ethiopian Prime Minister Meles Zenawi had resisted Summers' gambit in 1997, according to Stiglitz, the IMF cut off the cheaper loans it had earlier made available. Cross-conditionality also made Ethiopia ineligible for other low-interest loans and grants from the World Bank, the European Community, and aid from bilaterals.

Stiglitz waged war within the bank and Clinton regime, finally winning concessions, but he learned a lesson: 'There was clear evidence the IMF was wrong about financial market liberalisation and Ethiopia's macroeconomic position, but the IMF had to have its way.' Zenawi poignantly implored, at a mid-2003 Economic Commission for Africa meeting, 'While we will not be at the high table of the IMF, we should at least be in the room where decisions are made.'

The only reform project to deal with financial speculation was a bail-out mechanism which might save Wall Street from its own worst excesses, but also allow a 'workout' system for countries that had urgent repayment difficulties. In mid-2003, a debt arbitration mechanism was finally proposed by the IMF's current acting managing director, Anne Krueger, a Bush appointee. However, the plan came to naught, for as the *The Guardian's* Larry Elliott explained:

> Billions of dollars from the bail-outs ended up in the coffers of the big finance houses of New York and George Bush was told not to meddle with welfare for Wall Street. The message was understood: the US used its voting power at the IMF to strangle the bankruptcy code at birth.

Reforming from the Outside?

Under the prevailing balance of power, the top-down reform processes discussed above could not have worked. But what of other efforts at reform from the outside (ostensibly from below), particularly via international commissions in which the World Bank plays a crucial hosting and financing role?

The three major recent processes in which well-meaning civil society advocates went inside the bank were the World Commission on Dams, the Structural Adjustment Participatory Review Initiative (Sapri) and the Extractive Industries Review. In the first case, a bank water expert, John Briscoe, actively lobbied Southern governments to reject the findings of a vast, multi-stakeholder research team in 2001. According to Patrick McCully of International Rivers Network, 'The World Bank's singularly negative and non-committal response to the WCD Report means that the bank will no longer be accepted as an honest broker in any further multi-stakeholder dialogues.'

As for Sapri, hundreds of organisations and scholars became involved in nine countries: Bangladesh, Ecuador, El Salvador, Ghana, Hungary, Mexico, the Philippines, Uganda and Zimbabwe. They engaged in detailed analysis from 1997 to 2002, often alongside local bank and IMF officials. Bank staff withdrew from the process in August 2001. In April 2002, when the research, a 188-page report, 'The Policy Roots of Economic Crisis and Poverty', was tabled for action, civil society groups found that the bank ignored it.

The third case, the Extractive Industries Review (EIR), also nearly went off the rails when in April 2003 an incident in Bali, Indonesia delegitimised the exercise before a final report was drawn up. A meeting between the bank, international mining industry and civil society ended in an uproar when 15 environmental and human rights groups left in protest. According to the *New York Times*, 'The group of reviewers set up by the bank had already circulated its draft conclusions supporting the bank's oil, gas and mining investments, even though conferences organised to gather information from concerned groups and individuals in Asia, the Middle East and Africa had not yet taken place.'

In the meantime, the bank approved loans for two infamous pipelines, Chad–Cameroon and Caspian, despite objections from the environmental, human rights and social justice communities. By late 2003, civil societies indignation meant that the EIR leader, former Indonesian environment minister Emil Salim, encountered another legitimacy crisis for World Bank participation politics.

In response, Salim ensured the critique by social movements and environmentalists made it into the December 2003 draft report, including the recommendation that public funds should not be used to facilitate private fossil-fuel profits. The recommendations would have meant an end to World Bank coal lending by 2008; mandatory revenue sharing with local communities; extensive environmental and social impact assessments; 'no go' zones for mining or drilling in environmentally sensitive areas; no new mining projects that dump tailings in rivers; obligatory environmental restructuring; and increased renewable energy investments.

No one was surprised when lead bank energy staffer Rashad Kaldany disagreed with the recommendations. Several major environmental NGOs blasted the institution:

> One of the bank's most important environmental reforms of the 1990s was its more cautious approach to high-risk infrastructure and forestry projects. This policy is now being reversed. The World Bank recently announced that it would re-engage in contentious water projects such as large dams in what it refers to as a 'high risk/high reward' strategy. In 2002, the bank dismissed its 'risk-averse' approach to the forest sector when it approved a new forest policy. The World Bank is also considering support for new oil, mining, and gas

projects in unstable and poorly governed countries, against the recommendations of its own evaluation unit.

Starting from Scratch?

Civil society enthusiasts of such commissions should have been warned by well-meaning insiders who also failed to move the reform agenda forward. From a vantage point in the chief economist's office during the late 1990s and early 2000s, David Ellerman saw more than his share of reform gambits. Finally, Ellerman threw up his hands:

> Agencies such as the World Bank and the IMF are now almost entirely motivated by big power politics and their own internal organisational imperatives. All their energies are consumed in doing whatever is necessary to perpetuate their global status. Intellectual and political energies spent trying to 'reform' these agencies are largely a waste of time and a misdirection of energies.

Persuasion by reformists within the chief economist's office did not affect the institution, agreed William Easterly, a former senior staffer:

> There's a big disconnect between World Bank operations and World Bank research. There's almost an organisational feud between the research wing and the rest of the bank. The rest of the bank thinks research people are just talking about irrelevant things and don't know the reality of what's going on.

Abuse of power and dogmatic ideology were Stiglitz's long-standing justifications for his August 2002 call to consider replacing the IMF:

> I'm beginning to ask, has the credibility of the IMF been so eroded that maybe it's better to start from scratch? Is the institution so resistant to learning to change, to becoming a more democratic institution, that maybe it is time to think about creating some new institutions that really reflect today's reality, today's greater sense of democracy. It is really time to re-ask the question: should we reform or should we build from start?

At the same time, a Columbia University colleague of Stiglitz, Jeffrey Sachs, began arguing that low-income countries should not repay World Bank and IMF loans, and should redirect debt servicing directly towards health and education. Decapitalisation of the Bretton Woods Institutions through a new wave of sovereign defaults would be a sensible and direct closure tactic.

After all, Sachs insisted, no one:

> in the creditor world, including the White House, believes that those countries can service these debts without extreme human cost. The money should instead be rerouted as grants

> to be spent on more demanding social needs at home. Poor
> countries should take the first step by demanding that all
> outstanding debt service payments to official creditors be
> reprocessed as grants for the fight against HIV/AIDS.

The idea was not as outlandish as it appeared at first blush, according to the *Boston Globe*, for during the 1980s Bolivia and Poland both got away with this strategy: 'Because the two countries used that money for social causes both were later able to win debt forgiveness.'

Default may be the logical option, since so few HIPC resources are being allocated for debt relief. Argentina, Nigeria and Zimbabwe may have been the highest-profile defaulters since 2000, but there are many more that will eventually feel pressure from the grassroots, conduct a cost-benefit analysis, and decide that default – combined with internal financing of development using local currency to meet basic needs – is the common sense approach.

Solidarity and Strength

In parallel to Third World governments becoming more militant, pressure on the institutions from their main shareholders – Northern citizens via their governments – will be vital. An extraordinary new tactic will assist: the World Bank Bonds Boycott. US groups like the Center for Economic Justice and Global Exchange have been working with Jubilee South Africa and Brazil's Movement of the Landless, among others, to ask: is it ethical for socially-conscious people to invest in the World Bank by buying its bonds (responsible for 80 per cent of the bank's resources), hence drawing out dividends which represent the fruits of enormous suffering?

In even the conservative belly of the global economic beast, the USA, organisations endorsing the boycott included important US cities such as San Francisco, Milwaukee, Boulder and Cambridge; major religious orders; the most important social responsibility funds; and major trade union pension/investment funds. During late 2003, the world's largest pension fund, TIAA-CREF, sold its World Bank bonds as campaigners made it a special target.

Bank Boycott activists understand that the institutions' waning legitimacy – and hence threats to funding by socially-responsible investors and eventually angry taxpayers – is the only target that most Third World social movements can aim at. They have done so in recent years with an increasingly militant perspective that worries not about the fund and bank's 'failure to consult' or 'lack of transparency' or 'undemocratic governance' – all easy populist critiques, whose reformist ambitions are terribly weak. (What difference, after all, would it make if Trevor Manuel were the first non-European IMF MD?)

Most of the attention that the leading activists pay to the Washington Consensus ideology is to the core content: commodification, whether in relation to water, electricity, housing, land, anti-retroviral medicines and health services, education, basic income grant support or other social services, ideally all at once and in cross-sectoral combinations. It is there, in grassroots movements to decommodify the goods and services which the World Bank and IMF increasingly put out of reach, that the only feasible alternative strategy can be found.

A longer version of this article appeared in Capitalism, Nature, Socialism, *June 2004.*

The Rains Do Not Fall
on One Person's Roof...

Interview with Rudy Amenga-Etego
Pambazuka News 171, 26 August 2004

THROUGHOUT THE GLOBAL South, public goods or services such as water, electricity, education and health care have become the subject of privatisation under a free market ethos pushed by international financial institutions. This ethos dictates that allowing private companies free rein is the only sure way to 'development'. The privatisation of water is one of the hotly contested areas where activists who argue that water is a human right have squared up against water barons represented by powerful transnational companies. In Ghana, the National Coalition Against the Privatisation of Water has fought against a major water privatisation project backed by the World Bank in a campaign that has wide resonance for movements against water privatisation worldwide. In this question and answer article, Rudolf Amenga-Etego from the National Coalition Against the Privatisation of Water, answers questions from Pambazuka News.

Pambazuka: First of all, why is privatisation of water wrong?

Rudy Amenga-Etego: Water is about life. The saying that 'water is life' cannot be more appropriate. Privatising water is putting the lives of citizens in the hands of a corporate entity that is accountable only to its shareholders. Secondly, water is a human right and this means that any philosophy, scheme, or contract that has the potential to exclude sections of the population from accessing water is not acceptable both in principle and in law. Privatisation has that potential because the privateers are not charities: they are in for the profit. Price therefore becomes an important barrier to access by poor people. Water is the collective heritage of humanity and nature. The rains do not fall on one person's roof so why should a few shareholders appropriate it to line their pockets? Water must remain a public good for the public interest.

Pambazuka: How does privatisation – and the problems with access to water – impact on the lives of Ghanaians?

RAE: Market principles were introduced into water provisioning. A social service to tax paying citizens and their dependants suddenly became a business returning profits to a greedy few. Those who cannot afford safe water turn to unsafe sources such as rivers, ponds and dams for their supply. The health implications are obvious. Take the northern region of Ghana for example. As soon as the World Bank came in and introduced their demand-driven policies, which meant safe water went only to the communities that paid for it, guinea worm increased drastically in the poorer communities who could not afford to pay. Ghana, which was on the way to eradicating guinea worm, over a span of only two years became the second most endemic country in the world, second only to the Sudan which we all know is at war with itself. Ghana is not at war, the blame is squarely on the head of the World Bank that arm-twisted the Ghanaian government into accepting the demand-driven policy. The worst impacts have been on women and children (especially girls) who now walk long distances to access safe water from government and charitable institutions and individuals who let them draw water free.

Pambazuka: What do you believe to be the World Bank and International Monetary Fund's agenda in pushing for the privatisation of water?

RAE: These institutions were originally set up to help reduce poverty on earth and help nations withstand post-war difficulties and grow their economies. They have become instruments in the hands of the United States government acting through its treasury office and are used to compel non-industrialised countries to adjust their economies to suit the US hegemonic agenda. The other Western powers profit by this (French, German, British and Dutch corporations are into the multi-billion water trade) and they therefore turn a blind eye. The World Bank and the IMF are also acting ideologically. Public bad, private good is the message in the Washington Consensus. They go to great lengths to present the private as the 'engine of growth'. But it is basically robbing the people (public) to pay the private. For example, the World Bank gives a loan to the government of Ghana to expand and rehabilitate its water sector and then through the imposition of conditionalities compels the government to hand over the facilities to private multinational companies to run for profit. The loan agreement then becomes a mere book transaction between the government and the World Bank – the private corporations go dancing to the bank to cash cheques, reaping where they have not sown.

Pambazuka: Your profile on the Goldman Environmental Prize (which you won earlier this year) website says: 'The World Bank and IMF have offered to loan Ghana $400 million to rebuild the publicly owned and controlled water system – but with a catch: the Ghanaian government must abandon its practice of making wealthy and industrial customers subsidise the cost of water to poor communities. In addition, water must be sold at full market rates.' With this in mind, what is the current status of water privatisation in Ghana? Is it true that the government has backtracked on its privatisation plans?

RAE: Not really. They wanted originally to hand over the water supply to two multinational corporations through a lease arrangement. The Coalition Against the Privatisation of Water (CAP of Water) stopped that in January

2003. But the World Bank has a privatisation fixation. So they have come up with a new strategy to grab Ghana's water. They have changed the country director in Ghana. The new man is trying to get soft-speaking Ghanaians to accept a five-year management service contract, which will roll back into a lease at the end of the term. The lessor (the government of Ghana) may however terminate the service contract after two years and lease the assets out immediately. So you see, they are taking one step backwards in order to take two steps forward. Not yet UHURU!

Pambazuka: If privatisation of water is not the answer, what alternative model do you propose?

RAE: The alternative is simply an accountable public system. The privateers came and met a system – a public system – which they have sought to convince us is not working. But they have failed to convince us that privatisation is better. Privatisation globally has led to an increase in water tariffs beyond the pockets of most people, it has led to low water quality (private companies are always cutting costs in order to maximise profit) and like in Cochabamba in Bolivia; uprising, repression and death. For small rural communities, community owned and managed systems are worth trying. Some such systems exist in Ghana and are fairly successful. In Ghana we are also experimenting with a variant called 'Public-Community Partnership'. A state provider supplies metered bulk water to a community which does the distribution (retailing) to households and institutions with public standpipes for the poor (who are assessed and listed by a water and sanitation committee which also serves as the management board for the community). Through this arrangement the governance issues of accountability, transparency and participation are addressed.

Pambazuka: To what extent has the National Coalition Against the Privatisation of Water linked up with other organisations in Africa fighting water privatisation? How important do you see this in building a united front?

RAE: The links are under development. Don't forget Africa is a huge continent – effective networking costs money but we are at it. We have links with a significant number of civil society groups in Africa. Our links with the Anti-privatisation Forum in South Africa and ORCADE in Burkina Faso has been very useful. We had a Pan-African conference on the right to water in Accra in May 2003. A committee was set up under my interim stewardship to work towards a meeting in South Africa, which will set out an agenda for a Pan-African Network on Essential Services. We are working at it.

Pambazuka: How can activists in the rest of Africa support your cause?

RAE: It is not my/our cause. It is the cause of Africa, of all those at the screwing end of corporate globalisation and US monoculture [Washington

Consensus]. The way to support is to start an anti-water privatisation cell in your own backyard and then link up with us.

Pambazuka: What strategies have you used in fighting water privatisation that have been particularly effective?

RAE: A combination of actions or methods: mass protest, leafleting, sign-on letters, petitions, and public awareness campaigns using radio, TV, and the print media. Also screening documentaries about struggles in other countries for mass viewing. We also organise seminars from time to time to review and upgrade our strategies.

Pambazuka: You have been frequently jailed for your political activities. What motivates you?

RAE: Those who produce the wealth must share in its benefits. So long as a neighbour (neighbour here is not defined geographically) is denied water, electricity, education, healthcare, etc because of their station in life I will remain in my trench!

This interview was conducted by email.

Global Apartheid Continues
to Haunt Global Democracy

Charles Mutasa
Pambazuka News 172, 9 September 2004

GLOBAL APARTHEID, like globalisation, is a buzzword that has evolved to describe a new global paradigm. Put simply, global apartheid is an international system of minority rule that promotes inequalities, disparities and differential access to basic human rights, wealth and power. Global apartheid is the opposite of global democracy. People like South Africa's president Thabo Mbeki, Fidel Castro of Cuba and the scholars Ali Mazrui, Richard Falk, and Patrick Bond, among many others, have used this concept in an effort to describe the global or economic injustice of our time.

Current manifestations of global apartheid are exhibited in the dominance of bilateralism and the hegemonic behaviour of the United States, the unbalanced and undemocratic processes in the World Trade Organisation (WTO), and the disproportionate power of multinational corporations and the Washington-based international financial institutions (IFIs).

In today's world apartheid is reflected in 'who gets what, when and how?' in the global system. Global apartheid offers explanations for the North-South polarisation, the peripherisation of Africa, the breakdown of WTO trade talks in Seattle (1999) and Cancún (2003), terrorism, endless conflicts and wars, problems with the free movement of labour between the South and the North, increased wealth in rich countries while resources are drained from poor countries, as well as the denial of life-saving medicines and care for people living with AIDS.

Debt and Global Apartheid

Debt oppresses poor countries and it has taken on proportions so as to render its repayment almost impossible. The debt has become a self-perpetuating vicious circle where new loans are taken to pay off the interest on standing ones. It is clearer than ever that the debt is not an economic problem, but a political one, and it is as such that it must be resolved.

Global apartheid through the bondage of debt fuels cycles of poverty and plagues many poor countries in Africa. The debt issue is no longer confined to the economic and financial spheres; as is demonstrated through the application of conditionalities attached to loans and debt relief. These conditionalities were historically introduced through World Bank structural adjustment programmes (SAPs) that were 'designed to rescue debtors', but were in reality driven by the desire to assure that ailing debtor economies did everything possible to pay back their debts.

Like apartheid in South Africa, SAPs entrenched great disparities in wealth, living conditions, life expectancy and eroded national sovereignty in the majority of sub-Saharan Africa. The introduction of conditionalities such as higher user fees in public facilities, subsidy cuts and lowering of budgetary allocations to social services has resulted in increased poverty and unemployment.

In fuelling global apartheid, the IMF and World Bank have special functions to play: they police and facilitate global apartheid while they simultaneously assist governments in adapting to the process of globalisation, helping them cushion the impacts of these policies felt by the poor. One chief economist was quoted as saying 'it is important to send the "ambulances" (social programmes) after the "tanks" (SAPs) have rolled through a country'. If a government strays from the path of globalisation the 'seal of approval' to borrow from public and private creditors is withdrawn by the IMF and World Bank, causing the governments' sources of credit to eventually dry up.

Countries that implemented SAPs became accustomed to operating under an 'external policy command', which discourages national dialogue on societal reform. This process has destroyed the social contract fundamental to ensuring government policies work effectively. Like former apartheid policies in South Africa, SAPs have been imposed upon the marginalised and materially deprived citizens of the global South, eroding their capacity to develop their own development programmes.

Debt has eroded the hard earned independence of African states. A crushing debt burden hampers poverty reduction and constrains development. Africa's debt crisis absorbs resources and energies that should be used to tackle urgent social problems.

Oloko Onyango's 1993 study of Uganda reveals that technocrats in the Ministry of Planning drew up national budgets that had to be endorsed by donors before their own parliament examined them. But even then, parliament merely acted as a rubber stamp. Since the introduction of SAPs as a way of resolving the debt crisis, independent policy-making and national economic management has diminished and narrowed considerably. Like in apartheid South Africa, in which blacks had no say in the rules that governed their country, global apartheid strips autonomy from the state and its people.

IFIs continue to put pressure on African development through their conditionalities, using development aid and loans as a lever to impose the neo-liberal paradigm of privatisation and deregulation, liberalisation and increased interest rates to control inflation. Under the newer Poverty Reduction Strategy Papers (PRSPs), set up to replace the old SAPs, they impose the same neo-liberal framework through the Poverty Reduction and Growth Facility (PRGF).

Studies done by AFRODAD on the PRSP process demonstrate how the IMF and the World Bank imposed their macro-economic framework on the process. This meant that the PRSPs could not be reshaped at the level of macro-economic policy as the framework was already fixed. Thus the link between PRSP and SAPs is a continued imposition of the neo-liberal macro-economic framework. Segregation in policy formulation and standards of living was a key feature of the apartheid system in South Africa. This is reflected in the current global apartheid paradigm with unrealistic IFI conditionalities, stifling African development goals, especially when the now-developed countries in the North used these now prohibited strategies for their own development process.

Many development agencies and sceptics have expressed widespread doubts regarding the heavily indebted poor countries (HIPC) initiative launched in 1996 to achieve the promised objective of a 'robust exit from the burden of unsustainable debts' for developing countries. Problems associated with the design and implementation of the initiative suggest that the HIPC initiative has not succeeded in providing adequate response to the Third World's debt overhang. The segregated and selective nature of apartheid is also seen in HIPC. It is interesting to observe that although Nigeria's debt stock is the largest in West Africa and the country is experiencing growing poverty, the country is not recognised as a HIPC eligible country simply because it produces oil.

Despite the many arguments against the conditionalities attached to multilateral lending and development assistance from bilateral donors, the conditions have intensified. It has become increasingly clear that there is a hidden agenda for control by those who propagate such conditionalities. This cannot be anything less than global apartheid. The whole process has been much slower than expected and the HIPC initiative is suffering from problems of under funding, excessive conditionality, inadequate debt relief and cumbersome procedures and eligibility restrictions. Creditors have not put sufficient political will, resources and serious analysis into the debt reduction operations.

Aid and Global Apartheid

Within global apartheid structures and systems, aid has always been connected to politics. During the Cold War, for example, investment flows, development efforts and humanitarian assistance tended to reflect the changing pattern of superpower alliance and competition. It has been pointed out that tying aid to politics translates into 'choice less democracy.' Thus, aid is a means of inducing policies and programmes favourable to the donor countries, even though promoting economic performance of recipient countries is the given rationale for doing so. According to a World Bank report, 'Aid can be the midwife of good policies'.

Aid to developing nations has not always been targeted towards genuine economic development efforts. Rather, in most cases, it has been given as an instrument of control under the global apartheid system. The current aid regimes undermine governance at the national level and impose conditionalities that lead to human rights violations. Adding to this, it is reliably estimated that for every dollar given in official development aid, three go back to the rich countries in debt service payments. Under the auspice of mandating policies for the good of the countries, aid actually decreases the level of control the government has over domestic expenditure allocation (both domestic and external).

Conclusion

The world has enough resources for everyone if we find the political will to eradicate poverty and hunger as well as put human life before profits. The debt must be cancelled to free up resources for equal development in both the North and the South. Kofi Annan's 21st Century Action Plan speech summed up what it will take if we are to replace global apartheid with global democracy, when he said:

> I would go a step further and propose that, in future, we consider an entirely new approach to handling the debt problem. The main components of such an approach could include immediate cancellation of the debts owed by countries that have suffered major conflicts or natural disasters, expanding the number of countries in the HIPC scheme by allowing them to qualify on the grounds of poverty alone.

In the name of global democracy, the international community needs to negotiate new measures that go beyond existing initiatives in order to resolve Africa's debt crisis and end global apartheid. The debt is unpayable and rescheduling will only postpone the problem. The debt bondage is the new face of colonialism or even slavery. Debt is used as an instrument of domination. It is also an instrument used to plunder and exploit indebted countries' resources. Ultimately, debt is at the heart of the unequal power relations between the North and the South.

Recommendations

1. The total cancellation of Third World illegitimate debts (as proposed for Iraq by the US) is a starting point in ending global apartheid.

2. There is an urgent need to address issues of unfair trade within the World Trade Organisation.

3. Europe and the United States should stop using aid as a means of neocolonialism or advancing their selfish ambitions.

4. There is a need to treat people of different geographical locations, race and origin equally when it comes to addressing global issues.

5. America's hegemonic wings need to be curtailed to ensure that it works within the framework of the United Nations.

6. The World Bank and the International Monetary Fund's role needs to be revisited and redesigned so as to make these institutions people centred and pro-poor in their economic development policies. There is need to put an end to the comodification of human lives through imposition of neo-liberal policies that value markets/ profits before people.

Ignoring the EIR :
How Industry, Government and the Bank
Chose Profits Over People

Abdulai Darimani
Pambazuka News 173, 16 September 2004

THE EXTRACTIVE INDUSTRIES Review (EIR) final report was particularly critical of the World Bank's role in policy reforms in the extractive industry sector, which have led to negative impacts on communities, the environment and human rights abuses. It recommended that the bank radically change its approach to funding such projects and even stop supporting some.

The president of the World Bank Mr James Wolfensohn set up the EIR secretariat under the chairmanship of Dr Emil Salim, former Environment Minister of Indonesia. The EIR secretariat was tasked to assess the impacts of the World Bank's intervention in the extractive industries, and to recommend its future role in the oil, gas and mining industries. The secretariat was specifically tasked to identify the negative impacts of the bank's operations in extractive industries; assess whether the bank's activities in these sectors can advance its mandate of poverty reduction through sustainable development; and recommend whether, or under what circumstances, the bank should continue to support extractive projects.

The review, a consultative process that included regional workshops, research projects, visits to four project sites, attendance at international conferences and informal consultations with a range of rights holders, released its final report following the final consultative meeting in mid-December 2003. The report affirmed the criticisms and concerns long expressed by African civil society and many other groups across the world.

The recommendations demanded that the bank adopt significant reforms including doing more to reduce poverty; immediately ceasing funding for coal projects worldwide and phasing out its support for oil production by 2008; enhancing human rights protection; acquiring prior informed consent for indigenous peoples and communities affected by extractive sector activity; and an end to support for destructive mining technologies.

The report also recommended that the bank should prepare and publish net-benefit analyses; update and fully implement the Natural Habitat Policy as a basis for clear no-go zones, and should not finance any oil, gas or mining projects or activities (including through policy lending and technical assistance) that might affect existing World Heritage properties, current official protected areas, or critical natural habitats or areas planned in the future to be designated by national or local officials as protected.

Some African governments and mining industry representatives and their associations viewed these recommendations with scepticism, calling them anti-development indicators for mineral-endowed African countries. During the consultative process some governments and industry tried to water down many of the progressive recommendations. However, facts could not be beaten and African civil society and their global colleagues worked hard to retain them in the report.

In the past years, the World Bank has promoted extractive sector reforms in Africa through support in trade and investment liberalisation; privatisation of state-owned companies; institution and capacity building; apparently to improve conditions for foreign direct investment in the extractive sector; and direct finances of private sector extractive industry projects through equity investments, loans and guarantees.

The World Bank affiliates have helped fund major but highly controversial private sector extractive projects in Africa. In the oil/gas sector the bank supported the Chad-Cameroon pipeline project. In the mining sector, the bank has supported highly controversial projects in Zambia, and Tanzania. Former artisanal and small-scale miners from Tanzania claimed that a Canadian company and the Tanzanian authorities forced tens of thousands of villagers away from the site of the Kahama Mines in the Bulyanhulu gold tract in 1996. The Multilateral Investment Guarantee Agency (MIGA), a private guarantee arm of the World Bank, supported this project three years later.

Early this year, a group of African ministers of mines meeting in Johannesburg, South Africa, expressed misgivings about the recommendations of the EIR final report. They called on the World Bank not to adopt all the recommendations of the EIR final report, which they believed could spell disaster for mineral endowed poor countries banking on mining projects in these sectors for development.

The ministers were reported to have indicated that the EIR final report had not given sufficient consideration to the fact that the extractive industries are essential to economic growth and poverty reduction, and that for some countries the extractive industries represent a very important means of creating revenue for government programmes. The ministers also expressed concern about the precondition of World Bank investment in countries that have robust and transparent governance criteria in place. They believed that a country's inability to meet World Bank governance criteria should not prevent that country from gaining access to the support, both financial and structural, that is required in order to develop such governance mechanisms. Otherwise, countries that are most in need of such developmental assistance could be excluded and would either remain mired in poverty or find less desirable paths to develop their extractive potential.

Two reasons could have influenced the ministers to present this view. The first is a response in self-defence. The second is the apparent influence from industry and their home governments. For a very long time, the extractive sector in Africa has been one of the areas for endemic corruption and abuse of power. The endemic corruption in the sector benefits those in power and the rich while marginalising the poor and local communities.

The unequal distribution of benefits also explains why many governments in Africa continue to supervise the abuse of community and citizens' rights, lowering of standards and net benefits of mining, oil and gas extraction on the continent. The EIR recommendations were a signal not just to the World Bank but also to all major players in extractive industries to put an end to the corruption and abuse of power. Even more so implementation of the recommendations would have set the stage for up-scaling similar recommendations for governments, which would have meant ripping governments of their dictatorial powers and minimising corruption in the sector.

The view of the African ministers was echoed by mining companies and mining industry associations, in particular the London-based International Council on Mining and Metals (ICMM) and the Mining Industry Associations of Southern Africa (MIASA), which groups chambers of mines from Botswana, Namibia, South Africa, Tanzania, Zambia and Zimbabwe.

These bodies argued that many of the recommendations in the EIR final report were not based on sound research and would, in fact, inhibit poverty alleviation and sustainable development. Mark Moody-Stuart, who served as a member of the EIR advisory group during the second half of last year, expressed the view that the net effect of the EIR final report's recommendations would be a virtual disengagement of the World Bank from mining, oil and gas.

The ICMM expressed concerns at the proposed governance prerequisites for World Bank investment, which included the quality of the rule of law and the absence – or even risk – of conflict. The council believed that these could be too demanding even for developed countries. The South African Chamber of Mines CEO Mzolisi Diliza shared the ICMM's concerns. Writing to the World Bank president, James Wolfensohn, on behalf of MIASA, he noted that much of the content of the EIR report undermined the legitimate role of governments.

They all concluded that adopting the EIR report's recommendations in their entirety would result in a massive reduction in foreign direct investment going to emerging markets, for which extractive-industries projects are sometimes their only available path to development. This is all industry rhetoric and manipulative tactics rooted in the narrow conception that the only path to economic development is foreign direct investment in the extractive sector. The current paradigm of mineral resource extraction does not benefit mineral endowed African countries. While foreign direct investment in extractive industries in Africa has increased over the last two decades poverty has not reduced, if anything it has increased in those countries.

Southern Africa is noted for its mineral potential and its long historical association with mineral extraction, yet the region's human development record has not improved. According to the 2003 edition of the United Nations Development Programme's Human Development Report, an estimated 20 million people – or 19 per cent – of the total population of the six MIASA countries live on less than a dollar a day, while 47 million people – or 44 per cent – live on less than two dollars a day. The current paradigm of mineral resource extraction in Africa is therefore exploitative.

Why was industry so concerned about the World Bank pulling out of extractive industries when the bank provides less than 5 per cent of the financing required for projects in the mining, oil and gas industries? It sounds amazing how when threatened the industry suddenly became the greatest advocate of the poor when ICMM's Kathryn McPhail (who used to research for the bank) said: 'What worries us most are not the implications for the mining industry as such, but the implications for development in emerging markets'. This argument was carried on by a letter from the Equator Banks, an investment group to the World Bank, that says: 'We believe that the EIR has not given sufficient consideration to the fact that the extractive industries are essential to global economic growth and poverty reduction.'

Two reasons explain why industry was concerned about the recommendations in the EIR's final report. First, the decision could be emulated by other financial institutions' withdrawal from the sector, which would drastically shrink lending to industry. Secondly, and even more important, was the fear of diminishing influence of the Breton Woods institutions on host governments' policies and practices which are critical to ensuring low standards for industry. The World Bank influences the development strategies and practices of developing countries by making them compromise their economic policies, investment regulations, and projects that benefit large transnational corporations.

The United States government is by far the most influential force in establishing the priorities of the World Bank. It can veto any significant shifts in policy and by custom appoints its president, who is usually a product of the financial sector. Given the new American imperialist offensive, under the so-called war on terror, the US has thrust Africa's extractive resources forward as a prize to be controlled as it seeks alternative sources of oil. Along the Gulf of Guinea, now referred to as the 'New Persian Gulf' the United States aggressively seeks military bases. Under these circumstances, it is not surprising that some African governments worked with the World Bank to roll back the progressive recommendations of the report.

Despite support for the recommendations made by the EIR gaining momentum worldwide, the bank's board decided in August to act on very few of the recommendations made in the report. It thus failed to change the way the bank does business in Africa, missing an opportunity to show a genuine commitment to respecting human rights and the needs of communities affected by extractive industries. Considering the World Bank's own vested interests, the opposition of powerful industry players, the complicity of African governments and the existing global political climate, the decision came as no great surprise.

This is an edited and updated version of an article that was published in African Agenda, *Vol. 7 no. 3, 2004.*

The International Monetary Fund and World Bank in Africa: a 'Disastrous' Record

Demba Moussa Dembele
Pambazuka News 175, 23 September 2004

THIS YEAR MARKS the 60th anniversary of the International Monetary Fund and the World Bank. Through their propaganda machines, both institutions will attempt to highlight their 'assistance' to Africa. But in reality, since the 1970s, these institutions have gradually become the chief architects of policies, known as 'the Washington Consensus,' which are responsible for the worst inequalities and the explosion of poverty in the world, especially in Africa.

Yet, when they began to intervene on that continent in the late 1970s and early 1980s, their stated goal was to 'accelerate development', according to a World Bank document, familiarly known as the Berg Report, published in 1981. But as the following editorial will show, the actual record is disastrous.

The main pretext for their intervention was to 'help solve' the debt crisis that hit African countries in the late 1970s, following the combination of internal and external shocks, notably sharp fluctuations in commodity prices and sky-rocketing interest rates. The remedy they proposed, known as stabilisation and structural adjustment programmes (SAPs), achieved the opposite, and contributed to worsening the external debt and exacerbating the overall eco-nomic and social crisis.

In 1980, at the onset of their intervention, the ratios of debt to gross domestic product (GDP) and exports of goods and services were respectively 23.4 per cent and 65.2 per cent. Ten years later, in 1990, they had deteriorated to respec-tively 63 per cent and 210 per cent! In 2000, the debt to GDP ratio stood at 71 per cent while the ratio of debt to exports of goods and services had 'improved' somewhat, at 80.2 per cent, according to the World Bank's Global Development Finance.

The deterioration in debt ratios is reflected in the inability of many African countries to service their external debt. As a result, accumulated arrears on principal and interests have become a growing share of outstanding debt. In 1999, those arrears accounted for 30 per cent of the continent's debt, compared with 15 per cent in the 1990s and 5 per cent for all developing countries. To compound the crisis, African countries are getting very little, in terms of new loans, except to pay back old debts. As a result, since 1988, the part of accumu-lated arrears in 'new' debt is estimated at more than 65 per cent.

Between 1980 and 2000, sub-Saharan African (SSA) countries had paid more than $240 billion as debt service, that is about four times the amount of their debt in 1980. Yet, despite this financial haemorrhage, SSA still owes almost four times what its owed more than 20 years ago! One of the most striking illustrations of this apparent paradox is the case of the Nigerian debt. In 1978, the country had borrowed $5 billion. By 2000, it had reimbursed $16 billion, but still owed $31 billion, according to President Obasanjo.

The Nigerian case is a good example of the structural nature of Africa's debt crisis and of the power imbalance that characterises world economic and financial relationships. It is this general context that allowed the IMF and World Bank to increase their influence in African countries. One good illustration of this has been the rapid rise in the share of the World Bank and its affiliate, the International Development Association (IDA), in SSA's debt. The combined share of both, which was barely 5.1 per cent of SSA's total debt in 1980, had jumped to 25 per cent in 1990 and to more than 37 per cent in 2000, according to the World Bank. In other words, the World Bank group has become the principal 'creditor' of many sub-Saharan countries, which explains the enormous sway it holds over these countries' policies.

One way they exercise this influence is through the imposition of stiff conditionalities on African countries in exchange for loans and credits. Financial liberalisation, aimed at attracting more foreign investments to compensate for shortfalls in export revenues, instead fostered more instability, due to the volatility of exchange rates resulting from speculative short-term capital flows. This, combined with higher interest rates, crowded out both public and private investments. For instance, investments as a percentage of GDP fell from an annual average of 23 per cent between 1975 and 1979 to an average of 18 per cent between 1980 and 1984 and 16 per cent between 1985 and 1989. They recovered somewhat in the 1990s, but averaged only 18.2 per cent between 1990 and 1997, according to UNCTAD. These statistics are consistent with those given by the World Bank, which show that the annual investment ratio averaged 18.6 per cent and 17.2 per cent in 1981–1990 and 1991–2000, respectively.

These low investment ratios resulted in a contraction of output. Real GDP growth, which averaged 3.5 per cent in the 1970s, fell to 1.7 per cent, between 1981 and 1990, according to the World Bank. However, this masks the sharp declines recorded in the 1980s, dubbed 'the lost decade' for Africa. This is better illustrated by the negative growth rates of both GDP and consumption per capita. They fell respectively by 1.2 per cent and 0.9 per cent a year between 1981 and 1990. It is estimated that in 1981–1989, the cumulative loss of per capita income for the continent as a whole was equivalent to more than 21 per cent of real GDP.

In a report released in September 2001, UNCTAD indicated that the average income per capita in SSA was 10 per cent lower in 2000 than its 1980 level. In monetary terms, average income per capita fell from $522 in 1981 to $323 in 1997, a loss of nearly $200. The same report said that rural areas experienced an even greater decline in income. These statistics were confirmed by the

World Bank, which says that income per capita in SSA contracted by a cumulative 13 per cent between 1981 and 2001.

The 2004 edition of the World Development Indicators says that SSA is the only region in the world where poverty has continued to rise since the early 1980s, that is at the onset of the IFIs' intervention. According to that document, in 1981, an estimated 160 million people lived on less than $1 a day. In 2001, the number had risen to 314 million, almost double its 1981 level. This means that approximately 50 per cent of Africa's population lives in poverty. When the threshold is $2 a day, the numbers rise from 288 million to 518 million, during the same period.

The Costs of Trade Liberalisation

According to the IMF and World Bank, one of the sources of Africa's crisis is its inward-looking trade system, characterised by the protection of domestic markets, subsidies, overvalued exchange rates and other 'market distortions' that made African exports less 'competitive' in world markets. In place of this system, they propose an open and liberal trading system in which tariff and non-tariff barriers are kept to a minimum or even eliminated. Such a system, combined with an export-led growth strategy, would put Africa on a solid path to economic recovery, according to both institutions.

The costs associated with trade liberalisation have largely offset any potential 'benefits' African countries were supposed to derive from that liberalisation. First of all, trade liberalisation has translated into substantial fiscal losses, since many countries depend on import taxation as their main source of fiscal revenues. Therefore, the elimination of, or reduction in, import tariffs has led to lower government revenues.

But one of the most negative impacts of trade liberalisation has been the collapse of many domestic industries, unable to sustain competition from powerful and subsidised competitors from industrialised countries. In fact, Africa's industrial sector has been among the biggest victims of structural adjustment.

From Senegal to Zambia, from Mali to Tanzania, from Cote d'Ivoire to Uganda, entire sectors of the domestic industry have been wiped out, with devastating consequences. Not only has the industrial sector contribution to domestic product continued to fall, but also the industrial workforce has continued to shrink dramatically. In Senegal, more than one third of industrial workers lost their jobs in the 1980s. The trend was accentuated in the 1990s, following sweeping trade liberalisation policies and privatisation imposed by the IMF and the World Bank, especially after the 50 per cent devaluation of the CFA franc, in 1994. In Ghana, the industrial workforce declined from 78,700 in 1987 to 28,000 in 1993. In Zambia, in the textile sector alone, more than 75 per cent of workers lost their jobs in less than a decade, as a result of the complete dismantling of that sector by the Chiluba presidency. In other countries, such as Cote d'Ivoire, Burkina Faso, Mali, Togo, Zambia, Tanzania, etc, similar trends can be observed.

In several annual and special reports, the International Labor Organisation (ILO) has documented the devastating impact of SAPs on employment and wages. The African Union seems to have come to grips with that devastation. It organised a special summit on employment and poverty, in the capital of Burkina Faso, on 9–10 September 2004. It was revealed during that summit that only 25 per cent of the African workforce is employed in the formal sector. The rest, 75 per cent, is either in the subsistence agriculture or in the informal sector. In light of this reality, the summit issued a plan of action aimed at exploring strategies to foster job creation. But such a plan will only be credible if African countries are ready to move away from IMF and World Bank recipes, which were harshly criticised during the summit.

UNCTAD has reported that more than 70 per cent of Africa's exports are still composed of primary products, more than 62 per cent of which are non-processed products. This helps justify the need for more liberalisation and deregulation to make African exports more 'competitive'. The second objective is to help justify the need for more liberalisation and deregulation to make African economies more 'competitive' and 'attractive' to foreign direct investments. This also explains the push for more privatisation.

In the name of 'comparative advantage', the export-led growth strategy forces African countries to compete fiercely for market shares, leading them to flood the same markets with more of their commodities. As a result, trade liberalisation has accentuated the volatility of African commodities, whose prices experienced twice the volatility of East Asian commodity prices and nearly four times the volatility that industrial countries experienced in the 1970s, 1980s and 1990s. This has contributed to worsening Africa's terms of trade.

According to UNCTAD, if Africa's terms of trade had remained at their 1980 level:
■ Africa's share in world trade would have been twice its current level
■ The investment ratio would have been raised by 6 per cent per annum in non-oil exporting countries
■ It would have added to annual growth 1.4 per cent per annum
■ It would have raised GDP per capita by at least 50 per cent to $478 in 1997 compared with the actual figure of $323 during that year.

The Costs of Financial Liberalisation

One of the main objectives of financial liberalisation is to make African countries 'attractive' to foreign direct investments. But as the experience of development shows, foreign direct investments follow development, not the other way around. In addition, despite all 'the right financial policies', foreign investments continue to elude Africa, with less than 2 per cent of flows to developing countries, despite having among the highest rates of return on investments in the world. And these flows are concentrated in a few oil-producing and mineral-rich countries, according to UNCTAD and the World Bank.

In reality, financial liberalisation has yielded little gains. For most African countries, it has been associated with huge costs. First, it entails higher levels of foreign exchange reserves to protect domestic currencies against attacks resulting from speculative short-term capital outflows. Second, financial liberalisation has increased the likelihood of capital flight, in part as a result of a greater volatility of domestic currencies. The high costs of trade and financial liberalisation further weakened African economies and opened the way to the privatisation of the continent.

The Privatisation of Africa

Privatisation, like financial liberalisation, is seen by the IMF and World Bank as an instrument to promote private sector development, which has been elevated to the status of 'engine of growth'. The privatisation of state-owned enterprises (SOEs), including water and power utilities, has been one of the core conditionalities imposed by the two institutions, even in the context of 'poverty reduction'.

Most of the foreign direct investments registered by African countries in the 1990s came as a response to privatisation of SOEs. No sector was spared, even those considered as 'strategic' in the 1980s, such as telecommunications, energy, water and the extractive industries. In 1994, the World Bank published a report assessing the process of privatisation in SSA. After complaining about the slow pace of privatisation throughout the region, it issued a warning to African governments to accelerate the dismantling of their public sector, accused of being 'at the heart of Africa's economic crisis'. The process of privatisation peaked in the late 1990s and ever since has levelled off, despite more deregulation, liberalisation and all kinds of incentives offered to would be investors.

To date, it is estimated that more than 40,000 SOEs have been sold off in Africa. However, the 'gains' from privatisation, projected by the World Bank and the IMF, have been elusive. In fact, many privatisation schemes have failed and contributed to worsening economic and social conditions. Almost everywhere, privatisation has been associated with massive job losses and higher prices of goods and services that put them out of reach of most citizens.

Building a Neo-liberal State

The concept of 'good governance' was promoted by the IMF and World Bank to explain the failure of SAPs. It tends to convey the idea that SAPs have failed, in large part, because African States are 'corrupt', 'wasteful' and 'rent-seeking' and because of the 'poor implementation' of policies. In other words, SAPs were basically 'sound'; it is the combination of 'rampant corruption' and lack of qualified personnel that led to the failure of these policies. Thus, 'good governance' means nothing else than the need to build a neo-liberal state, subservient to the IFIs, able to effectively implement, 'sound policies' and to protect the interests of foreign investors.

Indeed, one of the main goals of the IMF and World Bank has been to discredit state-led development strategies in favour of market-led strategies. This is why one of the main targets of these institutions has been the role of the African state in economic and social development. To discredit that role, a two-track strategy was adopted. The first track was to attack the credibility of the African state as an agent of development. To achieve that goal, an abundant literature has been published by the two institutions, highlighting the 'corrupt', 'predatory', 'wasteful' and 'rent-seeking' nature of the African state. To justify these epithets, the IFIs pointed to the 'mismanagement' of the public sector, accused of being an obstacle to economic growth and development. These attacks helped make the case for the sweeping restructure of the public sector, which, in many cases, led to its dismantling in favour of the private sector.

The second track in weakening the role of the state in development was to deprive it of financial resources. Trade and financial liberalisation achieved in part that goal. As already indicated, trade liberalisation not only led to a greater loss of fiscal revenues, following lower tariff barriers, but it also led to huge trade losses. This was compounded by financial liberalisation which entailed further fiscal losses resulting from tax holidays and low income tax rates. To make up for these losses, the African state had to resort to more and more multilateral and bilateral loans and credits, which further alienated its sovereignty.

As a result, many African states have been stripped of all but a handful of their economic and social functions. Cuts in spending mostly fell on social sectors. State retrenchment primarily aimed at eliminating subsidies for the poor, removing social protection, and abandoning its role in fighting for social justice through income redistribution and other social transfers to the most disadvantaged segments of society. This explains, among other things, the degradation of many basic social services and the explosion of poverty in Africa since 1981, as the World Bank itself has acknowledged.

While dismantling or weakening the economic and social roles of the state, the IMF and World Bank have sought to build or strengthen the functions most useful to the implementation of neo-liberal policies and the promotion of private sector development. This explains the insistence on 'capacity building' or on 'institution building', heard over the last few years. However, the institutions that the IMF and World Bank talk about are not for development, but for markets. In other words, they propose building institutions supportive of neo-liberal policies and in the service of the private sector, especially foreign investors.

Thus, the 'institution building' agenda promoted by the IMF and the World Bank has nothing to do with promoting democracy and protecting human rights. In fact, the neo-liberal conception of governance undermines both since it deprives representative institutions of their role in formulating public policies following open and democratic debates. They are reduced to implementing what the IMF and World Bank and their G8 masters decide for African countries and their people.

From Structural Adjustment to Poverty 'Reduction'

After producing poverty and deprivation on a massive scale in Africa and elsewhere, the IFIs' focus on 'poverty reduction' since 1999 could not be more suspect. But to make this shift a bit more credible, the IMF's Enhanced Structural Adjustment Facility (ESAF) was renamed Poverty Reduction and Growth Facility (PRGF) and the World Bank has set up a Poverty Reduction Support Credit (PRSC).

There is no doubt that the shift in the rhetoric of the IFIs amounts to an admission of failure of past policies, which put too much emphasis on correcting macroeconomic imbalances and 'market distortions' at the expense of economic growth and social progress. The disastrous record of SAPs and the continued deterioration in the economic and social situation of countries subjected to IMF and World Bank programmes put into question the credibility and even the legitimacy of these institutions. Their crisis of legitimacy was exacerbated by stepped up attacks by the Global Justice Movement and growing criticism from mainstream economists, especially from Joseph E. Stiglitz, former World Bank chief economist.

The Nature of the Poverty Reduction Strategy Papers (PRSPs)

The PRSPs are supposed to provide more freedom to developing countries in formulating their policies. This is what the bank and the fund call 'national ownership.' Representatives from the government, the private sector, civil society organisations – and even the poor – are supposed to 'participate' in drafting the PRSP of each country to decide on how to use the proceeds released by 'debt relief' to achieve 'poverty reduction'.

In reality, the macroeconomic framework that underpins the PRSPs is the same as that which underpinned the now discredited SAPs. That framework is non-negotiable and includes fiscal austerity, trade and financial liberalisation, privatisation, deregulation and state retrenchment, etc. In essence, despite the disastrous outcome of their past policies, the IMF and the World Bank still believe that those policies are in the 'interests of the poor'. In particular, they think that trade liberalisation and openness are the best – if not the only – road to growth, which they see as a 'prerequisite' for poverty reduction. Hence the export-led growth strategy advocated by the two institutions, but which has been a big failure in African and other developing countries.

A survey of 27 African PRSPs by UNCTAD in 2002 has demonstrated that all of them, without exception, contain the policies outlined above; policies which are at odds with both the wishes and the interests of the poor, observes the document. It is this straightjacket that ties up developing countries' hands and prevents them from achieving any substantial gain in poverty 'reduction'. Most of the time, countries have failed to implement these conditions, leading to the suspension of their programmes.

In fact, the IFIs' conception of poverty views it as an isolated aspect of overall economic and social development that should be dealt with by short-term measures. Hence, the emphasis in the PRSPs on more spending for primary education and health, among others. Thus, PRSPs contain some short-term measures aimed at mitigating the negative impact of macroeconomic policies and structural reforms on the most vulnerable groups, notably the poor. However, the tools the World Bank and the IMF have proposed to achieve this goal are the same as those already tested in the past and that have aggravated poverty and deprivation in much of Africa.

In reality, PRSPs are SAPs with more conditionalities and less resources. As already indicated, a new 'generation' of conditionalities have been added to old conditionalities, with the concept of 'good governance', analysed above. UNCTAD has revealed that between 1999 and 2000, 13 African countries had signed programmes containing an average of 114 conditionalities, 75 per cent of which are governance-related conditionalities. One can imagine the enormous human and financial resources needed to deal with such a number of conditionalities. For this reason, the degree of compliance with IMF and World Bank-sponsored programmes has significantly declined since the mid-1990s. For instance, the rate of compliance was estimated at about 28 per cent of the 41 agreements signed between 1993 and 1997, according to UNCTAD.

With the PRSPs, the IMF and the World Bank pursue three objectives. First, mislead world public opinion, especially in Northern countries, into believing that they are really serious about 'reducing poverty'. And the World Bank alone counts on a huge and sophisticated propaganda machine to achieve this. With the more than 300 staff of its external relations department – propaganda department, one should say – the bank has all the means it needs to 'explain' effectively its policies. It has achieved some success, since some big Northern NGOs, once very critical of SAPs, see the PRSPs as a 'positive shift' in the IFIs' policies.

The second objective of the PRSPs is to enlist broad support within each country to help rehabilitate discredited and failed policies. This is what 'national ownership' and 'participation' of civil society organisations are supposed to achieve. While insisting on the 'participation' of civil society organisations, their most vocal critics, the IMF and World Bank tend to sideline representative institutions, like national assemblies. This is another illustration of these institutions' contempt for the democratic process in Africa. Finally, with PRSPs, the IMF and the World Bank seek to shift the blame to African countries and citizens for the inevitable failure of these 'new' policies.

Conclusion

The IMF and World Bank have utterly failed in 'reducing poverty' and 'promoting development'. In fact, they are instruments of domination and control in the hands of powerful states whose long-standing objective is to perpetuate the plunder of the resources of the Global South, especially Africa. In other words, the fundamental role of the bank and fund in Africa and in the rest of the developing world is to promote and protect the interests of global capitalism.

This is why they have never been interesting in 'reducing' poverty, much less in fostering 'development'. As institutions, their ultimate objective is to make themselves 'indispensable' in order to strengthen and expand their power and influence. They will never relinquish easily that power and influence. This explains why they have perfected the art of duplicity, deception and manipulation. In the face of accumulated failures and erosion of their credibility and legitimacy, they have often changed their rhetoric, but never their fundamental goals and policies.

This is why they cannot be trusted to bring about 'development' in Africa. If the experience of the last quarter of a century has taught Africa one fundamental lesson it is that the road to genuine recovery and development begins with a total break with the failed and discredited policies imposed by the IMF and the World Bank.

In fairness to both institutions, we must recognise, however, the complicity of African leaders in the disastrous outcome of neo-liberal policies. Many governments and senior civil servants have bought into the agenda promoted by the IMF and World Bank. Therefore, they bear a great responsibility in the current state of the continent. Thus, to put an end to the influence of these institutions, African social movements and progressive forces must explore strategies aimed at promoting a new kind of leadership able and willing to challenge these institutions in favour of genuine alternative development policies.

A Happy Birthday?
the Chad–Cameroon Oil Pipeline One Year On

Akong Charles Ndika
Pambazuka News 175, 23 September 2004

ON FRIDAY, 10 OCTOBER 2003, before African head of states and foreign dignitaries in Kome, Chad, President Idriss Deby symbolically turned the tap that opened the flow of 225,000 barrels of oil. The $3.7 billion crown jewel project of the World Bank is the biggest foreign investment in sub-Sahara Africa. For the next 25 years, approximately 900 million barrels of oil will be pumped from 300 oil wells drilled in Doba, south of Chad, along a 1,070km pipeline to Cameroon on the Atlantic coast.

World Bank financing, which totalled just 4 per cent of the cost, was crucial to the project. The oil consortium comprising of Exxon, Petronas, and Chevron considered the participation of World Bank as a necessary political risk insurance, which enabled them to raise more money on international capital markets. Meanwhile, the World Bank embraced the project as an unparalleled opportunity for land-locked Chad to lift its 6.5 million population out of acute poverty, and for ocean-bordered Cameroon to generate much needed revenues.

Some months after Chad, the world's fifth poorest country, entered the pantheon of Africa's petro-states, it is worth taking stock of the project's overall impact now that the exploitation phase has started. Has the project broken free from the traditional gap between the expectations and dismal realities of oil exploitation? Better still, has the oil been a weapon of mass poverty (WMP) or a weapon of mass development (WMD) to Chad and Cameroon?

The background to any petroleum project is key in determining the development outcomes. In fact, the underlying development problems associated with the extraction of black gold are not inherent in the resource itself. However, there is little disagreement on the ability of oil to ratchet up pre-existing conflict in a society; oil can become the very rationale for starting war. In this light, the socio-political environment in which the World Bank approved the project was a potent recipe for poor development outcomes.

There is an endemic mix of corruption and civil strife in Chad and Cameroon. For instance, Chad, since independence, has been marred by a vicious cycle of conflicts and war. Besides the absence of basic ingredients for the growth of civil society, elections are shamelessly rigged, fraud is rife, and the regimes have shown a predilection to violently repress dissenting voices.

For example, villagers were coerced to give their accord to the project in consultations prior to its approval. Tales in Kome, where villagers were consulted in the presence of government forces and rebels, are all too glaring. The village chief was imprisoned for his unfavourable attitude, and the oil company representative arrived accompanied by military police. Given this background, most people were too intimidated to speak out against the project.

Given that Cameroon has consecutively crowned Transparency International's ratings of the most corrupt countries in the world, it was no surprise that a bellicose climate of non- information disclosure concerning the project was the norm.

International civil society organisations in 1997 argued for the project's postponement to ensure the two countries upgrade their governance capacities. Contrarily, the World Bank in June 2000 discounted the burgeoning corruption and civil strife in Cameroon and Chad respectively to approve the project. Shortly after, civil society partners were proved right when the Chadian government, on receiving $25 million from the project consortium as a signature bonus, admitted to having used the money to procure arms to quell a rebel insurgence in the north of the country.

More recently, soon after the project's official inauguration last October, the government closed down the country's only independent radio station, FM Liberté, which had close ties to the country's human rights organisations. Then residents of the capital city, Ndjamena, witnessed the first public executions in more than a decade after court trails which human rights groups described as a mockery of justice. They were a signal to critical voices in the country to stay quiet.

It is worth noting that the World Bank's own operations and evaluation department (OED) review commissioned in 2001 finds the bank wanting on issues of governance. The review points out that while the World Bank is aware of the underlying causes of the underperformance of resource-rich countries, it has yet to formulate and implement viable approaches to address them. The recently released report of the World Bank sponsored Extractive Industry Review, primed the role of governance in shaping development outcomes of oil projects. Unequivocally, it recommended the World Bank to stop support for petroleum projects in areas of conflict or at high risk of conflict.

Broken Livelihoods and Promises

Approximately 880km of the pipeline traverses Cameroon's fragile ecological zones. These include one of Africa's unique coastal rainforests, home to several indigenous peoples. Before the commencement of the construction phase, thousands of affected peoples living in villages and communities along the route of the pipeline were identified for eventual compensation. One hundred and fifty families were singled out for resettlement. Many village lands were expropriated, crops and plants destroyed and water sources polluted. The compensation plan, which included individual and communal compensations, was very limited in scope and inadequate to restore or improve broken livelihoods.

Despite compensation being paid to replace agricultural land, most of the funds did not go into agricultural production or reinvestment to make provision for the future. The affected communities have been left alone with little or no skills to face the long-term impacts: funds have not generated new livelihoods for villagers; prices have increased due to shortage of labour and agricultural goods on the market; the rural–urban exodus has increased and conflicts between locals and migrants attracted by the new found wealth have also increased.

The communal compensation plan, which had as its objective to compensate communities with social development projects, was very limited. Communities, who were supposed to identify projects themselves through consultations, were instead constrained to choose from a restrictive list of options proposed by the consortium.

The project thus raises a crucial issue: that of balancing profits with ecological and social principles in petroleum exploitation. Driven by the ethos of cost minimisation, the consortium was motivated to fast-track its operations, while time-intensive social and environmental components such as capacity building lag behind. To what extent, therefore, can multinational corporations be constrained to synchronise the evolution of their exploitation operations with that of social and environmental safeguards?

Turning oil revenue into long-term benefits for the masses is the most contentious issue in resource-rich countries, particularly in Africa. Ultimately, this depends on the quality of public policy. The World Bank prides the revenue oversight mechanism in the Chad-Cameroon pipeline as an innovation to the extractive industry.

Under pressure from World Bank, the Chadian government decreed a petroleum management law in 1998. The law provides for the following division of the $2 billion royalties and dividends that are expected to accrue from the project in the next 25 years: 10 per cent would be set aside in a future-generation fund to prepare Chad for a post-oil future; the remaining 90 per cent would pass through an offshore petroleum revenue account, 80 per cent of which would go to five priority sectors (health, rural development, education, infrastructure, and environmental and water resources); 5 per cent would go to the Doba oil producing region; and the remainder would be used by the Chadian government to tackle pressing operational needs.

To mainstream transparency, accountability, and participation, an oversight committee, comprising representatives from civil society, government, administration, and the judiciary was created to monitor the flows and approve spending from the offshore account.

Undoubtedly, this initiative is laudable. However, there are some flaws, which incapacitate it. For instance, three months after Chad started to taste the oil revenues, the committee lacked basic office facilities. In addition, the 5 per cent allocated to the Doba region is inadequate. Worst of all, the allocations contained in the law can be changed by the government unilaterally after five years.

In addition, the law covers only direct revenues generated from royalties while indirect revenues such as taxes and customs duties are precluded. These could account for up to 45 per cent of the total oil revenues expected over the lifetime of the project.

Conclusion

Several conclusions about petroleum development in Africa can be drawn from the Chad-Cameroon pipeline project.

Firstly, oil corporations cannot be transformed into development agencies even with the best of intentions and monitoring mechanisms. Secondly, global wielders of development outcomes like the World Bank cannot exercise sufficient clout against the oil multinationals' penchant for profits. Thirdly, the World Bank is incapable of respecting even its own weakening safeguard policies, which are premised on controlling damage rather than avoiding harm.

Fourthly, the embryonic neo-liberal governance structures in Africa are incapable of constraining foreign direct investments, which are principally attracted by ground mineral resources, to respect ecological and social principles. The flawed contention of the World Bank is 'one cannot eat omelettes without breaking some eggs' but the broken eggs are usually the poor who end up with no livelihood opportunity and become even poorer.

Finally, Public Private Partnerships (PPP), the buzz paradigm of sustainable development, are fundamentally incapable of readdressing the unequal power relations between fattening multinationals, weakening states and the World Bank.

As it turns 60, it is time, therefore, to pressure the bank to retire from financing development and environmental disasters like the pipeline. In sum, just like the weapons of mass destruction in Iraq, the Chad-Cameroon pipeline is an illusive weapon of mass development. It is time to send some United Nations development experts to Chad and Cameroon to uncover weapons of mass poverty.

CHAPTER 8

THE ROAD HOME
FOR AFRICA'S REFUGEES

Protecting the
Rights of Refugees in Africa:
Beginning with the UN Gatekeeper

Barbara Harrell-Bond and Mike Kagan

Pambazuka News 182, 11 November 2004

> You talk of refugees as though human rights did not exist
> which are broader and more important. Once an individual, a
> human being, becomes a refugee, it is as though he has become
> a member of another race, some other sub-human group.
> (Rizvi 1984)

Introduction

The lack of attention to the ways in which refugees' rights are violated in host
countries is astonishing if one considers that the protection of the rights of all
people has been on the United Nations (UN) agenda since the adoption of the
Universal Declaration of Human Rights, and that refugees have formed an
important part of the UN's work since the Second World War. Refugees should
enjoy the same human rights as any other people. However, refugees have
traditionally been relegated to the category of 'humanitarian' problems, the
human rights dimension of their plight being generally ignored.

In practice, to enjoy the most basic human security, it is not enough today for
an asylum-seeker to be a human being. They must obtain the formal label
'refugee' to enjoy even legal recognition as a person in most countries. Without
this label, a person will find themselves in fear of the state rather than protected by a government. Living without documents, without UNHCR or government protection, places refugees at imminent risk of detention and refoule-

ment. It leaves them vulnerable to exploitations large and small by their neighbours, landlords, and employers.

After 'getting in' to a country, the determination of refugee status is the most critical challenge that people in danger face when they seek protection. There is a growing tendency in Africa to put individual refugees through the process of individual status determination, rather than group-based recognition.

The UN High Commissioner for Refugees (UNHCR) has said that 'the importance of these procedures cannot be overemphasised ... A wrong decision might cost the person's life or liberty'. For UNHCR, fair refugee status determination (RSD) procedures are 'essential' for full application of the 1951 Convention. The General Assembly has repeatedly referred to the need to establish 'fair and efficient procedures' in the asylum process (e.g. GA res. 51/75, 12 February 1997 and GA res. 50/152, 9 February 1996).

Being granted status is also the first step towards refugees taking an active part in governing their own lives and future. Determining their status is the responsibility of the state where they seek asylum. However, in over 60 countries – mainly in Africa, the Middle East and Asia – the local office of the UNHCR handles RSD, making it nearly the largest RSD decision-maker in the world. The fact that so many states have handed this responsibility over to UNHCR (more than half have ratified the 1951 convention) is indicative of how little some governments have done to implement the convention, shifting responsibility instead to the UN.

When UNHCR fills the gap, refugees and governments should be able to rely on UNHCR to perform such an essential role in keeping with the highest standards. When human rights groups raise alarm about a government's refugee policies, they usually call for UNHCR to have more access. UNHCR has given progressive, legally sound advice to governments about RSD. UNHCR is responsible for supervising refugee law, and refugees ought to be able to trust that in UNHCR's hands their rights will be respected. Yet, on RSD, UNHCR is saying one thing to governments, and doing something much worse.

UNHCR's RSD procedures have been assessed independently by lawyers, scholars, and human rights organisations in the Middle East, Southeast Asia and East Africa. Their conclusions are the same: UNHCR's RSD procedures lack the most basic safeguards for fairness, resulting in a high chance of mistakes in a field where there simply is no margin for error. There is an unacceptable risk that people in grave danger will be refused protection when they apply to UNHCR offices. Furthermore, by not following its own advice about RSD procedures, UNHCR sets a bad example for states. The system is broken and needs to be fixed.

What Exactly is Wrong with UNHCR's Refugee Status Determination?

The essential problem with UNHCR conducting refugee status determination is that by assuming the role of decision-maker, it compromises its role as protector of refugees with that of being 'judge and jury' of their claims. These are contradictory roles and wherever UNHCR places itself in this situation, it loses the trust of refugees. Secondly, its RSD practices lack procedural safeguards and fairness. They are hence at high risk of error, and can put people in danger of refoulement in fact if not refoulement in form.

Despite being absent from the text of the refugee conventions, UNHCR has issued fairly comprehensive specific procedural requirements for fair RSD. The earliest attempt conclusions of the Executive Committee of the UNHCR (Excom) – in particular conclusion 8 (XXVIII), 1977 – and the Handbook on Procedures and Criteria for Determining Refugee Status (UNHCR 1992a), set out basic procedural requirements. State practice has also over the years fleshed out standards of procedural fairness that apply to refugee status determination, both through case law and through statutes or administrative regulations (Verdirame and Harrell-Bond 2004). UNHCR has now issued more comprehensive advice to states about standards necessary for a fair and effective RSD procedure. In May 2001, as part of its Global Consultations on International Protection, UNHCR issued its most comprehensive guidance on RSD procedures to date, a background paper called 'Fair and Efficient Asylum Procedures'. UNHCR added to this guidance in February 2003 with comments submitted to the Council of Europe.

The standards UNHCR has set out are admirable. But, for whatever reason, UNHCR itself has not seen fit to follow them.

We detail a number of specific problems:

Secret evidence. Withholding evidence considered in an applicant's case – which the applicant involved cannot see or dispute – is a familiar (and very worrisome) part of military and state security trials, but with rare exception it should not be part of RSD. UNHCR told the Council of Europe: 'UNHCR [...] recommends that information and its sources may be withheld only under clearly defined conditions where disclosure of sources would seriously jeopardise national security or the security of the organisations or persons providing information' (UNHCR annotated comments on the amended proposal for a council directive on minimum standards on procedures in Member States for granting and withdrawing refugee status, COM(2002) 326 final of 18 June 2002, presented by the commission – commenting on Article 14).

But in its own RSD procedures, UNHCR offices withhold nearly all evidence from asylum-seekers, in accordance with a confidential August 2001 memorandum from the Department of International Protection. Evidence routinely withheld from asylum-seekers includes reports from mental health assessments and medical examinations, transcripts of their own interviews, statements by other witnesses, and country of origin information.

Reasons for rejection. UNHCR has advised governments that refused asylum-seekers 'should receive a written decision …[and] the decision should be a reasoned one' (UNHCR, Asylum-Processes: Fair and Efficient Asylum Procedures, May 2001). But when UNHCR refuses a refugee claim, its offices generally refuse to provide detailed written reasons that could be used in preparing an appeal. In some offices, the person receives a letter with just one or two sentences explaining the rejection. In other offices, rejected applicants get only a three-letter code, such as 'LOC' (lack of credibility). Some UNHCR offices give no explanation at all. At the same time, UNHCR offices write, and keep on file, detailed assessments of each case.

Independent appeals. Since 1980, UNHCR has called on governments to provide rejected asylum-seekers with access to an independent appeal. (OAU-UNHCR Guidelines for National Refugee Legislation and Commentary, 1980). In 2001, UNHCR said that this appeal must be to 'an authority different from and independent of that making the initial decision'([UNHCR, Asylum-Processes: Fair and Efficient Asylum Procedures, May 2001). But in most UNHCR offices, the only appeal is to a different staff member in the same office, usually a colleague of the person who made the original rejection, working under the same supervisors.

Right to counsel. UNHCR has advised governments that 'at all stages of the procedure, including at the admissibility stage, asylum-seekers should receive guidance and advice on the procedure and have access to legal counsel.'

In a few UNHCR offices, the principle of legal representation is accepted. But other offices resist the right to counsel. Some UNHCR offices refuse to accept submissions by lawyers. Others refuse to speak with lawyers about their clients' cases. Still others have questioned asylum-seekers about why they chose to seek legal assistance. In one UNHCR office in the Middle East, a protection officer recently insisted that an indigent refugee pay a significant fee to a notary in order to be represented by a lawyer in a hearing over whether UNHCR would withdraw his refugee status.

Behind these failures are fundamental questions of transparency and accountability. By withholding evidence and the reasons for rejection, UNHCR shields its actions from scrutiny. But this tendency toward secrecy goes beyond individual cases. UNHCR's RSD operating procedures are generally not released to the public. The Department of International Protection (DIP) memorandum instructing UNHCR offices to withhold evidence from asylum-seekers was never circulated to the public for comment, and to this day it is officially internal.

UNHCR has indicated that it is drafting a new handbook governing its RSD activities, but it has not yet asked for public comment. It is worrisome to think that procedural standards are being re-debated within UNHCR simply because this time UNHCR offices are meant to apply them. There is no plausible reason why the legal standards of UNHCR's RSD procedures should differ from the high standard that it recommends to governments. When UNHCR tells the public that certain standards are essential for refugee protection, these standards should automatically be implemented in UNHCR's own offices.

Prima Facie Recognition of Refugees and their Right to Identity Papers

Although reforming RSD procedures themselves in urgent, it is also important to reduce their importance. Individual RSD is, as a rule, intensive, burdensome on all involved, high stakes, and high risk for error. The more UNHCR and governments can find other ways to recognise refugee status, the better.

In cases of mass movements where it is impracticable to conduct individual status determination of refugees seeking asylum, governments may grant prima facie recognition to the group on the basis of nationality. Prima facie recognition may be granted either under the 1951 convention or the Organisation of Africa Unity (now African Union) convention (OAU).

This makes sense; it reflects the practice in post-Second World War Europe when all refugees were recognised on the grounds of nationality. When Nansen, appointed by the League of Nations, was first named Commissioner for Russian Refugees, all Russian refugees in Europe after the revolution were entitled to recognition. Similarly, everyone knows there is war in southern and western Sudan; people fleeing that war should simply have to 'prove' their nationality.

Decisions to grant prima facie recognition to particular nationalities should be 'gazetted', i.e. as legal decisions they must be published officially. This is only the first step; every adult refugee must be issued with an identity card (1951 UN Convention, Article 27). The Conclusion of the Executive Committee of UNHCR (Excom), in 1993, also reiterated the necessity of the issuing of personal documentation as a device to promote the protection of the personal security of refugees (No. 72 XLIV).

Nansen went much further. Realising that movement was necessary to find solutions to their plight, the Nansen Passport was introduced, allowing refugees to move to another country where they could find, for example, employment or education or re-join relatives. The Nansen passport thus served refugees as a passport, allowing them to travel between states. It was the forerunner of today's Convention Travel Document (CTD). Article 28 of the 1951 UN convention provides that contracting states shall issue travel documents, that is, CTDs to refugees lawfully in their territories for the purpose of travel outside their territories. (There are only two reasons for which contracting state can deny refugees this right: compelling reasons of national security or public order.)

In Africa, where most refugees are sent to camps or settlements, the only identification the vast majority receive is a family ration card, which usually includes only an indication of the size of the family with marks to punch when rations are received or non-food items are distributed, not their name.

What is being done?

At the International Consortium of Voluntary Agencies (ICVA) Pre-Executive Committee October 2004 meetings, four lawyers from Africa and the Middle East successfully lobbied for ICVA to call for an independent evaluation of UNHCR RSD. The following are excerpts from the final NGO Statement to UNHCR's Executive Committee on Evaluation and Inspection Activities:

> We would suggest that such an independent global evalua-
> tion be carried out by a team that includes international
> human rights lawyers, international and national NGOs
> working on refugee issues, academics, and legal aid practi-
> tioners. The issues that should be examined in the evaluation
> include an inventory of the RSD procedures that are applied
> in each UNHCR field office, with an examination of the pos-
> sible solutions to the political, financial, and human resource
> constraints that contribute to RSD procedures that do not
> fulfill practices advocated by UNHCR. The evaluation should
> recommend rights-based RSD procedures to be followed con-
> sistently by all field protection officers with a mechanism to
> ensure their implementation.

And from the Statement on Protection:

> Further, while recognising the important role played by
> UNHCR in asylum determination procedures in many coun-
> tries worldwide, NGOs have concerns that some of UNHCR's
> refugee status determination (RSD) practices in some coun-
> tries in Africa, the Middle East, and Asia do not always meet
> the standards of fairness to which UNHCR urges states to
> adhere ... UNHCR should not see its role in RSD as a substi-
> tute for government-run procedures. UNHCR should make it
> a priority that governments take over these activities and
> build their capacity to do so. We call on UNHCR to initiate
> public consultations on the new draft refugee status determi-
> nation procedures (from www.ICVA.ch – follow 'What's
> Hot').

It will be important to follow this initiative carefully over the next year and at the 2005 ICVA Pre-Excom meetings to ensure the issue is actively followed up.

What can you do?

The first step to change the situation for refugees is to inform yourself. While presuming that readers of *Pambazuka News* are committed to human rights, too few human rights organisations consider refugee rights as part of their mandate. In your country, as in so many, refugees are probably segregated in camps and those who manage to live elsewhere are usually trying to remain invisible to authorities for the reasons of lack of proper papers and the right to live outside of camps. Join the US Committee for Refugees' Anti-warehousing campaign and begin to study and expose the way refugee rights are being violated in your country. Lobby for their minimal right to freedom of movement (http://www.refugees.org/warehousing)

For those who think of refugees as 'just another problem among so many', remember that getting it right for refugees may be the best way to get rights for all. Is not the extent to which refugee rights are upheld a barometer for the extent that human rights are generally respected in any society? Human rights are indivisible and inter-related; focusing on the violations of the rights of refugees (who represent the most marginalised and unprotected population) is perhaps the most effective 'entry' point for improving the observance of human rights for all members of any society. Any investment in promoting the rights of refugees is an investment in a more just society.

Find out if there are any legal aid clinics in your country who would be in a position to represent refugee clients whatever their problems might be and encourage them to consider getting the necessary training to expand their clients to include refugees. The Forced Migration and Refugee Studies Programme (fmrs@aucegypt.edu) at the American University in Cairo (www.aucegypt.edu/fmrs) and AMERA Egypt, a refugee legal aid clinic (info@amera-uk.org) both provide training opportunities. Oxfam, through Reach Out also offers a Refugee Protection Training Project for all NGOs (http://www.reachout.ch/). Where legal aid clinics for refugees exist, support their work and see how you might get involved.

Clinics providing legal aid for refugees have been established in a few countries in the South and in Africa: the Refugee Law Project in Kampala (www.refugeelawproject.org); the Kenyan Refugee Consortium, Nairobi (refcon@connect.co.ke); AMERA-Egypt in Cairo (www.amera-uk.org). Others are the Frontiers Centre in Lebanon (frontierscenter@fastmail.fm) and the Istanbul Refugee Legal Aid Project in Turkey (isacaillol@hotmail.com).

If you are a lawyer, learn how to take refugee cases that have been unfairly dealt with by the legal system in your country to the Africa Commission. At its 35th Session the Africa Commission nominated a Special Rapporteur on Refugees and Displaced Persons in Africa. He is Mr Bahame Tom Mukirya Nyanduga. His address is: P. O. Box 7239, Dar es Salaam, Tanzania; his email: btn@ndr.omnisys.co.tz; btomn@yahoo.com

In the end, two points are absolutely essential. First, do not rely blindly on the UN. A strong UN is essential for a just and peaceful world, but that does not mean that UN agencies can be trusted any more than governments. They must be transparent, they must be accountable, and we must watch to make sure they practise what they preach.

Second, this entire discussion has been devoted to how we determine whether a person is a 'refugee' under the law. But we ought to remember: We do not need UNHCR or a complicated procedure to recognise another person as a human being. And that ought to be enough to give refugees the most essential human rights.

For details of references, see http://www.pambazuka.org/index.php?id=25612

World Refugee Day:
a Time to Celebrate?

James Milner
Pambazuka News 161, 17 June 2004

20 JUNE IS WORLD Refugee Day, a day to reflect on the state of the world's 12 million refugees. One of these 12 million is a young Somali student named Abass Hassan Mohamed.

Abass is the second oldest of six children. His family fled to Kenya, along with hundreds of thousands of other refugees, in the midst of the violent implosion of Somalia in 1992. He says very little about his early days in the refugee camp, apart from the fact that it was dusty, hot, violent, and that people died on a daily basis.

Twelve years later, he still lives in a refugee camp near Dadaab, in the Northeast Province of Kenya, just 80km from the border with Somalia, along with almost 135,000 other refugees.

This February, one year late, Abass received the results from his national secondary school exams. Competing against students from across the country, Abass sat exams in subjects as diverse as English, chemistry, commerce and Swahili. His results were extraordinary. He ranked first in the Northeast Province of Kenya, and eighth in the whole of Kenya.

Although he does not brag, Abass overcame incredible odds to achieve this remarkable result. Of the 44 students in his class, only 32 graduated. His days were full not only with the extracurricular activities like football, the debating club and the school environment club, but also with more demanding tasks, like standing in the blazing sun and 45°C heat for hours to receive the family's fortnightly rations of a few kilogrammes of maize. He learned to survive in one of the most violent camps in Africa, where rape, murder and armed robbery were almost daily occurrences.

There were only 300 desks in the whole school, so Abass had to share with two other students, with whom he also shared textbooks. He tried to work on his homework in the evenings, when the chores were done, but his family rarely had the fuel for the single kerosene lamp.

Abass now works as a teacher in one of the primary schools in his camp run by the aid agency CARE, earning 3,775 shillings a month, about £26. If a scholarship can be found, Abass plans to study medicine. In a community where there is only one doctor for 135,000 people, Abass feels that training in medicine is the best way that he can help his people, both in exile and when they return to Somalia. Abass believes that day will come.

Abass is but one example of the millions of refugees around the world, young and old, who have skills and abilities they want to contribute, but who are wasting away in isolated and insecure camps, trapped in a protracted refugee situation. The UN recently reported that, in Africa alone, there are over three million refugees who have spent over five years in the confines of a refugee camp, with no freedom of movement, dwindling donor support, and slim prospects of a solution for their plight.

This year's World Refugee Day celebrates the 30th anniversary of the entry into force of the Organisations for African Unity's (OAU) Refugee Convention. This convention is hailed by many as one of the most liberal refugee regimes in the world, expanding the refugee definition from those fleeing an individual fear of persecution to those also feeling civil conflict. But looking at the current state of refugee protection in Africa, there is little to celebrate.

Host countries across Africa continue to limit the quality and quantity of asylum they offer to refugees, fleeing both persecution and civil war. Refugees are increasingly 'warehoused' in remote camps, cut-off from local communities and fully dependent on international assistance. Unlike the 'golden age' of asylum in Africa, when refugees were allocated land to pursue self-sufficiency, host countries today often cite security concerns, environmental degradation and lack of support from donor governments as a justification for placing restrictions on the asylum they offer. In cases of mass influx, states are increasingly likely to try to close their borders to new arrivals or, as in the recent case of Darfur, hinder access to humanitarian agencies.

The result is a crisis in asylum in Africa.

This crisis is compounded by a reluctance on the part of Western governments to support the Office of the UN High Commissioner for Refugees (UNHCR) in fulfilling the mandate it received from the UN General Assembly in 1950: to provide international protection for refugees and to find a permanent solution to their plight. States have agreed, since 1951, that the granting of asylum places a heavy burden on certain states, and that the solution to the world's refugee problem cannot be achieved without international co-operation. Yet the West does little to cooperate.

When asylum seekers flee the insecurity of regions of refugee origin, they find increasing barriers to protection in Europe and North America. When the UNHCR appeals to donor countries to fund its programmes in Africa, insufficient contributions are made. The UNHCR has appealed for over $50 million to respond to the unfolding humanitarian emergency on the Chad/Sudan border, but has received only $18 million.

This funding crisis directly affects the level of protection that refugees across Africa receive on a daily basis. A lack of funds means that programmes will not be implemented to prevent the rape of refugee women, that protection staff will not be deployed to register new refugees, that education programmes will need to be cut, and that food assistance to refugees, already below internationally recognised standards, will need to be reduced.

A lack of donor engagement also inhibits the prospects of finding durable solutions to the plight of refugees. Three durable solutions have historically been used to resolve refugee situations. First, refugees have been able to integrate into their host community. Through the 1960s and 1970s, refugees fleeing wars of national liberation and civil wars in Africa were welcomed into their newly independent neighbours and encouraged, with the support of the international community and aid agencies, to settle on under-utilised land and rebuild their lives in a new country. Thousands were given citizenship, and many refugees were able to make significant contributions to their adopted countries. Such programmes are no longer possible in Africa.

Second, refugees have been able to voluntarily repatriate to their country of origin when the conflict has been resolved and when the mechanisms have been established to support their return and reintegration. With the end of the prolonged civil war in Mozambique in the early 1990s, almost a million refugees were able to return from Malawi. Sustained programmes ensured the success of their reintegration. In stark contrast, many instances of repatriation are less than voluntary. Many Burundian refugees are returning from Tanzania not because they believe that they will find peace in their homeland, but because they want to escape the unbearable conditions in the refugee camps. Many say that if they are going to die, they would rather die at home.

Even when the UN does believe that conditions in the country of origin could support large-scale repatriation and reintegration, the necessary funds are not forthcoming. In March 2004, the UNHCR appealed for donor support to lay the foundations for the repatriation of refugees to seven African countries. Two of these countries were Liberia and Sudan. While repatriation is not immediately possible to these countries, investment is essential in the coming months to ensure that the infrastructure is in place to support repatriation in the coming years. UNHCR appealed for $8.8 million for preparatory activities in Sudan. It has received $3 million. Likewise, it has appealed for $39.2 million to support operations in Liberia for the return and reintegration of both refugees and internally displaced persons. It has received only $3 million.

If a refugee cannot return to their country of origin, and if they cannot remain in their country of asylum, the only remaining solution for them is to be resettled to a third country. Resettlement is a long and demanding process, but it is the only possible durable solution for many refugees, especially refugees with special needs. Given the protracted nature of many of today's refugee situations and given the severity of many of the protection environments in which they survive, this durable solution is increasingly essential, but alarmingly scarce. While most of Africa's three million camp-bound refugees would qualify for resettlement, only 100,000 resettlement opportunities are made available by Western countries for resettlement programmes around the world. At the same time, UNHCR lacks the capacity and the institutional will to fill even this meagre quota.

But more money to UNHCR is not the answer to the plight of Africa's refugees. UNHCR is only part of the solution, and greater financial contributions without the backing of political will is wasted. Full funding for UNHCR's programmes is an important first step, but it is not enough.

A solution to the plight of the world's refugees must begin with the recognition that the problem of displacement is a global problem, and requires a global solution. The answer on the part of the international community should not be to pull up the drawbridges and sharpen the swords. The answer must be found in understanding how various aspects of foreign engagement – trade, aid, military, and foreign policy – can both cause refugee movements and affect the quality of asylum they receive.

Second, the leaders of the West must understand that it is in everybody's interest to resolve the world's protracted refugee situations. It is not only immoral to keep refugees warehoused in camps across Africa; it is uneconomical, can foster insecurity, and contributes to the growing resentment on the part of 'host' governments. Just as the plight of chronic refugee groups in Europe was resolved in the 1960s, there is urgent need for the political will and creative thinking to formulate comprehensive solutions for today's protracted refugee situations in Africa.

Finally, refugees themselves should be involved in the process of determining their future. Thirty years ago, refugees mattered. They were fleeing wars of national liberation in Africa or communism in Eastern Europe. In the context of the Cold War, they had political utility. Today, they are seen as hopeless and helpless, anonymous victims and huddled masses on our television screens.

But hopeless and helpless they are not. Like Abass, refugees have hopes and dreams for the future, and the ability, desire and skills to contribute to resolving the world's refugee problem. But contained in camps, they can do little. With the financial and political support of the international community, they could do great things.

The coming into force of the African Refugee Convention 30 years ago was a great step forward for refugees. Since then, we have taken many great leaps backwards. It is time to reverse the trend.

World Aids Day: the Clock is Still Ticking

Hein Marais
Pambazuka News 184, 25 November 2004

AIDS. IT KILLED ROUGHLY three million people last year, most of them poor, and most of them in Africa. Between 34 and 42 million people are living with HIV. Without antiretroviral therapies, AIDS will have killed the vast majority of them by 2015.

In such a world, time can seem a luxury, and the rigours of critical enquiry an indulgence. We need things done now, yesterday, last year. Indeed, an overdue sense of urgency has taken hold in the past five years – much of it thanks to relentless AIDS advocacy efforts. Along with sets of received wisdoms, a more or less standardised framework for understanding the epidemic and its effects has evolved, and a lexicon for expressing this knowledge has been established. All this has helped put and keep AIDS in the spotlight. It has popularised knowledge of the epidemic, countered the earlier sense of paralysis or denial, helped marshal billions of dollars in funding and goad dozens of foot-dragging countries into action. It has worked wonders.

But alongside these achievements are some troubling trends. There has emerged a roster of truisms that, in some respects, convey a misleading sense of certitude, and that might even be steering institutional responses in ineffectual directions. As well, awkward gaps are cleaving the AIDS world – gaps that threaten to detach the staples of advocacy from the riches of epidemiological and social research, and spoil the kind of multidisciplinary ferment that the struggle against AIDS dearly needs.

Strong advocacy tends to convey trim, crisp, unequivocal information. But in achieving this, vital complexity and ambivalence is often snipped and siphoned out. At times, research findings are casually interpreted or contradictory evidence is ignored. Sometimes intuitive reasoning is made to stand-in for absent empirical evidence. Much of the time, eclectic dynamics are jammed into simplistic, AIDS-centric frameworks.

All this occurs in good faith – and with the pressures of time and the palpable need to spur countries into action snapping at advocates' heels. But it should not stand in the way of doing the right things and doing them properly. And that is the danger we are flirting with at the moment.

Effective advocacy is not simply a neutral catalyst. It also invests activities with a specific content and character – all the more so when the advocacy carries the imprint and financial heft of key donors and multilateral agencies. This is not just a matter of how knowledge is being constructed and assimilated; it has very practical consequences. Big-gun advocacy often prefigures key elements and features of AIDS programming around the world. But we are seeing an unhappy antinomy develop between the streamlined demands of AIDS advocacy (and their translation into policy), and the generation and interpretation of reliable AIDS research and analysis.

Some examples

By the late 1990s it was widely assumed that conflict heightened the likelihood of HIV spread. Why? Because people are dislodged from their homes, their 'normal' rhythms of social organisation are disrupted, they lack access to many essential services, and women especially are vulnerable to sexual violence and might be forced to adopt, in the preferred euphemism, risky survival strategies (i.e. trade sex for favours, goods and services). It made good, intuitive sense. And by the early 2000s the view that conflict led to rising HIV rates was in wide circulation.

Evidence for these assertions was scant, though. Data from the Balkans showed no sign of significantly expanding epidemics there, for instance. In Africa, neither Angola, Sierra Leone, Sudan nor the Great Lakes region offered evidence that conflicts there were triggering rising HIV rates. (Instead, in northwestern Kenya, for example, the HIV infection rates in some refugee camps in 2002 were found to be much lower than they were in surrounding areas.) It now appears that chronic conflicts like that in Angola might actually have curbed the spread of HIV by limiting mobility (transport infrastructure was badly damaged, trading networks were truncated etc.). It might be that the threat of a surging epidemic is greater as peace is recuperated and as normality returns in post-conflict settings. The lesson? Assumptions, no matter how logical they seem, should be tested before they're paraded as facts.

Eclectic realities

Indeed, thanks to the massive output of AIDS impact literature in the past five years it has becoming increasingly evident how multifaceted and complex the responses of people and systems are to the epidemic – and not least in southern Africa, where AIDS is hitting hardest. Yet, the popularised knowledge of AIDS impact is, in some cases, as roughly-hewn as it is loud.

One example is the understandable temptation to distil generalised and ubiquitous 'truths' from very specific, usually highly localised research findings. Thus, labour losses attributed to AIDS on a single farming estate in Zimbabwe, for example, can end up being extrapolated to all of Zimbabwe (or even to 'Africa' as a whole). From this there might emerge a claim that, say, 'AIDS is cutting agricultural productivity by one-third in Africa'. In advocacy terms, of course, this has great currency – it is the stuff of headlines and sound bites that jolt. But it matters that the statement is inaccurate – and not just for didactic reasons.

The epidemic's socioeconomic impact is varied and complex, and operates as part of a web of other, richly varied factors. Neither the epidemic's effects nor the responses they elicit necessarily adhere to predictable, homogenous, linear paths. This has important bearing on the kinds of policies and interventions that are most likely to trump or at least cushion the epidemic's impact. Once such variety and contingency is scrubbed out – and reality is rendered as a mechanistic and predictable sequence of events – the effects can be both unhappy and wasteful.

Another example

There has emerged a palpable tendency to single out and over-privilege AIDS as a debilitating factor, as illustrated during the 2002–03 food crisis in southern Africa. There is ample evidence showing that the effects of AIDS in rural households, particularly those engaged in agricultural production, are pernicious. Where one or two key crops must be planted and harvested at specific times of the year, for example, losing even a few workers at the crucial planting and harvesting periods could scuttle production. But then came a grand leap of logic. With little but anecdotal evidence, a causal and definitive link was asserted between the AIDS epidemic and the food shortages.

The reasoning hinged mainly on reduced labour inputs (due to widespread illness and death of working-age adults). But these inputs figure among a wide range of variables needed to achieve food security – including marketing systems, food reserve stores, rain patterns, soil quality, affordability of seeds, fertilisers and pesticides, security of tenure, food prices, income levels, access to and the terms of financing, etc. It is difficult, perhaps even impossible to unscramble the effects of AIDS on rural communities and food security from economic, climatic, environmental and governance developments. The epidemic's apparent effect on food production occurred in concert with a series of other factors, including aberrant weather patterns and an ongoing narrative of unbridled market liberalisation, hobbled governance and wretched policy decisions.

Singling AIDS out as a primary, salient factor is a lot easier than fingering and tackling the other, more prickly factors – many of them tied to formidable interests and forces – that are at play. But it can be misleading and tempt shortsighted and ineffectual policy responses. When it comes to the epidemic's mangling consequences, policy responses are more likely to make a genuine difference if AIDS is made to take its place in the dock alongside the other culprits, which often include agricultural, trade and macroeconomic policies, land tenure and inheritance systems, and the capacity of the state to provide and maintain vital support services in rural areas. The over-privileging of AIDS lets decision-makers off the hook by endorsing fashionable courses of action that can fail to go to the heart of the matter.

The ground zero of this epidemic is where community and household life is built. And there is no doubt that, win or lose, the outcome of societies' encounters with AIDS ultimately depends on how communities and households are able to respond. This is widely recognised, hence the emphasis on so-called community safety nets and household 'coping' strategies in AIDS impact writing and policy outlines. There is the danger, though, that unless these mechanisms are buttressed with other, stout forms of structural support, we may end up fencing off much of the AIDS burden within already-strained households and communities. Yet, such forms of structural support have been systematically dismantled or neglected in many of the hardest-hit countries – typically as part of structural adjustments demanded by international financial institutions. Some of those same institutions are now enthusiastic fans of community resilience. Indeed, after years of scorched-earth social policy directives they are now casting the 'community' in an almost redemptive role. And this while much of social life has been subordinated to the reign of the market and the state shorn of its ability to fulfil societal duties.

The safety net and coping pieties sometimes skip around other important facets. Since many informal safety nets tend to centre on reciprocity, they run the risk of reproducing the inequalities that characterise social relations at community level. One study in Kagera, Tanzania, for example, found that the poorest households plunged deeper into debt because they lacked the wherewithal to enter into reciprocal arrangements. Women in particular found themselves sidelined. 'Communities' and 'the poor' are not homogenous.

Overall, a potentially treacherous distance is opening between the imperatives of advocacy and outlines of big-league programming, on the one hand, and rigorous epidemiological and social research and analysis, on the other. Part of this is a hazard of advocacy, which tends to favour declamation over explanation. Part of it is inflected with institutional 'cultures' and ideologies. Part of it is panic-induced; it is 2004, and we can count the national 'success stories' against the epidemic on one hand. Understandably, there's a rush on.

But part of the problem also lies in a failure to reconcile the schizoid aspects of AIDS – as a short-term emergency and a long-term crisis. It hass become second-nature to hitch the word 'AIDS' to 'development'. Google that phrase and the search engine will fling five million hits back at you. This implies a buzzing cross-pollination of expertise, inquisitiveness and knowledge building. That is an illusion, though. AIDS advocacy might have embraced some of the lingo, but it has assimilated very little of the critical knowledge built in development theory and practice over the past quarter century, not to mention other pertinent fields such as sociology, political geography and economics. There is precious little genuine, multidisciplinary rigour evident in AIDS discourse. And the smorgasbord feel of many AIDS programmes reflects this shortcoming. It is as if, once declarative truisms are achieved, serious reflection becomes a luxury. In a race against the clock, programmes and strategies must now be crafted. New insights or complicating information become a headache. And so the incipient interdisciplinary dialogue splutters into the intellectual equivalent of a one-night-stand. Do not call me, I will call you.

All this is unfortunate and, ultimately, counter-productive. Because AIDS advocacy is not just about sharing vital nuggets of knowledge, it is aimed also at promoting specific types of practice and forms of policy. If that knowledge is stunted, stripped of its riches and whittled into slim proclamations, we run a real risk of embarking on inadequate or inappropriate action. And all the while, that clock would still be ticking.

World Aids Day is on 1 December.

This article first appeared in the e-newsletter of the Isandla Institute, which can be visited at http://ww.isandla.org.za/.

Poverty, the Next Frontier
in the Struggle for Human Rights

Pierre Sané
Pambazuka News 186, 9 December 2004

POVERTY WILL ONLY cease when it is recognised as a violation of human rights and, as such, abolished.

One should be aware that the striking feature of our civilisation, as it globalises around the aspiration to unprecedented prosperity, is the persistence and even increase of poverty. It is an overwhelming fact: poverty affects half the world's population. It is spreading: the vast majority of the two to three thousand million human beings who will be added to the world's population before the end of the century will be exposed to it. It is putting alarming pressure on the environment and global equilibrium. The figures are apocalyptic: eight million children die each year because of poverty, 150 million children under the age of five suffer from extreme malnutrition, 100 million children live in the streets. Every three seconds, poverty kills a child somewhere. And our world puts up with it.

When, in 1994, 800 000 corpses of Tutsi and opposition Hutu victims of genocide in Rwanda were carried on rivers of blood through the country of a thousand hills, the world held its breath. We all felt guilty. We wished that action had been taken to prevent it. We all said, once again, 'never again!'. The United Nations established an international tribunal to establish the truth and hand down justice. 'We cannot bring back the dead, but the guilty shall pay. International law will prevail. Morality is safe'. But what about the eight million children who die each year from poverty-related diseases? We are well aware of these figures and they are probably underestimated.

What, then, is the basis of the ethical double standard which leads us to accept the poverty manufactured by our society, even though it kills more surely and methodically than machetes and militias? Is there a single moral or ethical justification for this central contradiction between the equality proclaimed in the granting of rights and growing inequality in access to life-giving resources? To address this question is essential for the preservation of our own humanity.

It would seem, however, that the famous 'standards of decency' are changing. Thus, the international community has set, as a priority for the millennium (the Millennium Development Goals – MDGs), to reduce by half in 15 years the number of people living in extreme poverty. This approach, however laudable in itself, does not exhaust the issue. For one thing, the intended goal will not easily be reached. But even if it were successfully achieved, the basic question would remain untouched: can persistent poverty be tolerated at all?

This problem has to be tackled from another angle. As long as we consider poverty as a quantitative, natural deficit to be made up, the political will to reduce it will not be energised. Poverty will only cease when it is recognised as a violation of human rights and, as such, abolished. This is why, and this is how.

When poverty is defined in relative terms, it is at once infinite and incurable. We are forced, at the same time, to consent to it indefinitely and to exhaust, in vain, unending resources in seeking to reduce it. This relativistic approach can only determine an arbitrary poverty line which is adopted as an artificial horizon. But such a bogus horizon remains unbearable: what do one or two dollars a day mean, and above all, what right do we have to make do with such a figure? For poverty is not a fate to be alleviated by international charity or aid. Nor does poverty reflect poor people's lack of self-reliance or their inability to compete in a free-for-all of supposedly equal opportunities. Poverty does not persist solely because of incompetent, corrupt governments that are insensitive to the fate of their population. No. Fundamentally, poverty is not a standard of living or even certain kinds of living conditions: it is at once the cause and the effect of the total or partial denial of human rights.

Of the five families of human rights – civic, political, cultural, economic and social – proclaimed by the Universal Declaration of Human Rights as inherent to the human person, poverty violates the fifth, always; the fourth, generally; often the third; sometimes the second, or even the first.

Reciprocally, the systematic violation of any one of these rights degenerates rapidly into poverty. As was recognised at the International Conference on Human Rights held in Vienna, in 1993, there is an organic link between poverty and violation of human rights.

And yet, human rights are indefeasible and inseparable. Their violation is a fundamental infringement of human dignity as a whole, and not a regrettable inconvenience to be endured by distant neighbours. It must therefore cease, and the imperative takes a simple form: poverty must be abolished. The claim sounds naïve, and may even bring a smile to your lips.

Condescension would, however, be misguided as well as inappropriate. There is nothing to smile at in distress, misery, dereliction and death, which march in grim parade with poverty. We should, indeed, be ashamed. But the issue is also substantive: the abolition of poverty is the only fulcrum that offers the leverage to defeat poverty.

Leverage, in this case, comes from investment, national and international reforms, and policies to remedy the deficiencies of all kinds that are the back-drop to poverty. Fortunately, humanity now has the means to answer the challenge: never have we been so rich, so technically competent and so well informed. But in the absence of a fulcrum, these forces cannot act as effectively as they might.

If, however, poverty were declared to be abolished, as it should with regard to its status as a massive, systematic and continuous violation of human rights, its persistence would no longer be a regrettable feature of the nature of things. It would become a denial of justice. The burden of proof would shift. The poor, once recognised as the injured party, would acquire a right to reparation for which governments, the international community and, ultimately, each citizen would be jointly liable. A strong interest would thus be established in eliminating, as a matter of urgency, the grounds for liability. This might be expected to unleash much stronger forces than mere compassion, charity, or even concern for one's own security. This would be more likely to result in benefits for others.

By endowing the poor with rights, the abolition of poverty would obviously not cause poverty to disappear overnight. It would, however, create the conditions for the cause of poverty to be enshrined as the highest of priorities and as the common interest of all – not just as a secondary concern for the enlightened or merely charitable. No more than the abolition of slavery caused the crime to vanish, no more than the abolition of domestic violence or genocide have eliminated such violations of the human conscience, the legal abolition of poverty will not, then, make poverty disappear. But it will place poverty in the conscience of humankind at the same level as those past injustices the present survival of which challenges us, shocks us, and calls us to action.

The principle of justice thus implemented and the force of law mobilised in its service are of enormous power. This, after all, is how slavery, colonialism and apartheid were ended. But while slavery and apartheid were actively struggled against, poverty dehumanises half the planet to a chorus of utter indifference. It is, undoubtedly, the most acute moral question of the new century to understand how such massive and systematic violations, day in, day out, do not trouble the conscience of the good people who look down upon them.

While equality of rights is proclaimed, growing inequalities in the distribution of goods persists and is entrenched by unjust economic and social policies at national and global level. To deal with poverty as a violation of human rights means going beyond the idea of international justice – which is concerned with relations between states and nations – towards the creation of global justice, which applies to relations between human beings living in a global society and enjoying absolute and inalienable rights – such as the right to life – that are guaranteed by the international community.

Such rights do not belong to the citizens of states but, universally, to human beings as such, for whom they are the necessary condition of life on the planet. The obligation to denounce violations and to ensure respect, protection and effective enjoyment of rights is incumbent on all, without distinction of race, country, or creed. The principle of global justice thus establishes the conditions for a fairer distribution of the planet's resources between its inhabitants in the light of certain absolute rights. Let us remember that, morally speaking, the right to property is not absolute: it follows that territorial sovereignty, which entails ownership of natural resources, cannot qualify as an absolute right, such as the right to life elsewhere.

What we must note is that nearly three billion people receive only about 1.2% of world income, while one billion people in the rich countries receive 80%. An annual income transfer of 1% from one group to the other would suffice to eliminate extreme poverty. In fact, the transfer continues to operate in the opposite direction, despite efforts towards debt reduction and development aid.

At the end of the day, there is a simple choice. Not between a 'pragmatic' approach, based on aid granted by the rich to the poor, and the alternative sketched here. The real choice is between the abolition of poverty and the only other way for the poor to obtain rights, which is for them to take them by force. Needless to say, the latter solution usually causes misery for all: social strife, rampant crime, mass uncontrolled migration, smuggling and trafficking are the only things to flourish. But what moral basis do we have to demand moral behaviour from people to whom we deny any opportunity to live a healthy life? What right have we to demand that they respect our rights? The sombre option will become increasingly likely if nothing is done – or too little, as tends to be the case with pragmatism, however deserving.

The options thus reduce to a single choice, which is the only one compatible with the categorical imperative to respect human rights: to abolish poverty in order to eradicate it, and to draw from this principle all the consequences that free acceptance of it implies.

No great programme will ensure the eradication of poverty. Its proclaimed abolition must, first, create rights and obligations, and thereby mobilise the true forces that can correct the state of a world plagued by poverty. By simply setting an effective and binding priority, abolition changes the ground rules and contributes to the creation of a new world. Such is the price to pay to give globalisation a human face; such is also the greatest opportunity for sustainable development that we can hope to grasp.

What are the implications for NGO activity? First, I would suggest that it is imperative to develop strategies that give tangible significance to the principles of indivisibility and interdependence of human rights. The unfortunate historical separation of human rights into civil and political rights on the one hand, and economic, social and cultural rights on the other, has tended to entrench the view that poverty was beyond the scope of human rights NGOs and to farm out poverty to market forces or development processes. Campaigns for ratification of international treaties must promote treaties on social, economic, and cultural rights, national legislations must be amended accordingly, and violations of such rights must be actionable. Furthermore, in the field, research techniques must be deployed to monitor the violations suffered by victims, fulfilment of their obligations by states and international actors, and reparations for injured parties.

Ultimately, the issue is to mobilise public opinion for a universal justice that is within our grasp. Its emergence has been lengthy – very lengthy. From the Universal Declaration of Human Rights to the Rome Conference that established the International Criminal Court, the emergence of universal justice has been defiled by acts of barbarity that have grossly infringed human dignity. Now, however, the legal instruments are there, and, step by step, experiments and initiatives give hope. It remains to energise political will by unceasing mobilisation, true thinking, the contributions of experts and support for victims and their families.

What promises does such global justice bear? Let me quote Nobel Laureate José Saramago:

> Were such justice to exist, there would no longer be a single human being dying of hunger or of diseases that are curable for some but not for others. Were such justice to exist, life would no longer be, for half of humanity, the dreadful sentence it has hitherto been. And for such justice, we already have a practical code that has been laid down for fifty years in the Universal Declaration of Human Rights, a declaration that might profitably replace, as far as rightness of principles and clarity of objectives are concerned, the manifestos of all the political parties of the world.

Such global justice is essential in order to ensure common welfare, and therefore international peace. To ensure freedom from poverty, a fundamental human right. To give dignity to the poor and the outcasts. But to succeed in the quest for justice, every single individual must be made aware of the issues at stake and mobilised.

The world will celebrate Human Rights Day on 10 December 10. What better day to remember the rights of the poor?

International Human Rights Day takes place on December 10.

CHAPTER 9

FOUR YEARS DOWN THE ROAD IN ZIMBABWE

Zimbabwe in March 2004:
Four Years on from the Beginning of the Plunge

Mary Ndlovu
Pambazuka News 146, 4 March 2004

TIME IS OUT Of joint in Zimbabwe. We have gone through the looking glass and live in a state of schizophrenia. We read one thing in the state media, and experience something quite different on the ground. The new farmers are said to be creating a revolution, but there is no farm produce in the shops, no agricultural goods to export. Our 'enemies' who want to sabotage our economy are feeding us, while our own rulers destroy productive capacity, pillage our natural resources, and even make money illegally exporting the food on which the people depend for survival.

Time moves too fast. In a day lives are turned upside down. A government decree quadruples tariffs on virtually every imported good, destroying businesses, crippling industries relying on imported components, wiping out the means of survival for hundreds of thousands of Zimbabweans who have been eking out a living through cross-border trade. In a week the only non-government daily newspaper is off the street, on the street and off the street again. In a month prices double in the shops, and 20,000 Zimbabweans die of AIDS. In a year inflation soars from 220 per cent to 620 per cent and your used car depreciates by doubling its Zimdollar value. And in a year the public mood changes from hope and expectation of relief from the madness to deep, debilitating despair.

On our side of the looking glass, the mounting catastrophe has political, economic, social and cultural components. Most objective observers would trace the economic problems back at least to the late 1980s. Certainly the introduction of structural adjustment at the beginning of the 1990s can be seen as the process which eroded the living standards of Zimbabweans, and spawned the first broad-based opposition party. It also generated pressure from interest groups such as war veterans and ambitious black businessmen who felt they had waited too long to share in the country's wealth. The government's response to these developments sent the country into the downward spiral which today ensnares us. Instead of taking the criticism and the pressure and sitting back to plan a coherent strategy of how to deal with the inter-related issues, ZANU PF panicked, saw their ruling position threatened, and from 1997 on have responded piecemeal, reactively and irrationally, bringing us to the tragedy which unfolds before our eyes.

They gave in to pressures from those groups with which they had racial and historical affinities, that is the 'indigenous businessmen' and the war veterans, while viciously attacking those in the political opposition and civil society who dared to demand policies that would serve the needs of the people at large. These were accused of wanting to sabotage the economy, acting as agents of foreign powers, fomenting discord and trying to reverse the gains of the liberation war. Because the government half believed their own fantasies, they became quite incapable of drawing appropriate strategies to handle the economic crisis, and became obsessed with simply retaining political power. Every economic policy became twisted to suit the immediate needs of ZANU PF, while the needs of the consumer, the producer, the employer and employee were disregarded. Basic economic sense was thrown to the winds, commonplace economic imperatives defied. ZANU PF returned to the militarist leadership and rhetoric of the liberation war.

The economic slide was precipitated by the 1997 surrender to the demands of war veterans, but it became a plunge from the beginning of the seizure of land from white commercial farmers in February 2000. Angered by the negative results of the referendum on a new constitution in that month, ZANU PF devised a malicious but brilliant strategy designed to recover domestic support, provide new sources of patronage, fulfil the promises of the liberation struggle and attract international support from traditional allies of the 1970s. In their panic they rushed headlong to seize agricultural land from white farmers by violent means, afraid to wait for a legal process to unfold. They justified this by the philosophy of armed struggle and the injustices perpetrated by colonisers in the hundred years before independence. Law was no longer necessary; the end justified any means.

It is exactly four years since the officially sanctioned land invasions began. During that time the economy has shrunk to less than half its previous size, while inflation has risen to 620 per cent. Added to the pre-existing economic crisis, the destruction of a substantial portion of commercial agriculture has brought a sharp decline in foreign exchange earnings, and severe food shortages. Government's attempts to manipulate prices, interest rates and foreign exchange rates have produced chaos – artificial shortages of price-controlled goods and a booming black market, illegal export of basic goods to neighbouring countries, closure of factories and other businesses, especially those related to agricultural production. The lack of foreign currency reduced ability to import essential consumer and capital goods and the general decline of the economy starved government of revenue. At the same time runaway inflation led to a need to print ever larger amounts of bank notes which government could not afford. The result was the crippling cash shortage in mid-2003. High inflation coupled with low interest rates impoverished pensioners and anyone else dependent on a fixed income, and initiated a flight of savings from banks into foreign currency. What could no longer be obtained in banks by any but the privileged few was readily available on many street corners in the major cities at up to eight times the official rate.

Those privileged few were having a heyday, amassing fortunes of gigantic proportions by accessing foreign currency from the banks at official rates and selling it on the black market. A new class of economic parasites was being created. We began to hear of 25-room mansions, stables of Mercedes Benz cars, cupboards full of designer suits. The owners did not hide; they boasted of their wealth in the face of the people whose situation was becoming daily more desperate.

The year 2003 was a dreadful one for most Zimbabweans. While the government tinkered at the edges of the economy and finally brought staple food-stuffs back to the shelves and solved the cash crisis by introducing bearer cheques as temporary legal tender, they failed to bring inflation under control. By the end of the year it had reached 600 per cent. And the economy continues to shrink. The October beginning of the 2003-04 planting season heralded new disasters in the future as agricultural inputs were simply not available to most of those wanting to farm. But the failures on the economic front were compensated for in the political arena. In spite of the ability of the opposition still to win local government elections in most urban areas, ZANU PF could make use of its new draconian security and media legislation, the support of a loyal army and police and national service militia to block out the opposition from rural constituencies. And in the urban councils held by the Movement for Democratic Change (MDC), ZANU PF has used its control of national resources to interfere and create havoc in local government, dividing and frustrating opposition controlled councils, particularly Harare, and making them lose public support. The mass action threatened by the opposition never got started in the face of government terror, and ZANU PF remains firmly in charge. The political tide running in favour of the opposition seems to have been halted. A combination of severe repression, patronage through allocation of land and positions that give access to public resources, and ever more strident racial and xenophobic rhetoric have kept the forces of opposition off balance and out of step.

Now, in March, 2004, four years on from the beginning of the plunge, where do we stand, and what is the outlook for the next 12 months?

Economically, we are still spiralling downwards. This year agriculture is expected to produce only one-third of the nation's staple maize requirements. Exportable crops such as tobacco and paprika, are down to a small fraction of what was previously produced. Industrial capacity deteriorates and unemployment rises. While donor aid feeds those people in rural areas whose own crops fail through poor rains and lack of inputs, an ever greater percentage of the urban population fails to cope, enters the ranks of the destitute and is in need of food aid even while food sits on the supermarket shelves.

Not only goods, but also services are either not available or unaffordable. Starved of government finance, social welfare has long ago collapsed as a point of last resort for the destitute. Hospitals have no equipment or medicines and few qualified staff. A patient with a fracture is told to bring plaster of Paris before his bone can be set. Schools have poorly functioning infrastructure, broken desks and toilets, paint peeling from walls, no laboratory equipment or books. Yet they charge fees that have forced many, in both rural and urban areas to withdraw their children. The mission boarding schools, once the pride of Zimbabwean education and the training ground for the professional classes, are deteriorating rapidly, unable to sustain quality with the fees that the dwindling middle classes are able to afford. Both the major state universities have been crippled by repeated staff and student strikes, and at present neither is holding classes.

While high fee-paying private schools manage to maintain reasonable standards, private health care is faltering on the brink of collapse. Doctors' fees, hospitals and medicines are unaffordable except for the elite and many procedures are no longer provided in the country. Employees on medical aid are no better off as the doctors and medical aid societies quarrel over rates and payment procedures, leaving the patients to pay cash and claim later. When a simple consultation, laboratory test and prescription may cost half a month's salary, or more, it will be rational for a worker to terminate medical aid subscriptions and it will not be surprising if all the medical aid societies collapse completely before this year is out, leaving health care accessible only to the very rich. Government's response to the failures of service providers was predictable – punish headmasters who try to keep their schools running by allowing fee increases in line with inflation, criminalise doctors who charge cash. It is hardly surprising that many educational and medical professionals have left the country.

They are not alone. A recent survey showed that 3.4 million Zimbabweans – a quarter of the population – lives outside the country. Professionals have left with their families to find work where there is greater security and they can command a higher standard of living. Young people have left to escape the dejection and boredom of joblessness and to find tertiary education which does not require the completion of a 'national service' which brutalises and indoctrinates. Mothers have left their children behind while they live in squalor and do menial jobs to send home the precious 'forex' which buys food, clothing and pays school fees. Pensioners go to do care work because they cannot survive on their pensions. Others have gone to earn the money to buy a house. They leave behind families broken, rudderless, a prey to the immorality which has gripped the country. Led by the orgy of violence and rape characterising the land seizures, national service training, and election 'campaigning', we – especially our younger generation – have lost the ability to distinguish right from wrong. Might is right; if you can exploit your fellow before he or she exploits you, fine. And then we have the example of our 'businessmen' who amass wealth without any skills, any work, by manipulating a corrupt system. Dealing is the name of the game, and he who plays it well prospers. 'Cry Beloved Zimbabwe', was the lament of the WOZA women who were stopped by the police from distributing roses on Valentine's Day. 'Let love overcome hate' was their stifled message that few were allowed to hear.

The new year produced a surprise as a new monetary policy announced by the Reserve Bank governor began to take effect. Suddenly we found members of the corrupt elite, even a designer-suit, 25-room mansion ZANU PF MP, behind bars on allegations of fraud and foreign currency dealing. Government announced a war on corruption. Was this an attempt to win favour among the people, with an eye to the 2005 elections or simply the public manifestation of a power struggle within ZANU PF as the succession issue hots up, or even a desperate need to raise foreign currency at any cost? The population is sceptical, and waits to see. A real war on corruption would have to bring down far more known crooks and thieves from their high places. At the same time, there has been an attempt to bring some sanity to the foreign currency market by introducing a state-controlled auction. This effectively devalued the currency by 75 per cent, bringing the official exchange rate up and the black market rate down, at least temporarily. But it has negatively affected exporters, importers and consumers and will certainly fuel inflation further. We are set for another round of catastrophic price rises. Where the problems are essentially political piecemeal policies cannot rescue us. A modern economy cannot thrive in the absence of political stability, without smooth linkages to the international players.

On the economic side then, 2004 is likely to bring us only misery. What of the political? It is encouraging that through all the intimidation and violence the opposition MDC has managed to survive, maintain its structures and has held together in spite of a wide internal divergence of ideological positions. It contains some individuals who have worked at great personal risk to bring change. Furthermore, they deserve credit for firmly adhering to principles of non-violence, restraining their youthful hotheads who would prefer to answer violence with violence. It is clear, however, that elections marked by state violence and terror will not bring change unless the electoral ground rules are completely rewritten, and that is certainly not going to occur in the present circumstances. What about the mass action route? Besides the opposition party, MDC, several civil society organisations have raised their voices against government policies. These include the labour federation, ZCTU, the National Constitutional Assembly, some of the churches, which have country-wide membership organisations, and several other NGOs. All of them, including the MDC, are divided between the activists, who want to take to the streets, and the lobbyists, who want to push for some kind of 'talks' with government.

Those in favour of street action are in a weak position. 2003 demonstrated that while people were prepared to protest by staying away from work, they were not ready to take to the streets and face the riot police and possibly the army. Activists watched events unfold in the Georgian capital Tbilisi with envy, but have been forced to admit that Zimbabweans are simply not yet willing to take the risk. Small demonstrations organised by the ZCTU, the NCA and WOZA, a group which organises grassroots women, invariably resulted in arrests or police brutality or both. The masses have shied away from such action, and without the masses, this tactic cannot shift ZANU PF in any way. But the bravery of the few, especially when they are women, keeps the opposition visible and raises sprits and hope.

Dialogue between ZANU PF and the MDC has been held out as the solution by neighbouring African countries, particularly South Africa. The purpose of such inter-party talks would be to agree to end human rights abuses, re-establish the rule of law, and rewrite the electoral rules so that a new election could produce a government accepted as legitimate domestically and internationally. Then a start could be made to repair the economic damage. Such talks would have to be brokered by foreign mediators.

For the MDC, talks would be the best solution, but so far they have proved elusive. For obvious reasons ZANU PF is not interested and has deliberately held out the impression to the South Africans that they were committed while doing absolutely nothing. But it is now becoming clear that in the end this is the only way that a solution will be found.

ZANU PF appears to think that they have outwitted the opposition and can hang on to power until 2005, when they will conduct an even more violent and dishonest election which will see them clear for another five years. Even now they are making preparations. A new presidential decree has introduced the power of detention without bail, on mere suspicion, where there is no evidence of wrong-doing. Youth militia training is being stepped up to provide a reserve of shock troops. The United Nations was asked to provide funding for the election, but the request was quickly withdrawn when they proposed to send a delegation to study the situation on the ground. The MDC, under severe constraint from forces of terror, unconstitutional laws, and a compliant

judiciary – and the unwillingness of their members to engage in civil disobedi-
ence – is hobbled. It can not do much more than hold its supporters together,
plan policies to implement if they do gain power, and work hard, as they are
now doing, to persuade African governments, particularly that of South
Africa, to apply the pressure for internationally accepted elections.

Hence the deep despair of the population. Most Zimbabweans face the year
with little hope for any early solution. But there are signs that the logic of economic failures may finally bring the whole edifice crashing down. Maybe
enough Zimbabweans will decide that 'enough is enough' and provide the
critical mass in the streets to topple ZANU PF. The 'war on corruption' has
now exposed the rot at the core and could develop into an uncontrollable
internecine struggle. The distortions in the Zimbabwean economy have
impacted heavily on the region. President Mbeki, like Obasanjo in December,
might finally decide that it is not worth the embarrassment of continuing to
support Robert Mugabe, whose galloping paranoia occasionally turns on
Mbeki himself. Or, a serious illness or even death of the 80-year-old Mugabe
might open an opportunity for a South Africa assisted return to legitimacy,
and an end to the madness. 'An idea whose time has come cannot be
stopped'.

The time for democratic change in Zimbabwe has not yet come. But time
does move fast in Zimbabwe. The unexpected occurs on a daily basis. While
today we may see little hope, tomorrow or next week will surely be different,
for ultimately time is on our side.

Open Letter to Nkosazana Dlamini-Zuma
and Other Women in the South African Cabinet

Everjoice J. Win
Pambazuka News 147, 11 March 2004

Dear sisters,

Happy International Women's Day to you. The 8 March is meant to be a day to celebrate how far we have come as women worldwide. But for us north of your border, we have no cause to celebrate. I am writing this letter to talk to you, woman to woman. I believe in other women. I don't buy into the now oft heard refrain that 'women don't support one another'. I celebrate your presence in the highest offices of your land, and I want to continue to have faith in other women.

But, I am making a lot of assumptions in writing this letter to you: that you are in leadership to promote and protect the rights of women. I assume that you feel for other women. Yes it is an assumption that those of us who have worked as feminists know so well. We vote for women to get into high offices and assume that they will stand up for our collective rights.

We think that because one woman has gone through a particular struggle she will easily identify with the struggles of others. That, like I said, is an assumption that has since been proved to be just that, an assumption. So I am writing this with these huge assumptions that you are interested in the rights of women wherever they are, whoever they are. If you aren't, stop reading here.

Sisters, you are letting us down. The women of Zimbabwe are hurting. Thousands have been physically abused, raped, are unable to survive from day to day, and millions are groaning under the weight of oppression.

Honourable Zuma, I am not talking about the British's 'kith and kin', that you like talking so much about. I speak only of *your* kith and kin. Black women.

Women who have never owned land in pre-colonial times or post-colonial times and who still have not been given any of the celebrated land that was redistributed.

But what all these women know is that their rights are violated day in and day out in the name of this land. Our president is on record as saying that women cannot be given land in their own capacity, unless they don't want to get married. On the former commercial farms all poor black women know is that they have lost their means of survival. You and I can argue from the safety of our good jobs that they were being exploited by the Rhodies. But to them it was a question of half a loaf is better nothing. Now it's a case of no bread is better than half a loaf! In the absence of alternatives they resort to commercial sex work, with all the dangers that it now entails (your government's denial-ism around HIV/AIDS not withstanding here. In Zimbabwe we are quite clear that one in every three people has HIV).

Hundreds of female nurses and teachers have fled from their rural posts since the 2000 elections, because of the politically motivated and organised violence that engulfed our country. Most of them are still unemployed as we speak, because the government refuses to allow them to 'transfer'.

Those who stayed continue to endure emotional and physical violence from so-called war vets and the Green Bombers. Young girls, some as young as nine or ten, have been raped and infected with HIV by gangs of marauding state sponsored thugs. There are no figures of how many black women and their families have been displaced from their homes.

Have you never wondered what life must be like for an ordinary black Zimbabwean woman right now? Let me share with you what I know, bearing in mind my class status. A packet of 10 sanitary pads costs Z$10,000. A domes-tic worker in Highfield township earns Z$15,000 if she is lucky. I leave the horrors of her monthlies to your active imagination. Saying hello to a doctor is now $50,000. Ten good pain- killers will cost you Z$15,000. A one- way trip into town from the nearest township by combi is $500.

Most walk back and forth every day. The woman still has to cook, clean and take care of everyone. Add to all this, the impact of the HIV crisis. It is women who still care for the sick, who have to care for their babies and who are still denied their reproductive rights. We are now back to the good-old system of pulling girls out of schools, because poor families can't afford to pay fees for both girls and boys. Our gender roles and rights questions haven't gone away simply because we are in a political crisis. They just get worse.

You have probably seen various videos and read countless stories about what is going on in Zimbabwe. I know many of you doubt the authenticity of these stories given the 'messengers' who put them out. But let me go back to the woman thing; you and I know the price that women pay for publicly speaking about any human rights violations that they suffer. We know the questions that are asked: What had she done? What was she wearing? Where was she going? Who is she? Can we really believe her? In the case of Zimbabwe's political violence against women add another set of questions: Which party is she from? Are you sure she wasn't paid by the British? Is it really true that Robert Mugabe, a whole liberation war leader, can do that? And in the case of the socio-economic crisis: Surely these figures are exaggerated?

Isn't this just Western propaganda?

That, my dear sisters, is why I said you are letting us down. We are dismayed, by the comments that some of you, particularly Nkosazana, have made about our situation in Zimbabwe. As any woman in a violent situation will tell you, there are no prizes awarded for speaking out. If anything you are ostracised by your own family/community. You are branded a bad woman, and worse you are violated several times over for daring to open your mouth.

Your public denials and accusations against those of us who dare to speak hurts. Telling us that what we are going through is 'British propaganda' is the same as accusing any South African woman who is raped of telling lies.

Your silence and quiet diplomacy does more harm to us emotionally than the physical wounds we carry. Those of you who have ever experienced domestic violence (and I am sure there are a few among you) or rape must be quite familiar with this; the pain you feel when your own family doubts your story. The anguish you go through when his and your own family accuse you of being the bad woman. The anger when they literally tell you to change your behaviour.

That is what you and your government are doing to the women of Zimbabwe.

Partly blaming the victims, mostly silencing them. As you celebrate International Women's Day, think about the women and girls of Zimbabwe. We are over six million nameless, faceless individuals. Go beyond Bob and Morgan. Talk to us. We are here. As our rights continue to be violated in the name of 'national sovereignty', all we ask of you is not to deny our pain. Don't silence us and deny us the space to name our violations and our violators. May none of what we are going through *ever* happen to any one of you or any woman of South Africa.

This letter was first published in South Africa's Mail and Guardian *newspaper. It is reproduced here with the kind permission of the author.*

Zimbabwe –
'The Government Wants the People
to Give Up Hoping'

Steve Kibble
Pambazuka News 155, 6 May 2004

'GIVE ZANU PF CREDIT, it has ridden the crisis, seen off the opposition and now all it has to do is manage the crisis and aim for re-election and then change the constitution' – Zimbabwean human rights lawyer, early 2004.

How are we to reconcile Zimbabwe's seemingly inevitable slide towards being a 'failed state' and the continued confidence within ZANU PF that they can handle the crisis and stay in power until after parliamentary elections due in 2005? More pertinently, what is the popular response to the multilayered crisis of the Zimbabwean state?

Since the government's defeat in the February 2000 constitutional referendum, ZANU PF has largely succeeded in re-imposing its control through a 'holistic strategy of repression'. A peace activist described the strategy as a sort of 'scorched earth policy in terms of social formations ... while it wants to hold elections so as to appear democratic it wants to prevent thought, communication, information, and analysis'.

Broadly speaking, the strategy entails a continuation of the militarisation/ securitisation of the country, under which these sectors are immune from the law and occupy increasingly prominent positions in intelligence, provincial administration, electoral administration and the like. Secondly, it includes the use of presidential powers – supposedly introduced as part of attempts to clamp down on corruption – allowing police to hold opponents of the regime in prison for up to a month without legal process on charges of 'subversion'. Thirdly, the regime continues its sustained attack on any focuses of independence or opposition.

This strategy has the following elements:

■ A state-driven violent land occupation process without resolving contradictions in the rural economy

■ The use of the police and security apparatus against opponents, including the use of sexual violence as retribution

■ The use of terror and judicial intimidation as well as ideological demonisation of the opposition to shut down space for independent voices

■ The 'restructuring' of the judiciary towards complete compliance

■ Legal and extra-legal harassment of the independent media, notably through the Access to Information and Protection of Privacy Act, which shut down the *Daily News*

■ Destabilisation of trades unions, NGOs and other civic bodies. The draft legislation already exists for NGOs to be the next target
■ Widespread torture and intimidation. The opposition has been softened up by four years of sustained repression and abuse. There has been a crackdown on the human rights sector, although brutal intimidation has often been replaced by more subtle forms
■ The co-option or denigration of religious leadership
■ The reorganisation of ZANU PF structures to ensure a strategy of coercive mobilisation
■ Use of violence as an election strategy with the bodies responsible for electoral administration firmly under government control including use of military personnel
■ The use of the land reform process, the indigenisation strategy, the stripping of state assets and the politically partisan use of government-controlled food as a 'primitive accumulation' tool to create a new economic bloc based on party affiliation and loyalty (although its sustainability is open to question)
■ An authoritarian economic nationalist ('anti-imperialist') rhetoric that has resonance in the region and continent, bringing together race, land and historical injustice in order to demonise the internal opposition and legitimise and maintain ZANU PF's rule through repression.

ZANU PF Rides Out the Crisis?

Since the decision in December 2003 by Harare to react to continued suspension by withdrawing from the Commonwealth, events have seemed to turn ZANU PF's way. There have been victories in by-elections marked by the usual violence and intimidation, including retaking the urban constituency of Zengeza in late March 2004.

The Reserve Bank governor Gideon Gono responded to recent dramatic collapses in the banking sector linked to endemic corruption by changing the foreign exchange system leading to an initial decline in inflation. This was combined with a drive against corruption. A prominent ZANU PF MP and proponent/symbol of black economic empowerment, Philip Chiyangwa, was briefly (and illegally) detained over charges of corruption. Indeed the anti-corruption drive in April 2004 claimed the arrest of the recently appointed finance minister but political lightweight Chris Kuruneri on charges of corruption in terms of illegally dealing in foreign currency.

Does this mean that after years of presiding over gross corruption, systemic human rights abuses, and spectacular economic and political decline, the Mugabe government is about to reform (as in the February cabinet 'reshuffle'), re-enter the 'civilised world' (as a victory for the 'quiet diplomacy' of the Mbeki government) and aim for clean parliamentary elections in 2005?

Certainly Thabo Mbeki has given June 2004 as a 'final deadline' for serious negotiations to be underway and (hopefully for him) lead to a government of national unity under a reformed ZANU PF, but not necessarily under Robert Mugabe. Few in the region and even fewer in Zimbabwe find this believable: so many promises, so many broken – and so many basically untrue claims from Mbeki that genuine talks are about to start.

Perhaps a greater indication of South Africa's stance was its backing at the UN Human Rights Commission in Geneva on 15 April 2004, just before South Africa's own elections, for a successfully carried African/Asian/Russian 'no action' resolution on the human rights situation in Zimbabwe – for the second year running.

Brian Kagoro, coordinator of the Crisis in Zimbabwe Coalition, said: 'It is disheartening ... that ... the human rights of the people of Zimbabwe have been reduced to the flexing of muscles between the global South and the global North.' As long as Mbeki still (in public at least) accepts the Mugabe rhetoric that the crisis is not about 'governance' and human rights but about resolving the triangle of race, land and colonial dispossession, serious pressure or ending of South African financial support seems unlikely.

The arrest of Chiyangwa is supposedly linked to the three factions fighting within ZANU PF over the succession to Mugabe – John Nkomo, party boss, Emmerson Mnangagwa, and Defence Minister Sydney Sekeramayi. Mugabe is thought to have removed his support for Mnangagwa after the latter was named in a recent UN report as heavily involved in the illegal diamond trade from the Democratic Republic of Congo. However both Mnangagwa and Sekeramayi are long term Mugabe allies and were involved in the massacres in Matabeleland in the 1980s. Conversely the Nkomo group are his key allies inside Matabeleland.

This is all part of what appears to be conflict between continuing the 'succession debate' on behalf of Mnangagwa and having no succession debate, meaning Mugabe stays in power. The easiest strategy is for Mugabe to put the succession on hold and proclaim he is staying out his period of office until 2008. This does little, however, to resolve internal and external questions of the legitimacy and sustainability of the regime or Mbeki's diplomatic strategy.

ZANU PF is likely to continue a strategic mix of coercion, bribery and electoral manipulation for the forthcoming 2005 parliamentary elections. According to the Justice in Agriculture Group there is likely to be a 'ring around the cities' with land being granted to pro-ZANU PF settlers in peri-urban areas plus some redrawing of urban constituencies to draw in rural dwellers under the party's control. The Harare government thus hopes to get a 'free and fair' verdict which would take the heat off, challenge the international community to lose interest and then be in a strong position to have the upper hand in post-election negotiations with the opposition Movement for Democratic Change (MDC).

In terms of negotiations after elections some elements of the MDC, weakened and weary of constant repression, infighting and lack of direction, may well be tempted to join a 'government of national unity'. Civil society would of course reject such a course given their demand for broad-based negotiations rather than elite deals but their capacity to push this demand is very limited at present.

Another element of the ZANU PF strategy is the continued use of food as a political weapon in a situation where an estimated five million Zimbabweans will be reliant on food aid. The Famine Early Warning System estimates that Zimbabwe's 2004 season is likely to see a harvest of between 800,000 and 900,000 tonnes, 33 to 38 per cent below its cereal requirements. The government, however, has stockpiled 240,000 tonnes of maize, has supposedly bought 70,000 tonnes from South Africa and according to diplomatic sources has additional stocks that it has seized. Although the World Food Programme and international NGOs report little overt political interference, the grain at the government's direct disposal provides it with a powerful weapon at election time.

Nor have the Zimbabwean churches in what is a very religious society managed to present a united voice in response to the crisis (or crises). It seemed in mid-2003 that there had been a recovery of the prophetic voice when the leader of the Zimbabwe Council of Churches publicly apologised to Zimbabweans for not bearing witness to the crisis, but this has now been downplayed by the churches seeking to push a negotiations and peace building strategy. The church leaders' dialogue process with ZANU PF and MDC appears on and off – possibly depending on how much pressure ZANU PF feels itself under electorally, regionally and internationally (seemingly little at present).

Even if ZANU PF has the upper hand it has substantial problems. According to the IMF in April 2004:

> Zimbabwe's economy has experienced a sharp deterioration in the last five years. Real GDP has declined by about 30 per cent and is still contracting. Inflation doubled in each of the last three years to reach 600 per cent at the end of 2003 ... Unemployment is high and rising, poverty has doubled since 1995, school enrolment declined to 65 per cent in 2003, and the HIV/AIDS pandemic [affecting 25 per cent of the sexually active population] remains largely unchecked.

After a staff visit in March 2004, the IMF called for tripartite talks between government, business and the unions. This was in response to Kuruneri's attempt to reach accommodation with the IMF by making some small repayments to service debt. The IMF had suspended technical assistance in 2002 and in late 2003 initiated Zimbabwe's compulsory withdrawal due to Harare's lack of co-operation and unwillingness or inability to repay the US$273 million owed (53 per cent of its quota). Nor did Zimbabwe pay US$110 million owed to the Poverty Reduction and Growth Facility (PRGF) – the first and only country ever to have protracted overdue obligations to the PRGF.

It is unlikely that the dual interest rate regime, or the continuing fast track resettlement with its lack of recognition of property rights for either commercial farmers or the new settlers, will appeal to the IMF any more than Zimbabwe's chronic inability to pay its debts.

Nor is Gono's financial strategy guaranteed success economically or politically. Politically, big questions arise immediately – did the cabinet understand the strategy and will Gono have the heavyweight political backing to carry it through? As Lovemore Madhuku asked, what happens when key ZANU PF 'untouchables', such as those given licences to import oil without open tendering or favoured by other forms of party/state patronage, become dragged into the war against corruption?

There is little strategy either to address what a local activist in the Catholic church described as the country's simultaneous deprofessionalisation (driving professionals overseas and destroying the sector's autonomy) and decapitalisation. Fifteen to 20 per cent of the population (i.e. two to three million) is living outside the country, mostly as economic refugees, and 500,000, largely farmworkers, are internally displaced.

Even with all of its strategies for staying in power, most delivery systems have collapsed in Zimbabwe making it hard to sustain patronage systems, especially in the rural areas where ZANU PF needs to maintain its iron grip. And whilst the factions inside ZANU PF may have been temporarily silenced over the succession, the struggle remains ready to erupt again within the context of fighting over the Gono recovery strategy. Although renewed targeted sanctions against the elite are unlikely to have much material impact, the elite resents them, and they suggest not just (some) international disapproval, but also unwillingness to invest or lend money (not that Zimbabwe has much to offer at present).

There remains the possibility that Mbeki, freshly mandated from the April 2004 elections in South Africa and ready to concentrate on outside matters (although it would seem that peacekeeping in Burundi is of higher importance), will actually put more weight behind his June 2004 deadline. Few Zimbabweans I spoke to would, however, welcome a government of national unity, given that it would be a rerun of the Unity Accord of 1987 when ZANU PF forced PF-ZAPU into the shotgun marriage of a de facto one-party state.

Without substantial constitutional and electoral changes, any such government of national unity would be suicidal for the MDC. Whilst opposition forces including the MDC have weakened under sustained assault inside the country they appear to have some hope that they are regrouping internationally and in the region. The MDC are currently examining whether or not they should contest the next elections given the manifest impossibility of them being free and fair.

What Can Outsiders Do? What Does the Future Hold?

Many of Zimbabwe's problems are of long-term duration. The inheritance of violent colonial dispossession and dehumanisation with the response of (in Brian Kagoro's words) a 'violent and hegemonic struggle for decolonisation ... culminated in a largely symbolic independence devoid of material gain for the majority black population.' This meant an authoritarian elite unable or unwilling to transform the repressive state colonial structures into democratic institutions, and the emergence of neo-patrimonialism and clientelistic structures along with long lasting cultures of intolerance and impunity.

What development there was in the 1980s was concerned with state building rather than nation building, within the context initially of apartheid destabilisation, followed by structural adjustment. Once the post-apartheid, post-Cold War moments arrived the implications of this history in terms of repression, corruption and abuse became clearer (except of course for knee-jerk 'anti-imperialists').

So where do progressives go from here? There is still a massive ideological battle to be won between the prescriptions of what Patrick Bond has called 'exhausted nationalism' and global neo-liberalism, in line with many of the directions pointed to in the various world and regional social forums. Equally Bond points to an existing tradition inside Zimbabwe itself with work on alternate policies having in the past been pursued by the Zimbabwe Congress of Trade Unions (ZCTU), the coalitions on debt, the United Nations Development Programme, and not least the National Working People's Convention of 1999.

This may help to counter the pessimism of a Catholic Institute for International Relations (CIIR) partner who saw at present 'a dearth of "thinking", a sort of anti-intellectualism in nearly every quarter ... and essentially ... a kind of absence of politics in the real sense, of positions and ideological clarity and coherence, of strategic thinking and organising.' He added that it is 'very significant that there is a very deep malaise and unhappiness among a large proportion of traditional leaders and spirit mediums, about the disregard for tradition and cultural wholeness.'

Certainly Zimbabweans, while happy to observe stayaways, have not shown great keenness to face the overwhelming firepower of the state on the streets. The sheer struggle for survival and the fact that remittances from abroad are helping keep them alive (and as Gono is aware, the economy as well) cannot be discounted in terms of seeming passivity in the face of desperate circumstances.

There is little leadership either from the MDC – which in any case has done well just to survive itself – from the trade unions or indeed the churches. Although there have been calls, notably by Morgan Tsvangirai, for a much greater coherence amongst opposition forces, notably the ZCTU, the National

Constitutional Assembly and the MDC, the sector has great difficulty in doing this. It also has difficulty agreeing on tactics, including on mass action and what its aims are – overthrow Mugabe, force ZANU PF to the negotiating table, etc. One thing that is unlikely to occur is any kind of armed response.

Outside Zimbabwe there have been a number of initiatives regionally and North-South in bringing together activists and academics in understanding the nature of the crisis. A particularly resonant one was the bringing together of the Zimbabwean and South African diasporas in London. There could be much greater North-South solidarity in a number of forums – NGO, academic, church and use of links with southern African organisations. Outside organisations need to provide support for those in Zimbabwe and the region who are providing information about the human rights and general situation inside Zimbabwe, and those under threat standing up to repression.

There is continuing need for pressure on the ANC government including from within the region. Pressure also needs to be directed at the other elements in the tripartite alliance such as the trade unions and the Communist Party, given Pretoria's assurances to the outside world that Mugabe would step down and serious negotiations would commence. What is it about a transition to democracy inside Zimbabwe that worries them more than the 'chaos that they know'? The International Crisis Group believes that the focus should be on promoting a free and fair election for March 2005 rather than pursuing the chimera of inter-party talks.

There should also be pressure for the long-delayed African Commission on Human and Peoples' Rights report on Zimbabwe to be released as called for by Zimbabwean, regional and human rights organisations.

This article is a shortened version of a paper published in the Review of African Political Economy (ROAPE) *No. 100, of June 2004. Our thanks to the editors of* ROAPE.

Media Repression in Zimbabwe

Henning Melber
Pambazuka News 166, 22 July 2004

PARTICIPANTS IN THE United Nations Educational, Scientific and Cultural Organisation (UNESCO) seminar on Promoting an Independent and Pluralistic African Press, held in Windhoek, Namibia, from 29 April to 3 May 1991, declared: 'Consistent with Article 19 of the Universal Declaration of Human Rights, the establishment, maintenance and fostering of an independent, pluralistic and free press is essential to the development and maintenance of democracy in a nation and for economic development.'

This Windhoek Declaration marked a highlight in the so-called second wave (of democratisation) on the continent. Ironically, it was also at Windhoek – almost 13 years later (end of February 2004) – when Zimbabwe's Minister of State for Information and Publicity signed a co-operation agreement with his Namibian counterpart on closer collaboration, including a planned joint weekly newspaper on regional issues.

In an in-depth interview offered to the local state-funded newspaper *New Era* (5 March 2004), he praised the presidents of both countries 'as two leaders that have remained steadfast, committed, not only as nationalists but also as Pan-Africanists, and as global leaders'. He urged both countries to pursue the common task of 'doing justice to the kind of solidarity that was born during the liberation struggle, and which must be upheld today and in future'.

He further identified the following common challenges:

> We are here to cement these historic bonds and ties, and look at the new challenges that we are facing, as we in particular begin to consolidate the economic objectives of our liberation struggle, and identifying the critical role of information, information not only in terms of the press, the print media, but also the electronic media and other multimedia platforms that are new, that are being used and that are accessible to these generations that may be prone to losing the bigger picture of the essential story.

The honourable minister has not always used such language. As a Zimbabwean scholar still abroad he stated at a conference on Robben Island as late as February 1999 that:

> it would be a mistake to justify the struggles for national liberation purely on the basis of the need to remove the white minority regimes from power and to replace them with black majority regimes that did not respect or subscribe to fundamental principles of democracy and human rights. ruling

personalities have hijacked the movement and are doing totally unacceptable things in the name of national liberation. Being here at Robben Island for the first time, I am immensely pained by the fact that some people who suffered here left this place only to turn their whole countries into Robben Islands.

Only three years later, in March 2002, he – now a minister – praised the results of the presidential elections in his country as an impressive sign 'that Zimbabweans have come of age that they do not believe in change from something to nothing. They do not believe in moving from independence and sovereignty to new colonialism, they do not believe in the discourse of human rights to deepen inequality.'

Rhetoric of such calibre has earned Jonathan Moyo the label 'Goebbels of Africa'. This is certainly too demagogic itself, given the historically unique dimensions of the German holocaust with which the Nazi propaganda minister is associated. But name calling of this kind documents the degree of polarisation and level of dissent in Zimbabwean society today. The current clamp down on the independent media in Zimbabwe is certainly neither exclusively nor decisively the result of a personal vendetta by a previously progressive scholar.

Jonathan Moyo is just one – though admittedly due to his track record a notably exotic – example of relatively high-profile, high-calibre representatives of a post-colonial establishment seeking their own gains while using populist rhetoric to cover up their selfish motives. They have become part and parcel of a set of deep-rooted anachronistic values within a system of liberation movements in power. After seizing legitimate political control over the state, these turned their liberation politics, under the disguise of pseudo-revolutionary slogans, into oppressive tools. Their 'talk left, act right' seeks to cover their true motive, which is to consolidate their hold on the political commanding heights of society against all odds, preferably forever – at the expense of the public interest they claim to represent at a time of deteriorating socio-economic conditions for the once colonised and now hardly liberated (and even less emancipated) majority.

Sadly enough, it was the same Jonathan Moyo who at an early stage of the sobering post-colonial realities in Zimbabwe offered courageous and sensible analytical insights into these processes. While a lecturer at the Department of Political and Administrative Studies of the University of Zimbabwe, he presented thought provoking and painful reflections on the liberation war (chimurenga) with all its dubious ambiguity.

Read this from a paper in late 1992:

> There can hardly be any doubt that the armed struggle in Zimbabwe was a pivotal means to the goal of defeating oppressive and intransigent elements of colonialism and

racism. However, as it often is the case with protracted social processes of a conflict with two sides, the armed struggle in this country had a deep socio-psychological impact on its targets as well as on its perpetrators.. For the most part, the armed struggle in this country lacked a guiding moral ethic beyond the savagery of primitive war and was thus amenable to manipulation by the violence of unscrupulous nationalist politicians and military commanders who personalised the liberation war for their own selfish ends.. This resulted in a culture of fear driven by values of violence perpetrated in the name of nationalism and socialism.

Nowadays, the erstwhile critical scholar represents the same mindset he had questioned. According to a news report by the Media Institute of Southern Africa (MISA), he used a press conference on 30 April 2004 in Bulawayo to threaten, 'there was enough space in Zimbabwe's prisons for journalists caught dealing with foreign media houses'. As 'terrorists of the pen' they would be targeted next. The report quotes the minister as saying: 'President Mugabe has said our main enemy is the financial sector but the enemy is media who use the pen to lie about this country. Such reporters are terrorists and the position on how to deal with terrorists is to subject them to the laws of Zimbabwe.' This is tantamount to paranoia and indicative of the recent efforts to censor even private communication.

As the mere distribution of and access to information can be damaging to the security interest of those represented by the minister, the next onslaught is directed against the private internet service providers (ISPs). The state owned telephone-company announced early June 2004 that ISPs had to enter new contracts stipulating that they as service providers prevent or report to the authorities anti-national activities and malicious correspondence via their telephone lines. If they fail to do so, they will be liable, i.e. penalised.

This follows earlier appalling interferences resulting in the closing of independent newspapers and the imprisonment or expelling of journalists on a systematic scale. The government and its executive branches are eager to emphasise that this repression is in compliance with the existing (enacted for just such purposes) laws and hence fully 'legal' (which, of course, is a far cry from legitimate). This simply shows that the 'rule of law' can apply in the absence of any justice. It is the strategy of the ban that constitutes the rule of law. It does not even spare government-friendly media productions and displays the intolerant, all-controlling nature of the system.

One prominent example is the banning of the live broadcasted television production 'Talk to the Nation' in mid-2001, which was sponsored by the National Development Association (NDA). The explanatory statement by an official of the Zimbabwe Broadcasting Corporation (ZBC) is a remarkable example of the 'innocence' of a totalitarian mindset: 'Live productions can be tricky and dangerous. The setting of the NDA productions was professionally done but maybe the production should not have been broadcast live. You do not know what someone will come and say and there is no way of controlling it.'

Media operating independently or outside the direct control of government were increasingly hampered and closed down, as the prominent example of the Daily News showed. On the basis of an alleged breach of a legal clause under the notorious Access to Information and Protection of Privacy Act (AIPPA), the Media and Information Commission (MIC) closed The Tribune in June 2004 for at least a year. Its publisher, himself a former ZANU PF MP, was reportedly suspended earlier on by the ruling party for 'disrespecting' ZANU PF top structures because he had denounced AIPPA in his maiden address to parliament.

It therefore does not come as a surprise that the latest annual overview of the state of media freedom in the Southern African region by the Media Institute of Southern Africa – issued on World Press Freedom Day (26 April) – records that more than half of all 188 media freedom and freedom of expression violations in 2003 among the ten monitored countries were in Zimbabwe.

International agencies committed to the freedom of press and the professional ethics of independent journalism are in agreement that the situation in Zimbabwe is intolerable. It prompted the annual general assembly of the International Press Institute (IPI) on 18 May 2004 in Warsaw to adopt the unanimous decision 'to retain Zimbabwe's name on the "watchlist" of nations that are seriously eroding media freedom'. And the board of the World Association of Newspapers (WAN) condemned at its 57th World Newspaper Congress in Istanbul early June 2004 the 'attempts to silence independent media'. At a meeting in Windhoek during early June 2004 a total of 24 newspaper editors from eight countries in Southern Africa, organised in the Council of the Southern African Editors' Forum (SAEF), suspended its Zimbabwean wing.

The narrowing down of the post-colonial discourse to a mystification of the liberation movement in power as the exclusive home to national identity and belonging finds a corresponding expression in the increased monopolisation of the public sphere and expressed opinion.

Amanda Hammer and Brian Raftopoulos, co-editors of a recent volume on Zimbabwe's Unfinished Business summarised this in their introduction as 'efforts to control or destroy the independent media and to silence all alternative versions of history and the present, whether expressed in schools, in churches, on sports fields, in food and fuel queues, at trade union or rate payers' meetings, in opposition party offices or at foreign embassies'.

Such desperate initiatives to enhance control signal at the same time a lack of true support among the population, who otherwise could be allowed to speak out freely. The repression of public opinion beyond the official government propaganda is therefore an indication of the ruthless last fight for survival of a regime, which has lost its original credibility and legitimacy to an extent that it has to be afraid of allowing a basic and fundamental principle of human rights – the freedom of expression.

Nation, Race and History in Zimbabwean Politics

Brian Raftopoulos

Pambazuka News 168, 5 August 2004

Introduction

ONE OF THE CENTRAL features of the Zimbabwean crisis, as it has unfolded since 2000, has been the emergence of a revived nationalism delivered in a particularly virulent form, with race as a key trope within the discourse, and a selective rendition of the liberation history deployed as an ideological policing agent in the public debate. A great deal of commentary has been deployed to describe this process, much of it concentrating on the undoubted coercive aspects of the politics of state consolidation in Zimbabwe.

However the manner in which the ideological battle has been fought by ZANU PF as a party and a state is of particular importance in trying to understand the ways in which a beleaguered state is attempting not only to extend its dominant economic and political objectives, but also its 'intellectual and moral unity, posing all questions around which the struggle rages not on a corporate level but on a 'universal' plane, and thus creating the hegemony of a fundamental group over a series of subordinate groups' (Gramsci 1971: 182).

For the manner in which Mugabe has articulated the Zimbabwean crisis has impacted not only on the social forces in the country but also on the African continent and in the diaspora. Such an ambitious political outreach demands that we view the Zimbabwean state as more than a 'simple, dominative or instrumental model of state power,' but as a state with a more complex and multi-dimensional political strategy. (Hall 1996:429; and Hall 1980.)

In this multi-dimensional strategy, the state has monopolised the national media to develop an intellectual and cultural strategy that has resulted in a persistent bombardment of the populace with a regular and repeated series of messages. Moreover this strategy has been located within a particular historical discourse around national liberation and redemption, which has also sought to capture a broader Pan Africanist and anti-imperialist audience.

Moreover in articulating this ideological strategy the ruling party has drawn on deep historical reservoirs of antipathy to colonial and racial subjugation in Zimbabwe, Southern Africa and Africa more generally, and on its complex inflections in the diaspora. Thus the Mugabe message is no mere case of peddling a particular form of false consciousness, but it carries a broader and often visceral resonance, even as it draws criticisms for the coercive forms of its mobilisation.

Nation and Race

In Zimbabwe the state has a monopoly control over the electronic media through such laws as the Broadcasting Services Act and the Access to Information and Protection of Privacy Act. Through such instruments the ruling party has been able to saturate the public sphere with its particularist message and importantly to monopolise the flow of information to the majority rural population.

Thus, as a report on the ways in which Zimbabwe Broadcasting Corporation (ZBC) delivered views on the nation in 2002, concluded:

> ZBC's conceptualisation on 'nation' was simplistic. It was based on race: the White and Black race. Based on those terms, the world was reduced to two nations – the white nation and the black nation and these stood as mortal rivals. The black nation was called Africa. Whites were presented as Europeans who could only belong to Europe just as Africa was for Africans and Zimbabwe for Zimbabweans.
> (Gandhi and Jambaya 2002: 4)

For the Mugabe regime the emergence of the opposition MDC in 1999 was a manifestation of foreign British and White influence in Zimbabwean politics. This construction of the opposition thus placed them outside of a legitimate national narrative, and thrust it into the territory of an alien, un-African and treasonous force that 'justified' the coercive use of the state in order to contain and destroy such a force.

Having discursively located the opposition as an alien political force, the full coercive force of the state was brought to bear on those regarded as 'unpatriotic' and 'puppets of the West'. Deploying elements of the police, intelligence service, army, the war veterans, party supporters and the youth militia, the ruling party has inflicted enormous damage on the personnel and structures of the opposition.

Nation, History and Culture

Scholars have observed that the writing of history has often been used to 'legitimate' the nation-state, both in an attempt to 'naturalise' it as the central principle of political organisation, and to make it the 'subject and object of historical development (Berger, Donovan and Passmore, 1999:xv). In Zimbabwe there has been clear evidence of this process since 2000 in particular.

As part of the attempts to revive ZANU PF's political fortunes in the 2000 general election and the 2002 presidential election, the ruling party placed a strong emphasis on reviving the narrative of the liberation struggle in general and the heroic roles of ZANU PF and Mugabe in particular.

In this narrative of liberation, a common African history and Pan-Africanist solidarity, the land has played a determining role as the key marker of a common struggle. It has formed the centrepiece of the ruling party's construc-tion of belonging, exclusion and history. The official discourse on the libera-tion struggle has been marked by the translation of a multi-faceted anti-colo-nial struggle into a singular discourse designed to legitimate the authoritarian nationalism that has emerged around the land question since 2000 (Hammar, Raftopoulos and Jensen 2003).

During the 2002 presidential election this liberation rhetoric was accompa-nied by a cultural programme that saturated the public with liberation war films, documentaries and dramas, promoting ZANU PF generally and Robert Mugabe in particular, while also carrying strong messages against whites.

Amongst the most damaging aspects of the telling of this national narrative through a series of dualisms (black/white, British/Zimbabwean), and com-pressions of the various aspects of the anti-colonial struggle into a single field of force, has been the enormous loss of complexity of the colonial encounter. The complexity of the settler-colonial period (not least of which included the changing relations between the black elite and different settler regimes) has been flattened into a Mugabe/Blair colonial encounter (White 2003:97). While the demonisation of Whites has served the needs of authoritarian nationalist politics in Zimbabwe, it has prevented a more creative, tolerant and difficult dialogue on the European influences in the making of Zimbabwean identities.

The On-Going National Question

The Mugabe government has worked hard to generalise its model of resolving the national question, based largely on the model of land reform through violent land occupations, articulated through a Pan-Africanist and anti-impe-rialist discourse. Moreover in this model the human rights question and the democratic demands of civic groups are dismissed as an extension of Western intervention, with little relevance to the 'real issues' of economic empower-ment.

In South Africa the Zimbabwean debate has taken on a particular resonance, not least because of the apparent popularity of Mugabe amongst many South Africans. On a broader level there are many aspects of the history and politics of Zimbabwe that resonate in the current South African context (Phimister and Raftopoulos 2004; Southall 2003; Melber 2003). Zimbabwean commentators close to the ruling party have not hesitated to 'shame' the South African gov-ernment into taking more Africanist political positions.

Moreover, the 'spell' of anti-imperialism and the resonance of the race debate in Zimbabwe has found a broader canvas for its articulation in the diaspora. In addition to cementing the support of other liberation movements in Southern Africa, ZANU PF has actively cultivated linkages with a few black civic groups in the US, UK and Australia in an attempt to build Pan-Africanist solidarity around the Mugabe project.

Conclusion

A decade ago I wrote an article on 'Race and Nationalism' in Zimbabwe. In re-reading the piece in recent weeks what strikes me most about the analysis, apart from an underestimation of the potential for a revived nationalist project by the ruling party, was its strictly national focus, which even then was a limitation of the article. In 2004 it is impossible to confront this subject meaningfully without addressing the broader reach of its effects at both regional and international levels. Mugabe has not only defined the national project around a selective reading of nationalist history and an exclusivist construction of the nation, he has also sought to ensure that this message resonates in other black struggles both regionally and internationally.

ZANU PF has set itself the task of establishing a hegemonic project in which the party's narrow definition of the nation is deployed against all other forms of identification and affiliation. In this project the media and selected intellectuals have been used to provide a continuous and repetitive ideological message, in order to set the parameters of a stable national identity conducive to the consolidation of the ruling party. As Zimbabweans listen to the radio, watch television and read the daily newspapers, all controlled by the ruling party, they are being 'informed' about what it means to be a 'good Zimbabwean,' and a 'genuine African'. They are also being told who is the 'enemy' within and without and advised to confront such 'enemies' with ruthless exclusion if necessary. For the present this political assault has seriously closed down the spaces for alternative debates around citizenship and national belonging.

These are excerpts from a paper entitled 'Nation, Race and History in Zimbabwean Politics', presented at the University of Edinburgh's Centre of African Studies International Conference on States, Borders and Nations: Negotiating Citizenship in Africa, in May 2004. Please see http:\\www.cas.ed.ac.uk for further information.

For a list of references see: http://www.pambazuka.org/index.php?id=23675

CHAPTER 10

NAMING THE DARFUR GENOCIDE

The Sudanese Government's Gun Barrel Politics in Dafur

Eva Dadrian
Pambazuka News 143, 12 February 2004

ONCE AGAIN THE military regime of Khartoum has proved that old habits die-hard. Trying once again to solve the Darfur crisis through the barrel of the gun is a clear indication that Khartoum has learned nothing from the 20-year-old war it fought against its own citizens in Southern Sudan. Despite agreeing recently that a ceasefire is necessary to stop the bloodshed in Darfur, and despite claiming this week that the 'war in Darfur' is over, the regime has stepped up its military operations in the province and by the same token has rejected the invitation to a conference on Darfur proposed by the Centre for Humanitarian Dialogue, a Swiss non-governmental peace group, to be held 14 –15 February in Geneva.

While fighting the so-called 'insurgents' the Sudanese armed forces and other paramilitary units – the Popular Defence Forces – have simultaneously targeted civilians, allegedly accused of supporting the rebellion. More than 600,000 people have fled from their destroyed villages and have taken refuge in other towns in makeshift camps under trees with almost no food, water or shelter, while more than 100,000 fled to neighbouring Chad. Khartoum announced that major military operations in Darfur are over but villages are still being attacked and burned by the Janjaweed, the Khartoum-backed armed militias, and government Antonov planes continue to bomb indiscriminately villages as close as 60km from Al Fasher, the capital of Northern Darfur.

A ceasefire negotiated in neighbouring Chad (Abeche 1) seeking to end the conflict collapsed because the government has not kept its part of the deal, i.e. stop all its military operations and especially rein in the Janjaweed. In fact Osman Youssef Kibir, the governor of North Darfur, has admitted that militiamen acting in the name of the government executed civilians in his province, although he denied that the government bore any responsibility for their acts. Last week, the government overrun a number of camps held by the fighters of the Movement for Justice and Equality (MJE), one of the fighting factions in

Darfur. Then it turned its wrath against the other faction, the Sudan Liberation Army and has surrounded Jebal Marra, their stronghold, with the full might of its armed forces and its allies.

The situation in Darfur is far from being 'under control', as claimed by the Sudanese President Omar al-Beshir. The rebellion will continue as long as Khartoum refuses to acknowledge any political motivation for the unrest in the province and rejects a political solution to the crisis, blaming it instead on 'armed criminal gangs and outlaws', who it says are aided by tribes from Chad.

Much of the tension in Darfur results from the same issues that led Southern Sudan to take up arms back in 1983 – a central government that exploits local resources, imposes its cultural beliefs on the indigenous African population and consistently plays off local tribes and ethnic groups against each other for short-term gains. The Darfur Liberation Front – which later changed its name to the Sudan Liberation Movement/Army (SLM/A) – took up arms last February because the Khartoum government had 'introduced policies of marginalisation, racial discrimination and exploitation that had disrupted the peaceful coexistence between the region's African sedentary and Arab nomad communities'. Since the rebellion erupted the province is a war zone, with tremendous suffering inflicted on the civilian population by the army and the armed militias. SLA complains that the government in Khartoum, like all its predecessors, is dominated by the northern Arab elite and has ignored their needs. They argue that Darfur too should be offered a slice of a power-sharing deal and that its natural resources developed for the benefit of the local population. Calling for a separation of state and religion, the SLA/SLM have spelled out their objective 'to create a united democratic Sudan' where the unity of the country will ultimately be based on the right to self-determination of the various peoples of Sudan. Also, they are asking for the establishment of an economy and a political system that addresses the uneven development and marginalisation that have plagued the country since independence. Yet these claims have had no effect on the government. It continues to refuse to acknowledge the political motivation for the unrest and accuses Eritrea and the Sudan People's Liberation Army (SPLA) of supporting and arming the rebels.

Darfur is the most underdeveloped region in the country and is prone to drought and famines, two factors which have fuelled conflict between nomadic Arab tribes, armed by the government, militias and local African villagers. Libya, who backs the Zaghawa, 'a useful long term leverage weapon against N'djamena' according to Al Fazzan, the former Libyan ambassador to Cairo who is now representing his country in Damascus, has offered to solve Darfur's 'tribal dispute' by inviting the Arab herders and pastoralists of Darfur into Libya. There, they will receive new territories, pastures and water points and even Libyan nationality. Tripoli wants at all costs to unite with

Sudan and Egypt and recently Kadhafi has proposed a draft constitution for a tripartite union to form the Golden Triangle, his 35 year-old dream. Sudan may be an oil producer at the rate of 330,000 barrels per day, but the oil bonanza only began in 1999. With the exception of the capital, there is practically neither proper health services nor education and no communications infrastructure in the country. Neglected by successive governments, the peripheral regions – Darfur, Kordofan, the Nuba Mountains and the Eastern Province – can easily claim to benefit from 'sustained UNDERdevelopment'.

Parallel to the issues of neglect and underdevelopment, racial discrimination and exploitation have poisoned inter-tribal co-existence. Pastoralism and farming have historically been and remain the most viable economic sectors in the province. It could be argued that land has long been at the heart of many conflicts in Africa, either between the indigenous black African populations and new comers – the case of Zimbabwe – or between farmers and pastoralists like in Darfur. During British colonial rule, the conflicts over pastures and water points were solved through the local tribal administration. Good neighbourliness still prevailed in those days; the pastoralists were allowed to move into the grazing areas with their cattle, sheep and camels, only after farmers had harvested their fields. But at independence, in the rush to modernise the country and move away from 'old traditions', the new rulers of Sudan dismantled the local tribal administration and never replaced it. In the early 1980s, as drought and underdevelopment reduced pastures and water resources, the struggle for survival intensified for the nomadic pastoralists. During the 1986–9 premiership of Sadiq Al-Mahdi (Umma Party) the problem resurfaced when the nomadic tribes of the region, commonly known as the Baggara, moved indiscriminately into farming lands. These actions were made possible by deliberate government policy and with the tacit approval of local government officials. The Baggara were even given weapons to 'defend' themselves in case they were attacked by the indigenous farmers. Needless to say, often the weapons were used to take over land and water points from the indigenous farmers.

Since then, Darfur has been the scene of attacks by armed groups on indigenous farmers. The present government reacted by detaining incommunicado in various prisons around the country community leaders and alleged critics of its policies in the province. Following unrest in and around Geneina, Northern Darfur (2001) where hundreds of Massaleet were killed and dozens of villages burnt to the ground, special courts were established to deal with 'murders, armed attacks and banditry'. These courts have handed down death sentences and cruel, inhuman and degrading punishments – cross amputation, public flogging – after unfair and rushed trials.

Armed conflict and deliberate government strategies have largely been responsible for the long history of wars and of famines in Sudan. The current fighting, primarily along ethnic lines, is the result of that strategy. For almost 25 years, famine and a scorched earth policy have been regarded as the outcome of a political process that takes the resources of a region from the weak –the indigenous people – and transfers them to the politically strong – Khartoum northern elites.

Various armed militia groups, the Janjaweed in the case of Darfur and the Muraheleen in the Nuba Mountains and in Southern Sudan, have been the vehicles for the regime policies and have been used as proxies by Khartoum. Their task is to attack and plunder the people of a given region and take their reward – the war booty – in the form of looted cattle, crops, etc. A few years ago, these groups did not have any political agenda in Darfur, but today this has changed. Their political agenda is to assist the government in 'arabising' the region and taking over its natural resources – oil and minerals. The army and the security forces, the specially created Popular Defence Force (PDF), support these militias whose main task is to terrorise and isolate the local populations by forcibly preventing them from working in their fields and looking after their animals. By burning crops and looting cattle, the Janjaweed militias have created and maintained artificial scarcities of food, driving the farmers from their land and pushing them towards urban centres or to the arid, desolate parts of the province. It is true that the raiding, displacement, and asset destruction did not affect all parts of Darfur simultaneously but they have created a situation of extreme instability whereby ordinary economic activities and survival strategies became impossible.

In addition, the nature of inter-tribal clashes in Darfur has been exacerbated by an inflow of arms from neighbouring countries – Chad and the Central African Republic (CAR). Tribal groups, militias, dissidents, rebel groups as well as ordinary civilians have easy access to small arms. However, in this particular instance, local politicians as well as the central government have fuelled the rivalry between farming settlers and semi-nomadic communities. Neighbouring states also have interests in Darfur. The Zaghawa of Darfur helped Idriss Deby gain power in N'djamena in 1990 and with their kin tribe in Chad they form the backbone of Deby's army and security forces. Libya has its own agenda, especially since Col Kadhafi has turned its attention to Africa and to the mineral-rich Sahel countries. In Northern Darfur, bordering Egypt and Libya, lies Jebal 'Aweinat, one of the richest mineral regions of the entire Sahel with foreseeable deposits of uranium, while Southern Darfur is known for its oil, iron ore and copper deposits.

The government has come under serious criticism from humanitarian and human rights organisations about attacks on civilian targets and the deteriorating security situation in Darfur. There is no circumstance that justifies deliberate attacks on civilians or military operations that endanger civilian lives. These are all grave violations of human rights and the laws of war. But since the Sudanese leaders and their friends, especially Libya, which became a member of the UN Human Rights Commission last year, halted the work of the UN rapporteur for human rights in Sudan in April 2003 during the commission annual meeting in Geneva violations of human rights have doubled in Darfur. As early as November 2002, Gerhart Baum, the UN Special Rapporteur on the Situation of Human Rights in Sudan, expressed concern over the slow progress achieved by the Khartoum government in redressing the human rights situation. He referred particularly to the negative role of the nomadic Arab tribes (mainly the Baggara and Misariyyah) from which the government formed Muraheleen (nomadic) militias, which were deeply implicated in abductions and the targeting of civilians. Yet this has been crippling because civilians' cattle and grain are looted, agricultural land devastated, homes burnt, mills destroyed. Thousands of Fur, Zaghawa and Massaleet are unable to go back to their villages, plant or replace their herds.

During a consultative meeting that took place in Nairobi in January between Vice-President Ali Osman Taha and Ahmed Diraige, the leader of the Sudan Federal Democratic Alliance (SFDA) and former governor of Darfur (1980–83) the government accepted that a ceasefire would be agreed and implemented under the supervision of international monitors. Negotiations opened with the Darfur fighters in order to reach a political settlement to the issue. But it seems that diplomatic and political solutions have been put aside and the government will pursue its military policy.

Sudan: Calling Genocide
by its Rightful Name

Eva Dadrian
Pambazuka News 163, 1 July 2004

LIKE A MULTICOLOUR fireworks display illuminating the skies and sending ecstatic crowds cheering for a few moments, the Naivasha Peace Agreement has faded away. The short-lived jubilation is over and with a serious hangover, the international community is waking up to the new Sudanese reality in Darfur, asking how and why it allowed it to happen?

Neither the UN nor the US has learned anything from past mistakes – Rwanda, Liberia, Sierra Leone and the Democratic Republic of Congo. Less than a month ago, brushing aside the sound of machine guns coming over from Darfur, UN Secretary General Kofi Annan described the signing of the agreement as a 'major step forward'. Now, on a mission to Sudan he described the situation in Darfur as 'the world's worst humanitarian crisis'.

Before going to Darfur (as a matter of fact like Evita Peron 'I have never left it') I would like to stop a few moments in Naivasha and see who are the real beneficiaries of the protocols signed between the Khartoum government and the Sudan People's Liberation Movement/Army. Is it a genuine 'key deal' that would benefit the Southern Sudanese people?

The sad reality is that only three individuals will benefit from Naivasha. These three so-called men of peace have succeeded in cheating the international community, the United Nations and the 35 million Sudanese.

Beleaguered, embattled and an outcast for the past 15 years, President Omar el Beshir, who since staging his coup in 1989 has escalated the war in South Sudan and sent thousands of young Sudanese zealots to their death, can now claim high and loud that he is the Sudanese leader who took Sudan out of its international isolation and brought peace to the country.

One Nobel Prize to go to el Beshir! Hip, hip, hurray!!!

Fraught with dissent among his own people and justifiably tired after 21 years of fighting, Dr John Garang of the SPLA is taking control of Southern Sudan. Crowned with the blessings brought by the Naivasha deal, Dr Garang is ready to believe anyone who tells him that he is the paramount chief of the South.

Was it a mere slip of the tongue when he declared 'We have reached the crest of the last hill in our tortuous ascent to the heights of peace' or did he mean 'the heights of power?'

One Nobel Prize to go to Dr Garang! Hip, hip, hurray!!!

Last but not least, comes the Texan cowboy who occupies the Oval Room in the White House. Having waved carrots and sticks, sanctions and promises of aid to the Sudanese for almost two years, now George W. Bush can happily wave the Naivasha deal to his hysteria-driven supporters as he campaigns for a second term. Naivasha is meant to counter Bush's disastrous policy in Iraq.

One Nobel Prize to go to Bush! Hip, hip, hurray!!!

I do not know what are the criteria set up by the famous Swedish Academy for prize sharing but I dread to think that UN Secretary General Kofi Annan and US Secretary of State Colin Powell would join in to form the most famous peace quintet of this millennium.

At the end of his visit to war-ravaged Darfur, and having seen the devastation caused by the violent campaign backed by Khartoum against its African citizens of the region, Secretary of State Colin Powell said 'Let's not put a label on things'. The nub of the matter is that we have to call the atrocities in Darfur by 'their rightful name' as Donald Payne, Democrat member of Congress for New Jersey and of the Congressional Black Caucus said recently. According to Payne, the atrocities committed in Darfur 'meet the requirements of the 1948 UN Convention on the prevention and the punishment of the crime of genocide and therefore we have a legal obligation under international law to act'. So why is everybody stalling? Why is no real decision taken? Time is running out for the people of Darfur and the atrocious memories of Rwanda are being revised while the US refuses to say the word.

But let us not play with words, meanings and legalities. Genocide has taken place in Darfur and ethnic cleansing is still being perpetrated because one million people could die before the end of this year if the international community, the UN and the US fail to intervene immediately to stop the killing and the displacement. Secretary Powell claims that he knows what the situation is like and that the US knows what it has to do and is going to do it – in other words, take real action.

Instead the US has circulated a resolution to member nations of the UN Security Council calling for sanctions against the Janjaweed militias, blaming them for what has been described as a 'humanitarian catastrophe' in Sudan and taking no action against the government of Omar el Bashir, the instigator of the ethnic cleansing in Darfur.

The sanctions are ridiculously irrational. They call for an arms embargo and travel restrictions on the Janjaweed militias. Is the United States serious when it circulates these sanctions to member nations of the UN Security Council? Does the Security Council really believe that the Janjaweed need travel documents to move from village to village to kill, rape, burn and destroy? As for an arms embargo, do the members of the UN Security Council really believe that the Janjaweed buy their weapons on the open market, with proper contracts and stamped and approved shipping documents, and that they, the supremos of the Security Council could stop these contracts? Are we to believe once again that these good people are being misled by erroneous 'intelligence' reports?

The western Sudanese region of Darfur is bordered by Chad, Libya and the

Central African Republic, three states where gun running is child's play and where the Janjaweed face no arms embargo and need no license to buy their lethal weapons. In addition, as they have been provided with official Sudanese armed forces uniforms, one presumes they would also have free access to weapons and ammunition from the arsenals of the Sudanese army.

There is indeed a 'humanitarian catastrophe and a security crisis' in Darfur, as Secretary Colin Powell finally decided to acknowledge this week. But the humanitarian crisis is man made and its origins are political. The people of Darfur, like their compatriots on the peripheries (the South, Nuba Mountains and Eastern Sudan) have been marginalised by all the Sudanese regimes, which have taken power since independence in 1956. Democratic rule, as universally understood, was never on the agenda of these regimes. Dominated by the Northern elites, the centralised governments ruled from Khartoum, seldom interested in the plight of the regional people. Ironical as it may sound, the regional people of Sudan are in the large majority Africans – Nuba, Beja, Fur, Massaleit, Dinka, Nuer, Shilluk, Zaghawa and many others.

Because of the emergency of the humanitarian catastrophe, the political aspects of the Darfur crisis are being brushed aside. But, as many leading Darfur politicians have asked, the humanitarian intervention has to go hand in hand with a political solution so the 1.5million internally displaced people and refugees scattered on the Chadian borders can return safely to their farms and live in peace and security guaranteed by their constitutional rights as citizens of Sudan. While the ancestral lands of the African people of Darfur have to be restored to their rightful owners, there is no doubt that the Arab nomadic groups and the African settlers of Darfur have to live together, like they did for centuries and share the same resources – water and land – in an equitable way. This can be achieved if the political will is there. If Kofi Annan wants progress in 48 hours, this is what he should ask from the government and the Darfur factions who took up arms against Khartoum.

Darfur Beyond the Crossroads: Struggles of African Nationalism

Kwesi Kwaa Prah
Pambazuka News 172, 2 September 2004

I HAVE HAD A CHANCE to look at Farid Omar's article 'Darfur at the Crossroads: Caught Between Western Hypocrisy and Muslim Complicity'. (Read it online at http://www.nu.ac.za/ccs/default.asp?2,40,5,461.) My impression is that while I can agree with some of the arguments he makes I am also in disagreement about some factual and interpretative errors in his discussion. I am going through his piece almost paragraph by paragraph in order to lay bare the discrepancies and factual inadequacies.

For a start, the Arab League and the Organisation of Islamic Conference (OIC) have not been altogether silent about the genocide in Darfur, which is instigated, aided and abetted by the Khartoum government. In a recent report by the BBC, on 9 August 2004, entitled 'Arab League backs Sudan on Darfur', the reporter indicated that 'Arab Foreign Ministers at an emergency session in Cairo backed Khartoum's measures to disarm Arab militias and punish human rights violators. They called on the UN to give Sudan more time to resolve the conflict. And Sudanese Vice-President Ali Osman Taha said he thought the UN's end of August deadline was impractical.' In effect the report indicated that, 'the Arab League has rejected any sanctions or international military intervention as a response to the crisis in Sudan's Darfur region.' The Sudanese Vice-President Ali Osman Taha had indicated that, 'We are really committed to disarm whoever is acting outside the law'. But who armed the Janjaweed? He added that, 'comprehensive stability was only possible if both the Arab Janjaweed militia and rebel groups disarmed'.

It is possible to read into this, firstly, the indecisive and guarded complicity of the Arab League position on the tragedy of Darfur. Genocide is not something which can be given time to be reversed. The slaughter and butchery of 30,000 Furs (not Darfuris) is a matter which needs to be brought to a close immediately. In any part of the world today any extension beyond immediacy in terminating genocide would hardly be countenanced. In the present Sudanese conflict in Darfur with the Sudanese army plus the Janjaweed on one side and African nationalist rebels on the other, who are oppressors and oppressed?

Secondly, if you compare the stance of the Arab League to that of the United Nations you will notice an enormous gap in perception of the magnitude, dimensions and interpretation of the crisis. While some of us recognise genocide and ethnic cleansing in the crisis others see a question of disarming armed bandits and rebels as the heart of the matter. I am not aware of what the

OIC has or has not said, but I would agree with Farid Omar that they appear to be 'strangely silent'. If that is the case, then that certainly amounts to implicit complicity.

I share the view of Peter Takirambudde, chief of the Africa Division of Human Rights Watch, that Sudan is 'trying to manipulate opinion in the Arab world to hide the massive crimes it has committed against Sudanese citizens.'

Magdi Abdelhadi of the BBC has observed that:

> there were no surprises in the Arab League statement and Khartoum got what it wanted. The statement welcomed measures already taken by the Sudanese government to disarm the Janjaweed and bring those responsible for human rights violations in Darfur to justice. The Arab foreign ministers also pledged to assist Sudan and the international community in resolving the conflict peacefully. The statement was very much in line with a report by an Arab League's fact-finding mission to Darfur earlier this year, which largely exonerated the Sudanese government from responsibility and laid the blame on a combination of factors, including protracted drought, tribal conflict and under-development in western Sudan.

Of course human rights violators should be brought to book. Human rights violations are unacceptable in the modern world, whether such violators are Americans in the Abu Ghraib prison in Iraq, Arab authorities in the Sudan, or human rights criminals in the Great Lakes area.

True enough:

> While western hypocrisy on the situation in Darfur is really problematic, Muslim complicity in the Darfur mayhem is equally disturbing. The Muslim people and their allies around the world should stand up for Darfuris, denounce and expose western double standards and condemn the AL and the OIC for their inaction and failure to put pressure on Sudan to contain the crisis in Darfur.

There I have no problems with Farid Omar's views. But then he goes on to say that:

> The western media has presented the political and humanitarian crisis in Darfur and broader conflict in Sudan as a race or religious war. This is a false paradigm. The conflict in Sudan is not one pitting the so-called Muslim-Arab North and the so-called Christian/animist South, or between the Arab Janjaweed militia working in collusion with the Sudanese government and the Black Africans in Darfur. The people of Sudan are all Africans, be they Black-Africans or Arab-Africans.

Here I have a bone to pick with Omar. Certainly the various conflicts or the various fronts of war in the Sudan are not simply racial or religious. That is the crude and distorted simplification of the issue. But, we must not forget that the Fur are Muslims just like the Arabs in the Sudan. Therefore the conflict cannot be put down to religious differences. Then, what is it?

For years the Khartoum regime of Muslim fundamentalists have also been pursuing ethnic cleansing in the Nuba Mountains of Southern Kordofan with genocidal overtones against the Nuba who are also mostly Muslims. A similar tactic has been in place there, that is, using local Arab militias working hand in glove with Sudanese army units against the Nuba. In the South of the country the conflict is of much longer standing and can be said to have commenced in August 1955, with a period of low intensity conflict between1972 and 1983. Since 1983 over two million southern Sudanese have died as a result of the war.

In the case of the war in southern Sudan the international media has too often simplified the struggle as a conflict between a Christian and animist South against a Muslim North. The real fact of the matter is that it is a struggle between Arabs and Arabised Nubians and the Africans of the Sudan whether they are Fur, Zaghawa, Messalit and other similar groups in the west or the Ingessana in the east or the Beja/Hadendowa in the Kassala area adjacent to Eritrea. Some Nubians are now rejecting Arabism. The struggle in the Sudan is an age-old struggle between the forces for the Arabisation of Africans and African nationalism, which rejects Arabisation.

It is not simply a question of Islam against Christians and animists. I have in the past on many occasions indicated to friends in the Southern Sudan that they have for too long allowed their position to be sold short by playing to the international media and other interests which simply defined the struggle as one between Christians and animists in confrontation with Muslims. The explosion of media attention in the wake of the emergence of the Darfur crisis has underscored the falsity of the religious explanation of the conflict. If the Fur, Messalit, Zaghawa, Ingessana and Beja are Muslims certainly the struggle of the Sudan is not a religious conflict of Muslims and non-Muslims.

The history of the Arabs in the Sudan has been part of the history of the Arabs in Africa. Arabs entered Africa in the middle of the 7th century AD and have been steadily Arabising Africans starting with the Berbers of northern Africa, who to this day have to a degree been resisting Arabisation. The Sudan and Mauritania are possibly the most decisive flash points in this process. Will Africans steadily accept being culturally Arabised or will they resist Arabisation and remain culturally rooted in their histories?

This is the real question about the Sudan and Africa. I say that I believe Africans prefer to remain African and not to become Arabs. I say this without prejudice to Arabs or those Africans who have become Arabised and wish to remain so. Just as much as Arabs have the right to protect their identity, history and culture, Africans also have a similar right. Just as much as Arabs wish to see the realisation of Arab unity (*el watani el arabi*), Africans also most fervently wish to see the unity of Africans. The Arab League with all its weaknesses represents contemporary aspirations of Arabs for Arab unity.

As I have often argued, for as long as the pursuit of this ideal is conducted democratically for the freedom of Arab peoples, the ideal deserves the support of all progressive and well meaning people. But this must not be allowed to proceed geographically, politically, economically and culturally at the expense of Africans. Where do the borders of the Arab world end and who are the people beyond the borders of the Arab world? Africans need to answer this question for themselves.

Today on the maps of the Arab League the Arab world includes about a third of Africa's geographical area. There are some of us who say enough is enough. No further expansion at the expense of Africans is tolerable. The notion Arab-Africans is a term used in the Sudan to hide the realities of Arabisation. It is a concept which has become in some ways a Trojan horse for Arab expansionism in Africa. Culturally and otherwise, people will always mix and adopt new identities, but this must not become a one-way route to Arabisation and the cultural denationalisation of Africans.

In the broad historical experience of Africans two imperialisms can be pointed to, Arab and Western imperialism. Historically, Arab imperialism in Africa is older than Western imperialism by a millennium. The day Africans realise that Arabs are not Africans and Africans are not Arabs, but that the two peoples must live together in peace and with humanity towards each other, their recognition of an African identity will have moved one step further. They will have made a decisive conceptual move towards the ultimate achievement of African unity. The unity of Africa embraces historically, culturally and psychologically more directly the African diaspora than the Arab north of Africa. In this sense, the African diaspora is central to Pan-Africanism and African unity.

In a manuscript I am currently writing I have made the point that, if we want to maintain the rigour of the logic of the diaspora link, we must, as Africans, define our reality on a historical and cultural basis. In this respect, geography is only useful in as far as it helps us to understand the historical and social process. We can, therefore, hardly define the reality of contemporary Africa as a geographical expression; that is, Africans being all who live on the continent of Africa. The argument has a resounding and irresistible flip-side, which is that, all who do not live on the continent or were not born on the continent, are not Africans. This is the distorted logic which pushes out the African diaspora. We must not equate citizenship with nationality or cultural identity. A state may have people of different nationalities.

I do not agree that the so-called:

> race and religious analogy of the conflict is part of the ideo-
> logical ploy of US imperialism to generate anti-Arab hostility

among African-Americans and Black Africans, to win support of African-Americans and Black African Christians for the US neo-Conservatives/Christian right project against Arab and Muslim Africans, and in particular against Sudanese Muslims. It is also aimed at undermining the long standing Afro-Arab solidarity that has historically striven against the forces of Western imperialism, colonialism, apartheid and the occupation in Palestine.

Of course Western imperialism must be denounced but so also must the Arabisation of Africans be fought. It is ridiculous to bracket African-Americans with US neo-conservatives in this way. It is at best disingenuous and at worst mischievous. The point, which the Darfur crisis has forcefully brought home to many Africans in the diaspora, is that ultimately the definition and identity of Africans cannot be based on colour. In the Sudan it is not possible to differentiate African from Arab on the basis of colour and I am sure that with television available worldwide many Africans in the diaspora who have for centuries been faced with white racism find it difficult to digest the fact that most Arabs in the Sudan have black faces. The point I have elsewhere made is that amongst Arabs colours range from black to blonde. The same is true for Jews. In years to come this may be more clearly true for Europeans.

Ultimately what defines an African from an Arab are cultural and historical belongings, not nature but nurture, not biology but rather culture. The black colour which is common for most Africans happens to be a miraculous bonus, in the sense that whereas most other major peoples of the world have other attributes they share as groups based on culture, religion, language, history and geography, mixed to different degrees, in the case of Africans in the absence of clearly unifying language and religion, colour has become a most useful blessing which makes most Africans recognisable from a good distance. But, in the future increasingly there will be many Africans who are not necessarily black. This is the way the world is moving and this is the future of humanity.

From my viewpoint, part of the tragedy of Darfur is that African nationalism in the Sudan has been conveniently split between what is going on in the west, south, east and northeast. Africans have so far failed to find sufficient ground to realise that they are all fighting the same war. The Arabist rulers in Khartoum have been clever at creating convenient and tactical truces, and thereby silencing and truncating the Southerner's struggle from the Fur, Ingessana, Nuba and Beja. This amounts to success for the policy of divide and rule, which has been used in the past with great skill by successive Arabist regimes in Khartoum, who fear and deny the predominant African character of the Sudan. What al Bashir and the Khartoum clique fear most is that the Arabist minority may lose control of the Sudan; that the African majority may exert its preponderant character.

It is most doubtful if the Arab League, in its present form, would readily accept a thoroughly democratic solution to the national question in the Sudan. But Africans are waking up. Sooner or later the African character of the Sudan as a democratic expression of the society will triumph.

I am happy with Farid Omar's philosophically inclusive sense of humanity. But, I fear the persistence of the confusion of Arab and African on the continent and beyond. This confusion, on this specific matter, appears to be more prevalent among Africans than non-Africans. We still do not seem to know or understand who we are. I hope we do not go into another major Pan-African meeting/congress with this confusion. If this happens, we would not have made any real headway since the last one. Let us not try to foist an African identity on people who do not want to be so regarded and who reject the African identity; who continue to despise and enslave Africans. I agree with Farid Omar when he says that, 'the root causes of the Sudanese conflict are primarily political and can be located in totalitarian tendencies that have over time, suppressed the evolution of popular democracy.' While this diagnosis is right the point has to be seen in relationship to the long history of oppression, slavery, war, ethnic cleansing and now genocide.

The suggestion that external forces have fanned the Sudanese conflict is grossly exaggerated and misplaced. Blaming the conflict on American arms and money and right-wing evangelical groups in the US does not do credit to the Africans of the Sudan. The Africans of the Sudan are a group oppressed by the minority Arab elite in the country. As for the territorial integrity and national sovereignty of the Sudan, we must remember that the Sudan as it is geographically represented today is like all African states an artificial creation of European powers. The British were anxious to control the whole of the Nile Basin in order to supply Egypt with its lifeline, the Nile waters.

Omar's contention that 'the Sudanese government either has no interest in resolving the crisis or lacks the capacity to do so' is spot on. As for the AU I agree with Farid Omar that the about '300 peace monitors it has deployed in Darfur is grossly inadequate.' Again Farid Omar's observation is pertinent when he writes that, 'Like the Arab League and Organisation of Islamic Conference, the Muslim and Arab media have also maintained a strange silence.' In sharp contrast to events in the Middle East, coverage on the horrific Darfuri scene by Al-Jazeera and other leading Arab satellite television stations such as the Dubai-based Al-Arabiya is dismally marginal. The failure by Muslim and Arab media to adequately cover the grisly events in Darfur smacks of complicity.

Africans need to read the correct lessons in the behaviour and attitude of the Arab media. The simple truth about all the wars in the Afro-Arab borderlands is that at best we should be able to nationally coexist in peace. But if we cannot live together in peace, then we must go our separate ways without rancour,

pain and mutual torment. The members of the global community have fortunately agreed as a standing international protocol, since the Treaty of Versailles,
that in our times, nations and peoples have the right to self-determination.

This protocol applies equally to the African people of the Sudan.

How Can We Name the Darfur Crisis?
Preliminary Thoughts on Darfur

Mahmood Mamdani
Pambazuka News 177, 7 October 2004

HOW CAN WE NAME the Darfur crisis? The US Congress, and now Secretary of State Colin Powell, claim that genocide has occurred in Darfur. The European Union says it is not genocide. And so does the African Union.

Nigerian President Obasanjo, also the current chair of the African Union, told a press conference at the United Nations headquarters in New York on September 23:

> Before you can say that this is genocide or ethnic cleansing, we will have to have a definite decision and plan and programme of a government to wipe out a particular group of people, then we will be talking about genocide, ethnic cleansing. What we know is not that. What we know is that there was an uprising, rebellion, and the government armed another group of people to stop that rebellion. That's what we know. That does not amount to genocide from our own reckoning. It amounts to of course conflict. It amounts to violence.

Is Darfur genocide that has happened and must be punished? Or, is it genocide that could happen and must be prevented? I will argue the latter.

Sudan is today the site of two contradictory processes. The first is the Naivasha peace process between the Sudan People's Liberation Army (SPLA) and the government of Sudan, whose promise is an end to Africa's longest festering civil war. The second is the armed confrontation between an insurgency and anti-government militias in Darfur. There is need to think of the south and the west as different aspects of a connected process. I will argue that this reflection should be guided by a central objective: to reinforce the peace process and to demilitarise the conflict in Darfur.

Understanding the Darfur Conflict Politically

The peace process in the South has split both sides to the conflict. Tensions within the ruling circles in Khartoum and within the opposition SPLA have given rise to two anti-government militias. The Justice and Equality Movement (JEM) has historical links to the Islamist regime, and the Sudan Liberation Army (SLA) to the southern guerrilla movement.

The Justice and Equality Movement organised as part of the Hassan Turabi faction of the Islamists. Darfur, historically the mainstay of the Mahdist movement, was Turabi's major claim to political success in the last decade. When the Khartoum coalition – between the army officers led by Bashir and the Islamist political movement under Turabi – split, the Darfur Islamists fell out with both sides. JEM was organised in Khartoum as part of an agenda for regaining power. It has a more localised and multi-ethnic presence in Darfur and has been home to many who have advocated an 'African Islam'.

The SLA is linked to SPLA, which first tried to expand the southern-based armed movement to Darfur in 1990, but failed. The radical leadership of that thrust was decapitated in a government assault. Not surprisingly, the new leadership of SLA has little political experience.

The present conflict began when the SLA mounted an ambitious and successful assault on El Fashar airport on 25 April 2003, on a scale larger than most encounters in the southern civil war.

The government in Khartoum is also divided, between those who pushed the peace process, and those who believe too much was conceded in the Naivasha talks. This opposition, the security cabal in Khartoum, responded by arming and unleashing several militia, known as the Janjaweed. The result is a spiral of state-sponsored violence and indiscriminate spread of weaponry.

In sum, all those opposed to the peace process in the south have moved to fight in Darfur, even if on opposing sides. The Darfur conflict has many layers; the most recent but the most explosive is that it is the continuation of the southern conflict in the west.

De-demonise Adversaries

For anyone reading the press today, the atrocities in Sudan are synonymous with a demonic presence, the Janjaweed, the spearhead of an 'Arab' assault on 'Africans.' The problem with the public discussion of Darfur and Sudan is not simply that we know little; it is also the representation of what we do know. To understand the problem with how known facts are being represented, I suggest we face three facts.

First, as a proxy of those in power in Khartoum, the Janjaweed are not exceptional. They reflect a broad African trend. Proxy war spread within the continent with the formation of Renamo by the Rhodesian and the South African security cabal in the early 1980s. Other examples in the East African region include the Lord's Redemption Army in northern Uganda, the Hema and Lendu militias in Itori in eastern Congo and, of course, the Hutu militia in post-genocide Rwanda. Like the Janjaweed, all these combine different degrees of autonomy on the ground with proxy connections above ground.

Second, all parties involved in the Darfur conflict – whether they are referred to as 'Arab' or as 'African' – are equally indigenous and equally black. All are Muslims and all are local. To see how the corporate media and some of the charity-dependent international NGOs consistently racialise representations, we need to distinguish between different kinds of identities.

Let us begin by distinguishing between three different meanings of Arab: ethnic, cultural and political. In the ethnic sense, there are few Arabs worth speaking of in Darfur, and a very tiny percent in Sudan. In the cultural sense, Arab refers to those who have come to speak Arabic as a home language and, sometimes, to those who are nomadic in lifestyle. In this sense, many have become Arabs. From the cultural point of view, one can be both African and Arab, in other words, an African who speaks Arabic, which is what the 'Arabs' of Darfur are. For those given to thinking of identity in racial terms, it may be better to think of this population as 'Arabised' rather than 'Arab.'

Then there is Arab in the political sense. This refers to a political identity called 'Arab' that the ruling group in Khartoum has promoted at different points as the identity of power and of the Sudanese nation. As a political identity, Arab is relatively new to Darfur. Darfur was home to the Mahdist movement whose troops defeated the British and slew General Gordon a century ago. Darfur then became the base of the party organised around the Sufi order, the Ansar. This party, called the Umma Party, is currently led by the grandson of the Mahdi, Sadiq al-Mahdi. The major change in the political map of Darfur over the past decade was the growth of the Islamist movement, led by Hassan Turabi. Politically, Darfur became 'Islamist' rather than 'Arab.'

Like Arab, Islam too needs to be understood not just as a cultural (and religious) identity but also as a political one, thus distinguishing the broad category of believers called Muslims from political activists called Islamists. Historically, Islam as a political identity in the Sudan has been associated with political parties based on Sufi orders, mainly the Umma Party based on the Ansar and the DUP based on the Khatamiyya. In sharp contrast to the strongly Sudanese identity of these 'sectarian' and 'traditional' parties is the militant, modernist and internationalist orientation of the type of political Islam championed by Hassan Turabi and organised as the National Islamic Front (NIF). Not only in its predominantly urban social base but also in its methods of organisation, the NIF was poles apart from 'traditional' political Islam, and in fact consciously emulated the Communist Party. Unlike the 'traditional' parties, which were mass-based and hoped to come to power through elections, the NIF – like the CP – was a cadre-based vanguard party which hoped to take power in alliance with a faction in the army. The fulfillment of this agenda was the 1989 coup which brought Turabi's NIF into power in alliance with the Bashir faction in the army.

As a political identity, 'African' is even more recent than 'Arab' in Darfur. I have referred to an attempt by SPLA in 1990 to confront the power in Khartoum as 'Arab' and to rally the opposition under the banner of 'African.' Both the insurgency that began 18 months ago and the government's response to it are evidence of the crisis of the Islamist regime and the government's retreat to a narrower political identity, 'Arab'.

Third, both the anti- and the pro-government militia have outside sponsors, but they cannot just be dismissed as external creations. The Sudan government organised local militias in Darfur in 1990, using them both to fight the SPLA in the south and to contain the expansion of the southern rebellion to the west. The militias are not monolithic and they are not centrally controlled. When the Islamists split in 1999 between the Turabi and the Bashir groups, many of the Darfur militia were purged. Those who were not, like the Berti, retained a measure of local support. This is why it is wrong to think of the Janjaweed as a single organisation under a unified command.

Does that mean that we cannot hold the Sudan government responsible for the atrocities committed by Janjaweed militias that it continues to supply? No, it does not. We must hold the patron responsible for the actions of the proxy. At the same time, we need to realise that it may be easier to supply than to disband local militias. Those who start and feed fires should be held responsible for doing so; but let us not forget that it may be easier to start a fire than to put it out.

The fight between the militias on both sides and the violence unleashed against the unarmed population has been waged with exceptional cruelty. One reason may be that the initiative has passed from the communities on the ground to those contending for power. Another may be the low value on life placed by the security cabal in Khartoum and by those in the opposition who want power at any cost.

What is the Solution?

I suggest a three-pronged process in the Sudan. The priority must be to complete the Naivasha peace process and change the character of the government in Khartoum. Second, whatever the level of civilian support enjoyed by militias, it would be a mistake to tarnish the communities with the sins of the particular militia they support. On the contrary, every effort should be made to neutralise or re-organise the militia and stabilise communities in Darfur through local initiatives. This means both a civic conference of all communities – both those identified as Arab and those as African – and reorganised civil defence forces of all communities. This may need to be done under the protective and supervisory umbrella of an African Union policing force. Finally, to build on the Naivasha process by bringing into it all those previously excluded. To do so will require creating the conditions for a reorganised civil administration in Darfur.

To build confidence among all parties, but particularly among those demonised as 'Arab', we need to use the same standard for all. To make the point, let us first look at the African region. The UN estimates that some 30,000–50,000 people have been killed in Darfur and another 1.4 million or so have been made homeless. The figure for the dead in Congo over the last few years is over four million. Many have died at the hands of ethnic Hema or Lendu militias. These are Janjaweed-type militias known to have functioned as proxies for neighbouring states. In the northern Ugandan districts of Acholiland, over 80 per cent of the population has been interned by the government, given substandard rations and nominal security, thus left open to gradual premeditated starvation and periodic kidnapping by another militia, the Lord's Redemption Army (LRA). When the UN Secretary General, Kofi Annan, flew to Khartoum recently, I was in Kampala. The comment I heard all around was: Why didn't he stop here? And why not in Kigali? And Kinshasa? Should we not apply the same standards to the governments in Kampala and Kigali and elsewhere as we do to the government in Khartoum, even if Kampala and Kigali are America's allies in its global 'war on terror'?

Internationally, there is the daunting example of Iraq. Before the American invasion, Iraq went through an era of UN sanctions, which were kept in place for a decade by the US and Britain. The effect of the sanctions came to light when UNICEF carried out a child mortality survey in 1999 at the initiative of Canada and Brazil. Richard Garfield, professor of Clinical International Nursing at Columbia University and chair of the Human Rights Committee of the American Public Health Association calculated 'on a conservative estimate' that there had been 300,000 'excess deaths' of children under 5 in Iraq during the sanctions. But the sanctions continued. Today, the US does not even count the number of Iraqi dead, and the UN has made no attempt to estimate them. Iraq is not history. It continues to bleed.

This backdrop, regional and international, should prompt us to ask at least one question: Does the label 'worst humanitarian crisis' tell us more about Darfur or about those labelling and the politics of labelling? Are we to return to a Cold War-type era in which America's allies can commit atrocities with impunity while its adversaries are demagogically held accountable to an international standard of human rights?

Some argue that international alignment on the Darfur crisis is dictated by the political economy of oil. To the extent this is true, let us not forget that oil influences both those (such as China) who would like continued access to Sudan's oil and those (such as the USA) who covet that access. But for those who do strategic thinking, the more important reason may be political. For official America, Darfur is a strategic opportunity to draw Africa into the global 'war on terror' by sharply drawing lines that demarcate 'Arab' against 'African', just as for the crumbling regime in Khartoum this very fact presents a last opportunity to downplay its own responsibilities and call for assistance from those who oppose official America's 'war on terror.'

What Should We Do?

First of all, we the civilians – and I address Africans and Americans in particular – should work against a military solution. We should work against a US intervention, whether direct or by proxy, and however disguised – as humanitarian or whatever. We should work against punitive sanctions. The lesson of Iraq sanctions is that you target individuals, not governments. Sanctions feed into a culture of terror, of collective punishment. Its victims are seldom its target. Both military intervention and sanctions are undesirable and ineffective.

Second, we should organise in support of a culture of peace, of a rule of law and of a system of political accountability. Of particular importance is to recognise that the international community has created an institution called the International Criminal Court to try individuals for the most heinous crimes, such as genocide, war crimes and systematic rights abuses. The US has not only refused to ratify the treaty setting up the ICC, it has gone to all lengths to sabotage it. For Americans, it is important to get their government to join the ICC. The simple fact is that you can only claim the moral right to hold others accountable to a set of standards if you are willing to be held accountable to the same standards.

Finally, there is need to beware of groups who want a simple and comprehensive explanation, even if it is misleading; who demand dramatic action, even if it backfires; who have so come to depend on crisis that they risk unwittingly aggravating existing crisis. Often, they use the call for urgent action to silence any debate as a luxury. And yet, responsible action needs to be informed.

For the African Union, Darfur is both an opportunity and a test. The opportunity is to build on the global concern over a humanitarian disaster in Darfur to set a humanitarian standard that must be observed by all, including America's allies in Africa. And the test is to defend African sovereignty in the face of official America's global 'war on terror.' On both counts, the first priority must be to stop the war and push the peace process.

CHAPTER 11

READERS LETTERS

Deep Disappointment

Kathleen Beatty

I READ WITH INTEREST the editorial and letter concerning the election of George W Bush (Pambazuka News 181, 4 November 2004). I am a citizen of the USA who did not vote for him. In my circle of friends and acquaintances who did not support him there is an overwhelming feeling of depression and dread, and of deep disappointment in the number of our fellow countrymen who actually went to the polls and selected him. Please know that there are many of us here who are appalled by the actions of our government. And there are many of us who expect the rise of fascism in our country, and know that even voicing our opinion in the future will be dangerous. This is a very difficult time...

I am currently studying modern African history in one of the few such undergraduate courses offered in our country (and offer an apology on behalf of my country for the part we have played in making life a hell for so many Africans). It is true that Americans are for the most part abysmally ignorant of the rest of the world – a common misconception is that Africa is a country.

Our educational system and our media are largely responsible for this sad state of affairs. The seductions of material comfort play their part, also – but I suspect that the latter is not a peculiarly American weakness – it's just that we as a whole have had the opportunity to be so seduced, while in many other countries it is only the leaders who are offered the same temptation. I take comfort in knowing that throughout the world there are, and have always been, people who care about freedom and justice and who dream of peace. We are probably always the minority – but what a dreadful world it would be without us! Thank you for your excellent site. Peace.

No Trespassing

J. Depelchin

FROM THE EDITORIAL to the comments on the Darfur piece earlier to the piece on the UN vote on ending the embargo in Cuba, to the essay on the squeeze on land by Robin Palmer, thank you (Pambazuka News 180, 28 October 2004).

All of the essays and comment point in the same direction and lead one to ask one question: why and how do we (i.e. those who side with those without land, work, health, clean air, etc.) manage not to unite?

The bi-centenary of Haiti is passing us by (1804–2004) as if it never happened. In contrast, remember how 1492–1992 and 1789–1989 were celebrated?

President Bush, almost at the same time American and French troops were kidnapping President Aristide, in a speech meant to defend 'American freedom' concluded 'there can be no compromise between freedom and slavery'.

Is it possible to say that our problem can be described as 'failure (hesitation, resistance?) of fidelity to the freedom achieved by the slaves who overthrew slavery in Haiti?'

Could that failure be explained by our inability (reluctance, hesitation?) to maintain Atlantic (and oriental) slavery and the wiping out of Native Americans as crimes against humanity against the dissolving effect, on our collective conscience, of what these crimes gave birth to: capitalism as we know it today, in which everyone is free to torture, maim, kill in order to maintain what is described as the one and only triumphant socio-economic system of all times.

Following the success of the slaves in 1804, the enslavers'-capitalists' motto has remained the same and can be summarised as follows: 'the discovered can never ever discover anything, and if they try, the most severe punishment shall be dispensed'. No one has been able to document the terror suffered by those who were kidnapped and shipped across the Atlantic, no one can imagine the terror suffered by those whose land was robbed.

It is easy to see wars in various parts of the planet as driven by the search to monopolise resources. Has it changed from the time when land and labour were the keys to opening up the promised land of capitalism?

Not many media referred to it, but Aristide's crucial faults (from the point of view of the US and the French governments) were not only putting an end to the army, asking for the French to repay what the Haitian governments paid between 1825 and 1947, more than 20 billion. More serious was the fact that Haiti was resorting to Cuban doctors and teachers to resolve its health and educational problems.

Cuba is seen as one of the trespassers of the 'No Trespass' sign, and has been punished ever since. (There are other many examples.) I agree with Tajudeen that Africans should unite (not just the governments) with the Cubans and all those who, since and before 1804 said no to slavery in any form, degree or shape.

The crisis of landlessness is not recent. It is genetically tied to the early beginnings of capitalism which has multiple roots and not just medieval Europe.

Debating the Darfur Crisis (1)

Tom Geepo

MANY THANKS FOR publishing Professor Mamdani' s brilliant analysis of
the situation in the Sudan (Pambazuka News 177, 7 October 2004). But the
Ugandan intellectual should have included his nationality instead of just
telling his readers that he is an eminent professor at Columbia University.
Hence, Dr Mamdani, in spite of what is happening in Africa, ought to be
proud of not only his Asian roots but also his birthplace – Africa (Uganda).

Debating the Darfur Crisis (2)

Amel Aldehaib

I HAVE BEEN IN South Darfur for the last two weeks, and was there when I
received the article 'How can we name the Darfur crises?' (Pambazuka News
177, 7 October 2004). I read the article with great interest. While in South
Darfur I have been listening to the views and analysis of some intellectuals
from the area, some tribal leaders and civil society actors. They all stressed:

*The ongoing conflict has nothing to do with a conflict over natural resources;
it has nothing to do with tribal conflict; it is a political conflict between the
government and the rebels, in which the government used the Janjaweed to
fight the rebels.

* The people of Darfur have been living together for hundreds of years.
There have been intermarriages between all tribes. The people of Darfur have
mixed blood. They told me that when Darfuria people go to central or north
Sudan they are called westerners. When people in the north label you a west-
erner they mean that you are not Arab. So the so-called Arab from Darfur is
not considering to be an Arab in north and central Sudan.

* The international experts, especially those who are now working in deliver-
ing humanitarian assistance in Darfur, are all driven by a Western mentality;
most of them mistrust the Arab staff. As a result a new culture has developed
in the camps (for which some international agencies should be held partly
responsible). When people in the camps want to say their prayers they just
pretend that they are not doing so, for they think that they might cause anger.

But when you discuss this issue in Khartoum (even with intellectuals), their
analysis and accordingly their proposal for intervention is misleading. In
Khartoum even now most are saying that either it is either a conflict over

natural resources or a tribal conflict with political interference. Sometimes it is hard for me to convince people or even to continue discussing it, for the media in Khartoum is continuously sending the message that the conflict is over natural resources.

I am happy that I found most of my thoughts in your paper, which is really talking to the minds of the people (it is not an emotional article, as some others are). I have sent the article to as many people as possible. Thanks a lot for providing us with such a rational and deep article, which really represents the reality.

How Can Information Reach Out to the Poor?

Francis Banda

THE ARTICLE BY Riaz Tayob of the Southern and Eastern African Trade Information and Negotiations Institute (Seatini) in South Africa is very educative and informative (Pambazuka News 178, 14 October 2004). One wonders whether some African leaders read this kind of literature. It would help them understand how to deal with their fellow leaders from the North. Institutions like the World Bank and IMF have literally taken over the roles and responsibilities of the states in Africa through pushing down the throat of high indebted countries in Africa a bitter pill aimed at underdeveloping them. As Riaz says, this is done through imposing free trade and liberation policies. Northern countries, who appear to control these IFIs, did not adopt these policies for themselves when they were developing.

My observation is that the sort of information that Riaz is sharing with us must reach out to more people in Africa, especially the poor. The challenge remains how to do this given the underdeveloped information communication systems. Even the language used is of the oppressor, which very few urban based intellectuals can access. Who can use it for themselves and not widely share this knowledge in order to empower the African people? This is one big weakness with our 'educated' Africans. How, then, do you think Pambazuka could help to popularise such information and widely communicate it to others.

I believe this could be one way of liberating Africa from social and economic bondage. If the people of Africa are empowered with information and knowledge and their anger evoked, they would control their destiny with or without the elite, whose interests appear to compromise with the oppressor as 'consultants' opportunists at the expense of the poor and Africa as a whole.

Darfur and the African Union

Waranya Moni

I HAVE BEEN FOLLOWING the insightful and comprehensive discussion on the issue of genocide that has been taking place in Pambazuka (Pambazuka News 177, 7 October 2004). I am now more informed of the causes and the challenges facing those seeking solutions to the crisis in the Western Sudan region of Darfur. I have also closely followed the actions being taken by the African Union and have been very disappointed to note that so far its intervention has been chaotic. I have no doubt that if the AU continues being the lead organisation seeking a solution to the Darfur crisis the results will be catastrophic for the Darfurans. I have come to this conclusion after hearing the statement of Mr Sam Ibok, the AU Director of Peace and Security, distancing the AU from US Secretary of State Collin Powell's statement that genocide is taking place in Darfur. Mr Ibok went further and not only challenged the US to take action, as required by international law, but also confirmed that the AU would not declare what is happening in Darfur as genocide until it had carried out its own investigations! I think we have now reached a point where we need to determine whether the AU is becoming an obstacle to the solution of the Darfur crisis. Its erratic actions and statements so far point to only one thing: its incapability to solving the problem in Darfur. I hope voices are raised to challenge the AU's incompetence and calls are made for more forceful international intervention.

Darfur Article: One of the Most Progressive Views I Have Come Across

Zaki El-Salahi

JUST TO SAY thank you: first to Mahmoud Mamdani, and secondly to Pambazuka News (Pambazuka News 177, 7 October 2004). I have been reading a lot on Darfur recently, and this is one of the most comprehensive, progressive views I have come across. This article is invaluable, at a time when the 'urgent crisis' our British news broadcasters were chatting about less than a month ago seems to have suddenly become un-news worthy ... reminds me of the two minutes Palestine, Afghanistan and Iraq seem to get regularly now.

Genocide: Debate of the Era?

Floris Beta

WHAT QUALIFIES AS genocide (Pambazuka News 177, 7 October 2004)? Let us not be selective. When it happens in some countries it is called 'genocide' and everyone agrees with the label. But then when other countries experience something even worse, it is put to analysis. So before an organisation can to respond to an emergency, to a horrible act, we need to debate whatever it is a genocide or not. Any way one looks it, after wasting time debating on the issue, it becomes a genocide. Is this a good way to handle an emergency?

Comparing Darfur to Uganda and DRC

Joe Ochogwu

THE DARFUR CRISIS in Sudan is one among other evil currents enveloping Africa (Pambazuka News 177, 7 October 2004). While I agree with Mamdani on the similarities of the Darfur crisis with those of Uganda and DRC, the former cannot compared to the latter. The large population of Displaced Persons in Darfur given the very short time frame of Janjaweed operations in the Darfur region requires further interrogation. Mamdani will do well to visit Chad and some other IDPs camp for the Darfur Victims, then a proper understanding of the humanitarian condition will be further intellectually comprehended.

Debating FGM (1)

David Mushabe

LET ME TAKE THIS opportunity to add my voice to those opposed to female genital mutilation (FGM) (Pambazuka News 173, 9 September 2004). I have read with great care the debate and/or exchange between Doreen Lwanga and Faiza Jama Mohammed regarding FGM, and my observations are presented below.

Ms Lwanga quoted the language of Article 5 relating to the 'Elimination of Harmful Practices', defined in Article 1(g) as '… all behaviour, attitudes and/or practices which negatively affect the fundamental rights of women and girls, such as their right to life, health, dignity, education and physical integrity'. She maintained, 'What is not clear [to her] is what forms of Female Genital Mutilation (or cutting) fall under this category as "harmful"?'. For crying out loud, couldn't Ms Lwanga realise that the operative words are 'harmful practices' and 'Female Genital Mutilation'? Clearly and in the context of the contentious article:

a) **harmful**: This means damaging, injurious, destructive, detrimental, hurtful, unsafe, etc. To that extent, the article would not bar practices that don't fit in any of the above. However, for the practice to be protected it ought to be demonstrably unharmful and ought to be backed by empirical evidence rather than emotional submissions and/or attachment thereto.

b) **mutilation**: This refers to disfigurement, defacement, damage, marring, injury, maiming, etc. I was disturbed by Ms Lwanga using mutilation and transformation interchangeably when she stated, 'In different African cultures, there are different forms of female genital transformation, some of which have never been harmful to the girl child or woman'. Whereas 'transformation' may not be harmful, mutilation is definitely harmful. The equivalent of transformation is merely 'makeover', 'alteration', 'renovation' none of which connote 'disfigurement', 'injury', etc.

When she states: 'I do not want to sound pretentious that there are no incidences where the FGM practices have produced harmful results, however, that does not make the norm harmful by itself. Malpractice could occur because an unsterilised instrument is used, or just like any other accident happens. The results may be harmful, such as profuse bleeding, genital injury or death, although that does not make the norm harmful. Thus, there is a need to emphasise that there is a difference between a 'norm' and a 'practice'.'

Well, whereas we have an admission as to the harmful nature of female genital mutilation, with all due respect to her sincere contribution, our friend did not offer any safe alternative. Had she advocated the legalised monitoring of 'transformation', which I don't doubt would provide a solution, it would have offered us food for thought, but she did not.

Article 17 of the protocol promotes a 'positive cultural context'. This, she says, she does not understand and wonders how it relates to the cultural rights of women as human beings. She, understandably, is opposed to any society codifying people's cultural practices and labelling them 'harmful'. She vehemently asserts that it is wrong to assume that you can take a 'broad brush' of one group (anti-FGM/C or pro-monogamous) and sweep away aspirations and traditions. What she missed though is that when the language of the article provides for a 'positive cultural context' it implies that the contemplated laws must consider the contextual environment. I submit that if this approach is adopted it would not amount to 'a broad brush' per se.

Assuming that the protocol would 'criminalise women's cultural lives', which is not true, but it is what is argued by Lwanga, the effect, if the law is contextually tailored, would be to reflect people's aspirations to transform society for the better. There are societies where children (little boys and girls who have not had their monthly periods yet) are sacrificed to the 'gods.' To those who believe in cleansing society of its curses by offering up these innocent children it is 'good practice' and a 'virtue'.

However, all common law jurisdictions classify this as murder. Can these people present any compelling argument in their defence? I think not! To that extent mutilation cannot be defended as a virtue whatsoever, and does not add value to the value or integrity of a woman. I shall not discuss the right of a woman to choose because Faiza Jama Mohammed already responded to that.

However, my question is what is the validity of a little girl's 'consent' amid cultural pressure to be 'a woman'? Lwanga cited examples where mothers may be forced to sneak out of cities and take their daughters for genital mutilation! These are the desires of the mothers and not of the daughters. Often, mothers want their daughters to walk the 'cultural journeys' which they themselves walked because they are still slaves of their past! What is disturbing is Lwanga's statement that such a protocol would 'deny them a chance of becoming women'. Gender is not defined by mutilation but by natural endowment.

Africa's dilemma is not its uneducated and/or illiterate population but rather her highly revered elite who, notwithstanding their Western exposure, continuously labour to strike a balance between 'intellectualism' and/or 'enlightenment' vis-à-vis cultural preservation. Whereas we may be tempted to resist 'undue Western influence' we should keep in mind that we have a duty to re-evaluate our cultures and rid them of vices, especially those that tend to suggest that you are not a full human being unless and until your genitals are mutilated.

Lastly, my apologies go to my sister Lwanga if my tone was harsh, because such must have been unintentional. Nonetheless, I can assure you that I was refuting the ideas in the article and not rejecting the wonderful individual who has actually ignited a healthy debate.

Debating FGM (2)

Yeno Thorli

IN BALANCING THE space for women rights and the space for respecting cultural practices Doreen Lwanga may not be entirely wrong in arguing that 'legislation aimed at protecting women's rights should also include the right to practice a certain culture, even if that might include FGM' (Pambazuka News 174, 16 September 2004). It is an accommodation of the right for cultural space. Is that so wrong? As cultures change and evolve, hopefully FGM will be left behind in time. My only concern in legislating against FGM is the criminalisation of our elders who wholly believe that it is an 'unharmful' cultural practice.

If two leading feminist activists who have the time and the brain power cannot arrive at a consensus on how we balance 'rights and culture' what hope is there for us lay women who want to believe and do the right thing, but at the same time do not want to disrespect our cultural practices.

My grandmother without, the benefit of Western education, rejected this piece of culture, so my mother was not done. My mother in turn rejected this piece of culture and I thankfully was spared. I have not had a daughter, but I do have a son, and he had to be circumcised in line with the cultural wish of the family. Was I wrong? Should I be criminalised (if for argument's sake male circumcision is outlawed)?

Debating FGM (3)

Ezekiel Mwenzwa

THE ONGOING DEBATE on what has been called female genital mutilation is not only entertaining but also worrisome, especially reading the comments by Lwanga and Mohammed, two women activists who purport to be talking for women, but from two almost extreme sides (Pambazuka News 174, 16 September 2004).

Let me give a general comment on what the two have said from an outsider's perspective. Firstly, the discussion is about to get out of hand and if these two ladies were talking face to face, we might need to call the fire brigade, so bring the fire down. This is because the import of the emotions expressed by the two, particularly Mohammed, is not only unhealthy for women's empowerment, but also questionable. Forgive me for saying that the two are trying to defend their positions in the name of women. For Lwanga, it should be understood that her arguments are scholarly, from an academic, but nonetheless impractical as the analogies she uses are grossly wanting. But as a scholar she is entitled to that for scholarship is about argument that leads to more and more debate that may lead to generation of knowledge over time.

Mohammed is the executive of an NGO, indeed a lobby group, that would like to problematise every thing about women to get much needed funding to continue eating. For me, eradication of FGM is not a basic need for women for it adds no extra food on their table, but education is. Why can't these organisations focus on the education of girls and put more funds there without concentrating on issues that won't add food on women's tables?

Debating FGM (4)

Rachel Irura

FEMALE GENITAL mutilation is a human rights violation that cannot be justified in the name of culture (Pambazuka News 174, 16 September 2004). I beg to differ that celebrating African womanhood entails continuing to perpetuate practices that are used to subjugate women. Celebrating African womanhood means that we should embrace wholeheartedly African cultural norms that uplift women and they are many, but at the same time, we cannot defend human rights violations using the tool of culture.

FGM violates a woman's womanhood, the very essence, the very vital part of her that makes her a woman. If we African women continue to think in these terms, whom do we expect to defend and advocate our rights? It is tragic to hear such sentiments supporting FGM echoed by one who is obviously learned. Culture is a constantly evolving and changing thing and is actually determined by the people who practise it. For instance, wife inheritance was the norm in many societies but with the HIV/AIDS pandemic, societal norms have had to take cognisance of this and the practice is slowly dying away. Therefore to advocate for a practice like FGM in any of its forms given the attendant medical complications is quite unrealistic.

There are many alternative ways of passing education about being a woman to our children without resorting to mutilating them. Which form if any of FGM serves a purpose except to subjugate a woman's sexuality? The practices and norms that shape the rubric of a people's interaction are their culture. Culture evolves as society evolves. We have come too far in striving for the rights of African women to allow sentiments such as those advocating for FGM to drag us back.

No to Water Privatisation in Ghana and Africa

Okwa Morphy Enebeli

YOUR INTERVIEW WITH Rudy Amenga-Etego is worthy of commendation (Pambazuka News 171, 26 August 2004). I completely agree with him that the privatisation of water is not the best option for Ghana and Africa in general, which has no welfare provisions. It goes to show the failure on the part of African governments to provide for the people they are supposed to govern. The failure of these essential amenities are due largely to the corruption that has become endemic in governance in Africa. The privatisation of water will further impoverish the people who have no means of livelihood. The act should be resisted.

Human Rights are Women's Rights

Obiagali Adaure

THE PROTOCOL ON the Rights of Women in Africa is beyond doubt the missing link in the charter's protection of women (Pambazuka News 166, 22 July 2004). Its adoption not only anchors into African soil the message and recognition that the injustices plaguing African women will no longer be tolerated, but it also affirms that human rights are women's rights too.

Although it is a document of great conceptual wealth, without the co-operation, political will, and commitment required from the members of the AU, its ambition to 'ensure that the rights of women are promoted, realised and protected in order to enable them to enjoy fully all their human rights' will never come to fruition. It will be nothing more than a piece of paper with writing.

I thank the pioneers of this initiative, for their efforts on behalf of the larger half of humanity, from (in God we trust) saving the protocol from such a miserable fate.

Oil and Corporate Recklessness in the Niger Delta

Sokari Ekine

JOEL BISINA HAS written an informative article on the Niger Delta (Pambazuka News 167, 29 July 2004). However there are a few points I would like to add.

Apart from a very brief mention of Ken Saro-Wiwa and Odi, Bisina fails to mention the state sponsored violence that has been taking place for the past 14 years. Nor does he mention the issue of demands for autonomy and resource control made by all the ethnic nationalities (please let us throw the word tribe into the dustbin of colonialism) of the Niger Delta.

When he does mention violence it is in the context of 'inter tribal and inter communal conflicts'. This implies the conflicts are nothing to do with oil. On the contrary the federal government has used divide and rule tactics to fuel conflicts between the different ethnic minorities by favouring one community over another at different times, by redrawing boundaries between communities and by arming one community and instigating murder.

Bisina also fails to include any gender dimension to his article. He mentions the 'ethnic militias' and illegal bunkering done by a minority of people but fails to mention the many activist groups and organisations that are fighting to expose the crimes and human rights abuses of the multinationals and their partner, the Nigerian government.

Joel Bisina replies

THANK YOU, SOKARI Ekine. I fully and wholly agree with you that some of the issues you raised are fundamental and are worthy of mention, but I want you to appreciate the fact that the Niger Delta question is as old as the Nigeria federation and so are the issues and the facets to the issues. Any attempt in a singular write-up to address all will amount to writing an encyclopaedia. So you would excuse my brevity.

I need to state here that I am very conversant with and actively involved in the entire Niger Delta struggle at various levels in my professional capacity and as someone from the region who lives and works there. Just trying to look at state sponsored violence alone will produce volumes – from the days of King Koko of Nembe Brass to the most recent military invasion in Egbema communities of Ogbudugbudu, Idebagbene and Itsekiri communities of Orugbo. There are many more examples.

Debating the Niger Delta Region

Joseph Peter

I READ THE ARTICLE written by Joel Bisina (Pambazuka News 167, 29 July 2004) and it is an interesting and thought-provoking insight into the very ugly, sad and degenerating condition of Nigeria's Niger Delta Region.

There is a marriage of convenience between the Nigerian state and multinational oil companies operating in the delta areas of the country. This relationship is unhealthy and inimical to the well being of the delta people and the entire Nigerian people. It is a case of conspiracy with the majority ethnic power elites and a few Niger Delta elites in league with these oil companies to continue to accumulate petrol dollars from the region to the detriment of the people.

Much as this is the pathetic situation of the Niger Delta, several social and economic contradictions are arising which will slow the processes of positive change in the area. The Niger Delta people seem to be very hostile to people from other parts of the country especially other minorities residing and trying to eke a living in the Niger Delta. Niger Deltans need the support of these people and their peers across Nigeria to achieve social justice. It is not a struggle the Deltans can fight to win alone. They must proactively engage other minority groups in the country to push the agenda further.

The conflict in the Niger Delta is no different from those of the Middle Belt region, as they both have to do with so-called majority ethnic hegemony dominance of minority groups. While majority ethnic groups in Nigeria have aggressively closed their space against the minorities, they are increasingly encroaching on the space of the minority groups. Central to these problems is the law that gives the federal government complete ownership of the land of Nigeria. With federal power being controlled by majority ethnic groups, the struggle will be difficult. However, concerted efforts from the minority groups can change the tide. The problem is land ownership; if we can constitutionally wrestle it from the government, nearly all the conflicts in Nigeria would be solved.

Using Africa's Resources for Africa

Enock Kanyanya

YOUR ARTICLE ON the wise use of resources (Pambazuka News 167, 29 July 2004) reminds me of what is happening in East Africa.

The British have continued to mine soda ash in Kenya without certification. Now the local community is pressing for the revision of the agreements to ensure that their interests are taken care of but the government is going against the community. A similar thing is happening in Tanzania where mining of several minerals is now in the hands of South Africans with no agreements with the people who have made sacrifices to keep the minerals. Now they have been relocated through poorly negotiated agreements that favour multi-nationals at the expense of the local community.

I would like to commend you for the article and ask for NEPAD to ensure that we do not encourage companies to take advantage of local communities because of their lack of negotiation power.

I am a natural resource manager in Kenya and I am worried about the trends taking shape in Africa. We need to build the capacities of local communities so that they are able to renegotiate and come up with resource use arrangements that are morally right and that can contribute to the development of rural populations and African countries at large.

ABOUT FAHAMU

FAHAMU IS COMMITTED to serving the needs of organisations and social movements that aspire to progressive social change and that promote and protect human rights. We believe that civil society organisations have a critical role to play in defending human rights, and that information and communications technologies can and should be harnessed for that cause. We are committed to enabling civil society organisations to use information and communication technologies to promote social justice.

Established in 1997 as a not-for-profit organisation, Fahamu has played a pioneering role in using the new information and communication technologies to support capacity building and networking between civil society and human rights organisations. Fahamu SA was established in 2002 in Durban, South Africa as a separate registered trust under South Africa law.

Fahamu seeks to enable civil society organisations to use information and communications technologies to influence social policy by disseminating information about their work; managing effective websites; making their information available on online databases; keeping them up to date with news and information on development and social justice; and engaging them in debate and discussion on social policy. Fahamu also uses information and communication technologies to provide distance learning courses aimed at strengthening the capacity of human rights and civil society organisations to be effective in achieving their goals.

In short, Fahamu seeks to enable movements in Africa to use information and communications technologies to make a difference to the lives of ordinary people so that they become active citizens determining policies on the basis of their own priorities.

Fahamu comprises a small core of highly skilled and experienced staff based in Oxford (UK), in Durban and Cape Town (South Africa), working with a wide range of international partners. The organisation has a network of some 20 associates located in Africa, the UK and elsewhere, who regularly undertake work for Fahamu, assisted by committed volunteers and interns (for further details see: http://www.fahamu.org/).

In addition to publishing Pambazuka News, Fahamu works in the following areas.

Innovations in distance learning

FAHAMU HAS DEVELOPED, in collaboration with the University of Oxford, a range of distance learning courses on human rights and capacity building that have benefited more than 300 people from nearly 160 organisations in more than 30 countries in the past two years, including human rights and civil society organisations, human rights commissions, paralegal workers, and African diaspora organisations.

The courses Fahamu has developed include:
- Introduction to human rights
- Investigating, monitoring and reporting on human rights violations
- Advocacy and campaigning
- Campaigning on freedom of information
- Role of media in the Rwandan genocide
- Gender, violence and conflict
- Using the internet for research and advocacy
- Leadership and management for change
- Practical financial management for NGOs
- Fundraising and resource mobilisation
- JustWrite: effective writing skills

In a recent evaluation of the programme, the Cambridge based International Research Foundation for Open Learning, stated:

> The materials are genuinely innovative in the field they seek to serve. They provide, taken together, an excellent menu of materials designed to strengthen the functioning of civil society. Given all that is known about 'conventional' training approaches, particularly in relation to the ineffectiveness of one-off training events/workshops, it is quite clear that this approach breaks new ground. The evaluators are not aware of any other such comprehensive approach to both personal and organisational professional development. The key word describing the response of individuals to the courses is 'empowerment'.

The technology and methodology used has been adopted by the Office of the UN High Commissioner for Human Rights, Association for the Prevention of Torture, UN Staff Systems College, Article XIX and by the Africa Program of the UN-affiliated University for Peace in collaborative courses developed with Fahamu.

Online databases, websites and newsletters for social change

FAHAMU HAS BEEN involved in the development of several online databases, providing a web interface to databases of research, news and publications. These include:

■ An annotated bibliography of selected research on civil society and health developed on behalf of the World Health Organisation and the Zimbabwean Training and Research Support Centre (http://www.tarsc.org/WHOCSI/search.php)

■ The Zimciv website – developed to enable people and institutions to access information produced by and about civil society in Zimbabwe; and to strengthen the dissemination, analysis of and debate on issues and positions taken up by civil society (http://www.zimciv.org/)

■ Annotated bibliography and publications database on equity in health – developed for EQUINET, the Network for Equity in Health in Southern Africa (http://www.equinetafrica.org/)

■ Portal website for partners in equity and health (http://www.equityinhealth.org.)

Social policy research

FAHAMU UNDERTAKES social policy research including research on the role of NGOs in development; the information, communications and training needs of human rights organisations; information and training needs of community based organisations; the evaluation of IDRC (Canada) social policy programmes; and healthcare training and internet connectivity in sub-Saharan Africa. Copies of relevant publications are available on request.

Ongoing course development

FAHAMU IS CURRENTLY working with the Office of the UN High Commissioner for Human Rights (OHCHR), Association for the Prevention of Torture, and the UN Staff System College to develop distance learning training materials on the prevention of torture, conflict prevention, and establishing effective human rights commissions. Discussions on the development of courses on HIV/AIDS are currently taking place with OHCHR and UNAIDS.

Fahamu is developing, in association with the UN-affiliated University for Peace, pilot course materials on gender, conflict and violence, which will be continued as additional funding becomes available.

Our funders

SINCE ITS ESTABLISHMENT, Fahamu has received the support of:
■ AOL Community Innovation Awards ■ Article 19 ■ Australia Aid ■ Commonwealth of Learning ■ Commonwealth Secretariat ■ DANIDA ■ British Department for International Development (DFID) ■ European Union ■ Ford Foundation ■ Foreign and Commonwealth Office ■ Foundation for Human Rights ■ Geneva Foundation ■ Canadian International Development Research Centre (IDRC) ■ JG & VL Joffe Charitable Trust ■ New Field Foundation ■ NOVIB ■ Office of the High Commission for Human Rights ■ Open Society Initiative for Southern Africa ■ Oxfam GB ■ SIDA ■ TrustAfrica■ UnLtd Millenium Awards ■ University of Oxford ■ University for Peace ■ and many individual donors.

Fahamu Ltd is a company limited by guarantee (4241054) and Fahamu Trust is registered as a charity 1100304. Fahamu SA is registered as a trust in South Africa IT 372/01.

For further details, see http://www.fahamu.org/.

www.ingramcontent.com/pod-product-compliance
Lightning Source LLC
Chambersburg PA
CBHW061717270326
41928CB00011B/2015